PrimeFaces Cookbook
Second Edition

Over 100 practical recipes to learn PrimeFaces 5.x – the
most popular JSF component library on the planet

Mert Çalışkan

Oleg Varaksin

[PACKT] open source*
PUBLISHING   community experience distilled

BIRMINGHAM - MUMBAI

PrimeFaces Cookbook
Second Edition

First published: January 2013

Second edition: May 2015

Production reference: 1250515

Published by Packt Publishing Ltd.
Livery Place
35 Livery Street
Birmingham B3 2PB, UK.

ISBN 978-1-78439-342-7

www.packtpub.com

Credits

Authors

Mert Çalışkan

Oleg Varaksin

Reviewers

Ramanath Bhongale

Aristides Villarreal Bravo

Sebastian D'Agostino

Commissioning Editor

Akram Hussain

Acquisition Editors

Tushar Gupta

Llewellyn Rozario

Content Development Editor

Ajinkya Paranjape

Technical Editor

Humera Shaikh

Copy Editors

Sarang Chari

Sonia Mathur

Project Coordinator

Harshal Ved

Proofreaders

Stephen Copestake

Safis Editing

Indexer

Mariammal Chettiyar

Production Coordinator

Conidon Miranda

Cover Work

Conidon Miranda

Foreword

JavaServer Faces has come a long way since its initial release. This is mostly due to the big ecosystem around it that allows many third-party add-ons to contribute. The first major extension was Facelets that removed the burden of JSP-based views.

With 2.0, Facelets became standard, and along with Facelets, many other features, including AJAX, originated from the community. JSF 2.2 followed the same approach and integrated various enhancements, such as HTML5-friendly markup, resource library contracts, and Faces Flows. Considering the current landscape of modern web application development, a server-side component framework such as JSF is still a popular choice among Java developers; this is because JSF is flexible enough to keep up.

I started PrimeFaces back in 2009 to provide a new alternative component suite to the JSF ecosystem. As of now, PrimeFaces is the most popular framework and the de facto standard for JSF applications built with Java EE. During this time, the component suite has extended to an over-100-rich suite of components utilizing modern JavaScript and CSS techniques, integrating responsive design, and providing mobile and push modules.

PrimeFaces is documented well in *PrimeFaces User Guide*, and Showcase is considered to be a practical guide in itself. However, there are many cases that can only be seen when doing actual development and are not to be found in the guide or Showcase. *PrimeFaces Cookbook, Second Edition*, focuses on these cases in a practical way to provide best practices as solutions to common requirements.

I've known Mert and Oleg for a long time; both are power users of PrimeFaces and longtime contributors to the framework. Their expertise in PrimeFaces makes this book a great complementary resource when developing applications with PrimeFaces.

Çağatay Çivici

Founder and Lead Developer of PrimeFaces

Foreword

I consider it a great blessing to have been associated with the JavaServer Faces technology for such a long time. In the 11 years since JSF 1.0 was released, the little corner of the enterprise software world in which JSF plays has experienced an enormous amount of growth and change, but it is still the world of enterprise software. During this time, I have come to have a deep appreciation of the unique technical and nontechnical requirements of enterprise software. This appreciation has shown me that these two aspects are very closely linked, and any framework that wants to play in the enterprise software space must broadly and deeply address both of them. The fact that there is still demand for the continued evolution of JSF is a testament to the ecosystem behind JSF and also how well it addresses these aspects.

One of the key nontechnical requirements of enterprise software is the ability to build projects that have very long service lifetimes. To do this, enterprises need technologies that are good enough to get the job done while having the necessary market backing and support guarantees to be trusted with mission-critical applications. This is where Java lives and thrives, and the Java Community Process (JCP) is the engine to develop Java.

There is a tension between the long service lifetime requirement of enterprise software and the constantly evolving state of the art. One element of this evolution is the rise and acceptance of open source software (OSS). When JSF first came out, enterprises looked at open source with a high degree of suspicion. Can we trust it? Will it be there for us throughout the service life for which we need it? Over time, enterprises have come to accept OSS. As the first part of Java to be made open source, JSF has ridden the crest of this trend. This was entirely enabled by the evolution of the JCP with which JSF is developed. Without the opening of the JCP to the ideas of OSS, JSF would have already faded out into nonuse. One could argue that the JCP has helped make OSS for enterprises.

The opening of the JCP was also a key enabler for the creation of the JSF component ecosystem, in which PrimeFaces is now the biggest player. I'm very grateful to all of the component libraries in the JSF ecosystem, in particular to PrimeFaces, for taking the core ideas of JSF and building on them to create solutions that can ultimately deliver real business value. Just as PrimeFaces takes the core ideas of JSF, Mert's and Oleg's book takes the core ideas of PrimeFaces and puts them in your hands for quick and easy deployment in your applications. These ideas are presented with frequent *How to do it...* and *How it works...* sections, showing first the practice and then the theory of PrimeFaces. With this style of presentation, Mert and Oleg cover the breadth and depth of PrimeFaces, diving down to the core underlying JSF when necessary to drive the point home.

I'm confident you'll find the second edition of this book a valuable resource as you develop JSF applications with PrimeFaces.

Ed Burns

JavaServer Faces Specification Co-lead

About the Authors

Mert Çalışkan is a software stylist living in Ankara, Turkey. He has more than 10 years of expertise in software development with the architectural design of Enterprise Java web applications. He is an advocate of open source for software projects such as PrimeFaces and has also been a committer and founder of various others.

He is the coauthor of the first edition of this book. He is also the coauthor of *Beginning Spring* by Wiley Publications. He is the founder of AnkaraJUG, which is the most active JUG in Turkey that has been having monthly meetups for 3 years now.

In 2014, he was entitled a Java Champion for his achievements. He is also a Sun Certified Java professional since 2007. He does part-time lecturing at Hacettepe University on enterprise web application architecture and web services. He shares his knowledge at national and international conferences, such as JDays 2015, JavaOne 2013, JDC2010, and JSFDays'08. You can reach Mert via twitter at `@mertcal`.

First, I would like to thank my friend Oleg Varaksin for joining me on this journey. I would also like to thank Çağatay Çivici and Ed Burns for crowning our book with their forewords—without their ideas and inspiration on the JSF ecosystem, this book wouldn't exist.

My thanks also go to Ajinkya Paranjape, content development editor; Humera Shaikh, technical editor; and Llewellyn Rozario, acquisition editor, all from Packt Publishing. I would also like to thank our reviewers, Aristides Villarreal Bravo and Sebastian D'Agostino, for the great job they have done in reviewing this book. These people accompanied us during the entire writing process and made the publication of this book possible with their support, suggestions, and reviews.

Last but not least, I would like to thank my mother, my father, my Tuğçe, and especially my beloved fiancé, Funda, who gives me her never ending support and enthusiasm.

Oleg Varaksin is a senior software engineer living in the Black Forest, Germany. He is a graduate computer scientist who studied informatics at Russian and German universities. His main occupation and "daily bread" in the last 10 years has consisted of building various web applications based on JSP, JSF, CDI, Spring, web services, REST, jQuery, AngularJS, and HTML5. He has a deep understanding of web usability and accessibility.

Oleg is an experienced JSF expert and has been working with the PrimeFaces library since its beginning in 2009. He is also a well-known member of the PrimeFaces community and a cocreator of the PrimeFaces Extensions project on additional JSF components for PrimeFaces.

Besides the aforementioned technologies, he has worked as a frontend developer with many other web and JavaScript frameworks—Struts, GWT, Prototype, YUI library, and so on. He also implemented an AJAX framework before all the hype about AJAX began.

Oleg normally shares the knowledge he has acquired on his blog at
http://ovaraksin.blogspot.de.

I would like to thank my family, especially my wife, Veronika; our advisers from Packt Publishing, Llewellyn Rozario and Ajinkya Paranjape; our reviewers; and the PrimeFaces project lead, Çağatay Çivici. These people accompanied us during the entire writing process and made the publication of the book possible with their support, suggestions, and reviews.

About the Reviewers

Aristides Villarreal Bravo is a Java developer, a member of the NetBeans Dream Team, and a leader of Java User Groups. He is also the CEO of Javscaz Software Developers. He currently lives in Panamá.

Aristides has organized and participated in various conferences and seminars related to Java, Java EE, the NetBeans platform, free software, and mobile devices, both nationally and internationally. He writes tutorials and blogs about Java, NetBeans, and web development too.

He has given several interviews on sites such as NetBeans, NetBeans Dzone, and javaHispano and developed various plugins for NetBeans.

He was a technical reviewer on one more book about PrimeFaces, *PrimeFaces Blueprints*, *Packt Publishing*.

> I would like to thank my family for their support and patience.

Sebastian D'Agostino currently lives in Argentina and has earned his computer software engineering degree from the University of Buenos Aires (UBA). He has been developing with C, C++, and Java EE in a professional manner for 6 years. He worked for big multinational companies, such as Oracle, but also participated in freelance work. He was involved in different projects covering backend, middleware, frontend, and even functional analysis. His frontend experience includes Struts, PrimeFaces, and AngularJS. Presently, he is working for Banco Industrial (Bind, Industrial Bank) and studying for a master's degree in information technology and communications at Universidad Argentina de la Empresa (UADE).

This is his first book review, but he is currently also reviewing another book by Packt Publishing.

I would like to thank my parents and my family for their constant support in my life and career decisions.

I would also like to thank the authors for producing such a good reference book on a piece of technology that I am very fond of. My thanks also go to the Packt Publishing team for giving me the opportunity to participate in this project.

www.PacktPub.com

Support files, eBooks, discount offers, and more

For support files and downloads related to your book, please visit www.PacktPub.com.

Did you know that Packt offers eBook versions of every book published, with PDF and ePub files available? You can upgrade to the eBook version at www.PacktPub.com and as a print book customer, you are entitled to a discount on the eBook copy. Get in touch with us at service@packtpub.com for more details.

At www.PacktPub.com, you can also read a collection of free technical articles, sign up for a range of free newsletters and receive exclusive discounts and offers on Packt books and eBooks.

https://www2.packtpub.com/books/subscription/packtlib

Do you need instant solutions to your IT questions? PacktLib is Packt's online digital book library. Here, you can search, access, and read Packt's entire library of books.

Why Subscribe?

- ▸ Fully searchable across every book published by Packt
- ▸ Copy and paste, print, and bookmark content
- ▸ On demand and accessible via a web browser

Free Access for Packt account holders

If you have an account with Packt at www.PacktPub.com, you can use this to access PacktLib today and view 9 entirely free books. Simply use your login credentials for immediate access.

To mom, dad, and my little Tuğçe...

–Mert Çalışkan

Table of Contents

Preface

PrimeFaces Cookbook, Second Edition, is the most comprehensive book about PrimeFaces—the rapidly evolving and leading JSF component suite. The book provides a head start to its readers by covering all the knowledge needed to work with the PrimeFaces framework and components in the real world. It is a quick, practical guide to learn PrimeFaces, written in a clear, comprehensible style. *PrimeFaces Cookbook, Second Edition*, addresses a wide audience interested in modern, trendsetting Java EE web development.

What this book covers

Chapter 1, Getting Started with PrimeFaces, provides details on the setup and configuration of PrimeFaces, along with the core concepts for every web application powered by PrimeFaces. The chapter gives a sneak preview of the basic features of PrimeFaces, such as AJAX processing and updating, component referencing by keywords and selectors, partial submitting, handling with Internationalization and Localization, along with the right-to-left language support and resource ordering.

Chapter 2, Theming Concepts, introduces PrimeFaces themes and the concept involved. Readers will learn about the theming of PrimeFaces components. The difference between structural and skinning CSS, installing and customizing PrimeFaces themes, along with creating new themes, will be detailed. Readers will also see how to adjust the font family and the font size throughout the PrimeFaces components to provide a consistent look and feel. Discussions of two variants of theme switchers and integrating additional icons finish this chapter.

Chapter 3, Enhanced Inputs and Selects, explains how to work with the input and select components available in PrimeFaces. Such components are the main parts of every web application. PrimeFaces provides nearly 25 components for data input that extend the standard JSF component suite with user-friendly interfaces, skinning capabilities, AJAX interactions, Client-side Validation, and many other useful features.

Chapter 4, Grouping Content with Panels, covers various container components, such as panel, accordion, scrollPanel, tabView, and dashboard, which allow grouping of JSF components. Various settings to configure panel components are detailed in this chapter. Furthermore, the chapter explains how to create complex layouts with the layout component and also responsive layouts for mobile devices and desktops with Grid CSS.

Chapter 5, Data Iteration Components, covers basic and advanced features to visualize data with data iteration components provided by PrimeFaces, including dataTable, dataList, pickList, orderList, tree, and treeTable. The discussed features include sorting, pagination, filtering, lazy loading, and single and multiple selections. Advanced data visualization with the schedule and dataScroller components will be demonstrated as well.

Chapter 6, Endless Menu Variations, explains several menu variations. PrimeFaces' menus fulfill all major requirements. They come with various facets—static, dynamic, tiered, hybrid, iPod-styled, and so on—and leave nothing to be desired. Readers will face a lot of recipes that discuss the menu's structure, configuration options, customizations, and integration with other components. At the end of this chapter, readers will know what kind of menu to choose and how to put it on a page for a particular use case.

Chapter 7, Working with Files, Images, and Multimedia, provides ways of managing operations on files such as uploading and downloading, image operations such as capturing, cropping, and displaying images with galleria, imageSwitch, and contentFlow. Readers will learn basic as well as advanced configuration of components and use cases.

Chapter 8, Drag Me, Drop Me, explains how the drag and drop utilities in PrimeFaces allow you to create draggable and droppable user interfaces efficiently. They abstract developers from dealing with implementation details on the browser level. In this chapter, readers will learn about PrimeFaces' drag and drop utilities—Draggable and Droppable. AJAX-enhanced drag and drop and a special integration with data iteration components will be explained as well.

Chapter 9, Creating Charts and Maps, covers the ways to create visual charts with PrimeFaces' extensive charting features and create maps based on Google Maps. PrimeFaces offers basic and advanced charting with its easy-to-use and user-friendly charting infrastructure. Throughout the chapter, mapping abilities such as drawing polylines and polygons and handling markers and events are covered as well.

Chapter 10, Client-side Validation, gives advice on how to implement Client-side Validation (CSV) with PrimeFaces. PrimeFaces' Client Side Validation Framework is the most complete and advanced CSV solution for JSF. Readers will learn all CSV tricks—configuration, standard validation, instant validation, and integration with Bean Validation. They will also meet custom client-side validators and find out how to extend CSV with JSF validators and Bean Validation.

Chapter 11, Miscellaneous Advanced Use Cases, introduces more interesting features of the PrimeFaces library. You will learn about RequestContext—a helpful utility that allows marking components as updatable targets at runtime, adding AJAX callback parameters, opening external pages in dynamically generated dialog (Dialog Framework), and more. In this chapter, a number of real-world samples will be also developed—blocking UI during AJAX calls, periodic polling, focus handling, controlling from submission, sticking components, content caching, and targetable messages, to name a few. Furthermore, after reading this chapter, readers will be aware of the pitfalls of menus within layout units and nested panels as well as possibilities for exception handling.

What you need for this book

The PrimeFaces core functionality only requires a Java 5+ runtime. The PrimeFaces library is just one single JAR file. With the help of the Maven tool, you can easily get the artifact for the PrimeFaces library (for more information on installing Maven, visit `http://maven.apache.org`). Please note that Maven demands a Java Development Kit installed on your local environment instead of on the Java Runtime Environment. Alternatively, you can download the JAR directly from the Maven central repository (`http://search.maven.org`) and add it to the project's classpath.

The showcase to *PrimeFaces Cookbook, Second Edition*, is hosted on GitHub at `https://github.com/ova2/primefaces-cookbook/tree/second-edition`. The homepage on GitHub contains all the details on how to clone the Git repository with the source code and build and run the showcase web application in your local environment.

Who this book is for

This book is for everybody who would like to learn modern Java web development based on PrimeFaces and is looking for a quick introduction to this matter. Prerequisites for this book are basic JSF, jQuery, and CSS skills.

Sections

In this book, you will find several headings that appear frequently (Getting ready, How to do it, How it works, There's more, and See also).

To give clear instructions on how to complete a recipe, we use these sections as follows:

Getting ready

This section tells you what to expect in the recipe and describes how to set up any software or any preliminary settings required for the recipe.

How to do it...

This section contains the steps required to follow the recipe.

How it works...

This section usually consists of a detailed explanation of what happened in the previous section.

There's more...

This section consists of additional information about the recipe in order to make the reader more knowledgeable about the recipe.

See also

This section provides helpful links to other useful information for the recipe.

Conventions

In this book, you will find a number of text styles that distinguish between different kinds of information. Here are some examples of these styles and an explanation of their meaning.

Code words in text, database table names, folder names, filenames, file extensions, pathnames, dummy URLs, user input, and Twitter handles are shown as follows: "We can include other contexts through the use of the `include` directive."

A block of code is set as follows:

```
<repository>
  <id>prime-repo</id>
  <name>PrimeFaces Maven Repository</name>
  <url>http://repository.primefaces.org</url>
</repository>
```

When we wish to draw your attention to a particular part of a code block, the relevant lines or items are set in bold:

```
Data:javax.faces.partial.ajax=true&javax.faces.source=j_idt19&jav
ax.faces.partial.execute=name&j_idt19=j_idt19&mainForm=mainForm&bo
okTree_selection=0_6&name=mert&j_idt21=&j_idt22=&j_idt23=&j_id
t24=&j_idt25=&j_idt26=&j_idt27=&j_idt28=&j_idt29=&javax.fac
es.ViewState=-6151865609302284540%3A502720797990996178
```

New terms and **important words** are shown in bold. Words that you see on the screen, for example, in menus or dialog boxes, appear in the text like this: "When the button with the **Partial Submit (False)** label is clicked, the AJAX request that will be sent to the server will contain all the ID's of the input text fields that exist on the page."

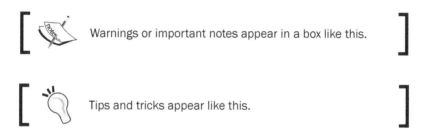

Warnings or important notes appear in a box like this.

Tips and tricks appear like this.

Reader feedback

Feedback from our readers is always welcome. Let us know what you think about this book—what you liked or disliked. Reader feedback is important for us as it helps us develop titles that you will really get the most out of.

To send us general feedback, simply e-mail feedback@packtpub.com, and mention the book's title in the subject of your message.

If there is a topic that you have expertise in and you are interested in either writing or contributing to a book, see our author guide at www.packtpub.com/authors.

Customer support

Now that you are the proud owner of a Packt book, we have a number of things to help you to get the most from your purchase.

Downloading the example code

You can download the example code files from your account at `http://www.packtpub.com` for all the Packt Publishing books you have purchased. If you purchased this book elsewhere, you can visit `http://www.packtpub.com/support` and register to have the files e-mailed directly to you.

Downloading the color images of this book

We also provide you with a PDF file that has color images of the screenshots/diagrams used in this book. The color images will help you better understand the changes in the output. You can download this file from: `https://www.packtpub.com/sites/default/files/downloads/34270S_Graphics.pdf`.

Errata

Although we have taken every care to ensure the accuracy of our content, mistakes do happen. If you find a mistake in one of our books—maybe a mistake in the text or the code—we would be grateful if you could report this to us. By doing so, you can save other readers from frustration and help us improve subsequent versions of this book. If you find any errata, please report them by visiting `http://www.packtpub.com/submit-errata`, selecting your book, clicking on the **Errata Submission Form** link, and entering the details of your errata. Once your errata are verified, your submission will be accepted and the errata will be uploaded to our website or added to any list of existing errata under the Errata section of that title.

To view the previously submitted errata, go to `https://www.packtpub.com/books/content/support` and enter the name of the book in the search field. The required information will appear under the **Errata** section.

Piracy

Piracy of copyrighted material on the Internet is an ongoing problem across all media. At Packt, we take the protection of our copyright and licenses very seriously. If you come across any illegal copies of our works in any form on the Internet, please provide us with the location address or website name immediately so that we can pursue a remedy.

Please contact us at `copyright@packtpub.com` with a link to the suspected pirated material.

We appreciate your help in protecting our authors and our ability to bring you valuable content.

Questions

If you have a problem with any aspect of this book, you can contact us at `questions@packtpub.com`, and we will do our best to address the problem.

1
Getting Started with PrimeFaces

In this chapter, we will cover:

- ▸ Setting up and configuring the PrimeFaces library
- ▸ AJAX basics with process and update
- ▸ PrimeFaces selectors
- ▸ Partial process and update with fragments
- ▸ Partial view submit
- ▸ Internationalization (i18n) and Localization (L10n)
- ▸ Right-to-left language support
- ▸ Improved resource ordering

Introduction

This chapter will provide details on the setup and configuration of PrimeFaces, along with the basics of the PrimeFaces AJAX mechanism. The goal of this chapter is to provide a sneak preview of some of the features of PrimeFaces, such as the AJAX processing mechanism, Internationalization, and Localization, along with support for right-to-left languages.

Setting up and configuring the PrimeFaces library

PrimeFaces is a lightweight JSF component library with one JAR file, which needs no configuration and does not contain any required external dependencies. To start with the development of the library, all we need is the artifact for the library.

Getting ready

You can download the PrimeFaces library from `http://primefaces.org/downloads.html`, and you need to add the `primefaces-{version}.jar` file to your classpath. After that, all you need to do is import the namespace of the library that is necessary to add the PrimeFaces components to your pages to get started.

If you are using Maven (for more information on installing Maven, please visit `http://maven.apache.org/guides/getting-started/maven-in-five-minutes.html`), you can retrieve the PrimeFaces library by defining the Maven repository in your **Project Object Model** XML file, `pom.xml`, as follows:

```
<repository>
  <id>prime-repo</id>
  <name>PrimeFaces Maven Repository</name>
  <url>http://repository.primefaces.org</url>
</repository>
```

> **Downloading the example code**
>
> You can download the example code files for all Packt books you have purchased from your account at `http://www.packtpub.com`. If you purchased this book elsewhere, you can visit `http://www.packtpub.com/support` and register to have the files e-mailed directly to you.

Add the dependency configuration as follows:

```
<dependency>
  <groupId>org.primefaces</groupId>
  <artifactId>primefaces</artifactId>
  <version>5.2</version>
</dependency>
```

At the time of writing this book, the latest and most stable version of PrimeFaces was 5.2. To check whether this is the latest available version or not, please visit `http://primefaces.org/downloads.html`. The code in this book will work properly with PrimeFaces 5.2. In prior versions or the future versions, some methods, attributes, or components' behaviors may change.

How to do it...

In order to use PrimeFaces components, first we need to add the namespace declaration to our pages. The namespace for PrimeFaces components is as follows:

```
xmlns:p="http://primefaces.org/ui"
```

That is all there is to it. Note that the p prefix is just a symbolic link, and any other character can be used to define the PrimeFaces components. Now you can create your first XHTML page with a PrimeFaces component, as shown in the following code snippet:

```
<html xmlns="http://www.w3.org/1999/xhtml"
  xmlns:h="http://java.sun.com/jsf/html"
  xmlns:f="http://java.sun.com/jsf/core"
  xmlns:p="http://primefaces.org/ui">
  <f:view contentType="text/html">
    <h:head />
    <h:body>
      <h:form>
        <p:spinner />
      </h:form>
    </h:body>
  </f:view>
</html>
```

This will render a spinner component with an empty value, as shown in the following screenshot:

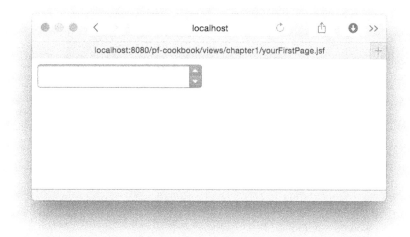

A link to the working example for the given page is given at the end of this recipe.

How it works...

When the page is requested, the `p:spinner` component is rendered with the `SpinnerRenderer` class implemented by the PrimeFaces library. Since the spinner component is an input component, the request-processing life cycle will get executed when the user inputs data and performs a post back on the page.

 For the first page, we also needed to provide the `contentType` parameter for `f:view` since WebKit-based browsers, such as Google Chrome and Safari, request for the content type `application/xhtml+xml` by default. This would overcome unexpected layout and styling issues that might occur.

There's more...

PrimeFaces only requires a Java 5+ runtime and a JSF 2.x implementation as mandatory dependencies. There are some optional libraries for certain features. All of these are listed in this table:

Dependency	Version	Type	Description
JSF runtime	2.0, 2.1, or 2.2	Required	Apache MyFaces or Oracle Mojarra
itext	2.1.7	Optional	`DataExporter` (PDF)
apache-poi	3.7	Optional	`DataExporter` (Excel)
rome	1.0	Optional	`FeedReader`
commons-fileupload	1.3	Optional	`FileUpload`
commons-io	2.2	Optional	`FileUpload`
atmosphere	2.2.2	Optional	PrimeFaces Push
barcode4j-light	2.1	Optional	Barcode Generation
qrgen	1.4	Optional	QR code support for barcode
hazelcast	2.6.5+	Optional	Integration of the `<p:cache>` component with hazelcast
ehcache	2.7.4+	Optional	Integration of the `<p:cache>` component with ehcache

 Please ensure that you have only one JAR file of PrimeFaces or a specific PrimeFaces theme in your classpath in order to avoid any issues regarding resource rendering.

Currently, PrimeFaces fully supports nonlegacy web browsers with Internet Explorer 10, Safari, Firefox, Chrome, and Opera.

The PrimeFaces Cookbook Showcase application

This recipe is available in the demo web application on GitHub (`https://github.com/ova2/primefaces-cookbook/tree/second-edition`). Clone the project if you have not done it yet, explore the project structure, and build and deploy the WAR file on application servers compatible with Servlet 3.x, such as *JBoss WildFly* and *Apache TomEE*.

The showcase for the recipe is available under `http://localhost:8080/pf-cookbook/views/chapter1/yourFirstPage.jsf`.

AJAX basics with process and update

PrimeFaces provides **Partial Page Rendering** (**PPR**) and the view-processing feature based on standard JSF 2 APIs to enable choosing what to process in the JSF life cycle and what to render in the end with AJAX. PrimeFaces AJAX Framework is based on standard server-side APIs of JSF 2. On the client side, rather than using the client-side API implementations of JSF, such as Mojarra or MyFaces, PrimeFaces scripts are based on the jQuery JavaScript library, which is well tested and widely adopted.

How to do it...

We can create a simple page with a command button to update a string property with the current time in milliseconds that is created on the server side and output text to show the value of that string property, as follows:

```
<p:commandButton update="display"
action="#{basicPPRBean.updateValue}" value="Update" />
<h:outputText id="display" value="#{basicPPRBean.value}"/>
```

If we want to update multiple components with the same trigger mechanism, we can provide the ID's of the components to the `update` attribute by providing them with a space, comma, or both, as follows:

```
<p:commandButton update="display1,display2" />
<p:commandButton update="display1 display2" />
<p:commandButton update="display1,display2 display3" />
```

In addition, there are reserved keywords that are used for a partial update. We can also make use of these keywords along with the ID's of the components, as described in the following table. Some of them come with the JSF standard, and PrimeFaces extends this list with custom keywords. Here's the table we talked about:

Keyword	JSF/ PrimeFaces	Description
`@this`	JSF	The component that triggers the PPR is updated
`@form`	JSF	The encapsulating form of the PPR trigger is updated
`@none`	JSF	PPR does not change the DOM with an AJAX response
`@all`	JSF	The whole document is updated as in non-AJAX requests
`@parent`	PrimeFaces	The parent of the PPR trigger is updated
`@composite`	PrimeFaces	This is the closest composite component ancestor
`@namingcontainer`	PrimeFaces	This is the closest naming container ancestor of the current component
`@next`	PrimeFaces	This is the next sibling
`@previous`	PrimeFaces	This is the previous sibling
`@child(n)`	PrimeFaces	This is the nth child
`@widgetVar(name)`	PrimeFaces	This is a component stated with a given widget variable name

The keywords are a server-side part of the PrimeFaces **Search Expression Framework** (**SEF**), which provides both server-side and client-side extensions to make it easier to reference components. We can also update a component that resides in a different naming container from the component that triggers the update. In order to achieve this, we need to specify the absolute component identifier of the component that needs to be updated. An example of this could be the following:

```
<h:form id="form1">
  <p:commandButton update=":form2:display"
    action="#{basicPPRBean.updateValue}" value="Update"/>
</h:form>

<h:form id="form2">
  <h:outputText id="display" value="#{basicPPRBean.value}"/>
</h:form>

@Named
@ViewScoped
public class BasicPPRBean implements Serializable {

  private String value;

  public String updateValue() {
```

```
        value = String.valueOf(System.currentTimeMillis());
        return null;
    }

    // getter / setter

}
```

PrimeFaces also provides partial processing, which executes the JSF life cycle phases—**apply request values**, **process validations**, **update model**, and **invoke application**—for determined components with the `process` attribute. This provides the ability to do group validation on the JSF pages easily. Mostly group validation needs arise in situations where different values need to be validated in the same form, depending on an action that gets executed. By grouping components for validation, errors that would arise from other components when the page has been submitted can be overcome easily. Components such as `commandButton`, `commandLink`, `autoComplete`, `fileUpload`, and many others provide this attribute to process partially instead of processing the whole view.

Partial processing could become very handy in cases where a drop-down list needs to be populated upon a selection on another dropdown and where there is an input field on the page with the `required` attribute set to `true`. This approach also makes immediate subforms and regions obsolete. It will also prevent submission of the whole page; thus, this will result in lightweight requests. Without partially processing the view for the dropdowns, a selection on one of the dropdowns will result in a validation error on the required field. A working example for this is shown in the following code snippet:

```
<h:outputText value="Country: " />
<h:selectOneMenu id="countries" value="#{partialProcessing
  Bean.country}">
<f:selectItems value="#{partialProcessingBean.countries}" />
  <p:ajax listener= "#{partialProcessingBean.handleCountryChange}"
    event="change" update="cities" process="@this"/>
</h:selectOneMenu>

<h:outputText value="City: " />
<h:selectOneMenu id="cities" value="#{partialProcessingBean.city}">
  <f:selectItems value="#{partialProcessingBean.cities}" />
</h:selectOneMenu>

<h:outputText value="Email: " />
<h:inputText value="#{partialProcessingBean.email}"
  required="true" />
```

With this partial processing mechanism, when a user changes the country, the cities of that country will be populated in the dropdown regardless of whether any input exists for the `email` field or not.

How it works...

As illustrated in the partial processing example to update a component in a different naming container, `<p:commandButton>` is updating the `<h:outputText>` component that has the `display` ID and the `:form2:display` absolute client ID, which is the search expression for the `findComponent` method. An absolute client ID starts with the separator character of the naming container, which is `:` by default.

The `<h:form>`, `<h:dataTable>`, and composite JSF components, along with `<p:tabView>`, `<p:accordionPanel>`, `<p:dataTable>`, `<p:dataGrid>`, `<p:dataList>`, `<p:carousel>`, `<p:galleria>`, `<p:ring>`, `<p:sheet>`, and `<p:subTable>` are the components that implement the `NamingContainer` interface. The `findComponent` method, which is described at `http://docs.oracle.com/javaee/7/api/javax/faces/component/UIComponent.html`, is used by both JSF core implementation and PrimeFaces.

There's more...

JSF uses `:` (colon) as the separator for the `NamingContainer` interface. The client IDs that will be rendered in the source page will be of the kind `id1:id2:id3`. If needed, the configuration of the separator can be changed for the web application to something other than the colon with a `context` parameter in the `web.xml` file of the web application, as follows:

```
<context-param>
    <param-name>javax.faces.SEPARATOR_CHAR</param-name>
    <param-value>_</param-value>
</context-param>
```

It's also possible to escape the `:` character, if needed, in the CSS files with the `\` character, as `\:`. The problem that might occur with the colon is that it's a reserved keyword for the CSS and JavaScript frameworks, like jQuery, so it might need to be escaped.

The PrimeFaces Cookbook Showcase application

This recipe is available in the demo web application on GitHub (`https://github.com/ova2/primefaces-cookbook/tree/second-edition`). Clone the project if you have not done it yet, explore the project structure, and build and deploy the WAR file on application servers compatible with Servlet 3.x, such as *JBoss WildFly* and *Apache TomEE*.

For the demos of this recipe, refer to the following:

- ▸ *Basic Partial Page Rendering* is available at `http://localhost:8080/pf-cookbook/views/chapter1/basicPPR.jsf`

- ▸ *Updating Component in a Different Naming Container* is available at `http://localhost:8080/pf-cookbook/views/chapter1/componentInDifferentNamingContainer.jsf`

- ▸ An example of *Partial Processing* is available at `http://localhost:8080/pf-cookbook/views/chapter1/partialProcessing.jsf`

PrimeFaces selectors

PrimeFaces integrates the jQuery Selector API (`http://api.jquery.com/category/selectors`) with the JSF component-referencing model. Partial processing and updating of the JSF components can be done using the jQuery Selector API instead of a regular server-side approach with `findComponent()`. This feature is called the **PrimeFaces Selector (PFS) API**. PFS provides an alternative, flexible approach to reference components to be processed or updated partially. PFS is a client-side part of the PrimeFaces SEF, which provides both server-side and client-side extensions to make it easier to reference components.

In comparison with regular referencing, there is less CPU server load because the JSF component tree is not traversed on the server side in order to find client IDs. PFS is implemented on the client side by looking at the DOM tree. Another advantage is avoiding container limitations, and thus the `cannot find` component exception—since the component we were looking for was in a different naming container.

The essential advantage of this feature, however, is speed. If we reference a component by an ID, jQuery uses `document.getElementById()`, a native browser call behind the scene. This is a very fast call, much faster than that on the server side with `findComponent()`. The second use case, where selectors are faster, is when we have a lot of components with the `rendered` attributes set to `true` or `false`. The JSF component tree is very big in this case, and the `findComponent()` call is time consuming. On the client side, only the visible part of the component tree is rendered as markup. The DOM is smaller than the component tree and its selectors work faster.

In this recipe, we will learn PFS in detail. PFS is recognized when we use `@(...)` in the `process` or `update` attribute of AJAX-ified components. We will use this syntax in four command buttons to reference the parts of the page we are interested in.

How to do it...

The following code snippet contains two p:panel tags with the input, select, and checkbox components respectively. The first p:commandButton component processes/updates all components in the form(s). The second one processes / updates all panels. The third one processes input, but not select components, and updates all panels. The last button only processes the checkbox components in the second panel and updates the entire panel.

```
<p:messages id="messages" autoUpdate="true"/>

<p:panel id="panel1" header="First panel">
  <h:panelGrid columns="2">
    <p:outputLabel for="name" value="Name"/>
      <p:inputText id="name" required="true"/>

    <p:outputLabel for="food" value="Favorite food"/>
    <h:selectOneMenu id="food" required="true">
    ...
    </h:selectOneMenu>

    <p:outputLabel for="married" value="Married?"/>
    <p:selectBooleanCheckbox id="married" required="true"
      label="Married?">
      <f:validator validatorId="org.primefaces.cookbook.
        validator.RequiredCheckboxValidator"/>
    </p:selectBooleanCheckbox>
  </h:panelGrid>
</p:panel>

<p:panel id="panel2" header="Second panel">
  <h:panelGrid columns="2">
    <p:outputLabel for="address" value="Address"/>
    <p:inputText id="address" required="true"/>
```

```
    <p:outputLabel for="pet" value="Favorite pet"/>
    <h:selectOneMenu id="pet" required="true">
    ...
    </h:selectOneMenu>

    <p:outputLabel for="gender" value="Male?"/>
    <p:selectBooleanCheckbox id="gender" required="true"
    label="Male?">
    <f:validator validatorId="org.primefaces.cookbook.
    validator.RequiredCheckboxValidator"/>
    </p:selectBooleanCheckbox>
  </h:panelGrid>
</p:panel>

<h:panelGrid columns="5" style="margin-top:20px;">
  <p:commandButton process="@(form)" update="@(form)"
    value="Process and update all in form"/>

  <p:commandButton process="@(.ui-panel)" update="@(.ui-panel)"
    value="Process and update all panels"/>

  <p:commandButton process="@(.ui-panel :input:not(select))"
    update="@(.ui-panel)"
     value="Process inputs except selects in all panels"/>

  <p:commandButton process="@(#panel2 :checkbox)"
    update="@(#panel2)"
    value="Process checkboxes in second panel"/>
</h:panelGrid>
```

 In terms of jQuery selectors, regular input field, selection, and checkbox controls are all inputs. They can be selected by the `:input` selector.

The following screenshot shows what happens when the third button is pushed. The p:inputText and p:selectBooleanCheckbox components are marked as invalid. The h:selectOneMenu component is not marked as invalid although no value was selected by the user.

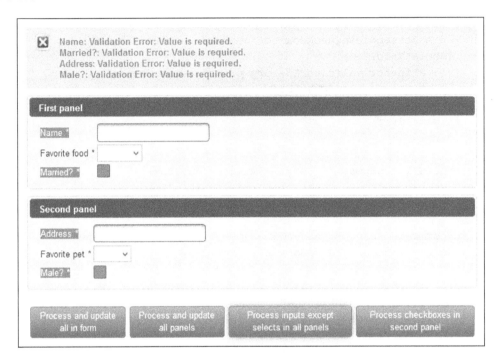

How it works...

The first selector from the @(form) first button selects all forms on the page. The second selector, @(.ui-panel), selects all panels on the page as every main container of PrimeFaces' p:panel component has this style class. Component style classes are usually documented in the *Skinning* section in *PrimeFaces User's Guide* (http://www.primefaces.org/documentation.html). The third selector, @(.ui-panel :input:not(select)), only selects p:inputText and p:selectBooleanCheckbox within p:panel. This is why h:selectOneMenu was not marked as invalid in the preceding screenshot. The validation of this component was skipped because it renders itself as an HTML select element. The last selector variant, @(#panel2 :checkbox), intends to select p:selectBooleanCheckbox in the second panel only.

In general, it is recommended that you use Firebug (`https://getfirebug.com`) or a similar browser add-on to explore the generated HTML structure when using jQuery selectors.

A common use case is skipping validation for the hidden fields. Developers often hide some form components dynamically with JavaScript. Hidden components get validated anyway, and the form validation can fail if the fields are required or have other validation constraints. The first solution would be to disable the components (in addition to hiding them). The values of disabled fields are not sent to the server. The second solution would be to use jQuery's `:visible` selector in the `process` attribute of a command component that submits the form.

There's more...

PFS can be combined with regular component referencing as well, for example, `update="compId1 :form:compId2 @(.ui-tabs :input)"`.

The PrimeFaces Cookbook Showcase application

This recipe is available in the demo web application on GitHub (`https://github.com/ova2/primefaces-cookbook/tree/second-edition`). Clone the project if you have not done it yet, explore the project structure, and build and deploy the WAR file on application servers compatible with Servlet 3.x, such as *JBoss WildFly* and *Apache TomEE*.

The showcase for the recipe is available at `http://localhost:8080/pf-cookbook/views/chapter1/pfs.jsf`.

Partial process and update with fragments

For enhanced AJAX capabilities, PrimeFaces offers the `<p:fragment>` component, which offers partial processing and updating with the AJAX request triggered by a component that resides inside the fragment itself. This component is useful and easy to use when multiple sections exist for a form with a different action for each section since there'll be no need to specify ID's for component processing and updating.

How to do it...

Let's define two fragments to retrieve data for registering a user into a system, one for user name input and the other for user address input. The definition of these two fragments would be as follows with the respective input fields marked with the `required` attribute:

```
<p:fragment autoUpdate="true">
  <p:fieldset legend="Basic Info">
```

```
  <p:outputLabel for="name" value="Name:" />
  <p:inputText id="name"
    value="#{fragmentBean.userName}" required="true" />
  <p:commandButton value="Save"
    actionListener="#{fragmentBean.saveUserInfo}" />
  </p:fieldset>
</p:fragment>
<p:fragment autoUpdate="true">
  <p:fieldset legend="Address">
    <p:outputLabel for="address" value="Address:" />
    <p:inputText id="address"
      value="#{fragmentBean.address}" required="true" />
    <p:commandButton value="Save"
      actionListener="#{fragmentBean.saveAddressInfo}" />
  </p:fieldset>
</p:fragment>
```

How it works...

When we click on the **Save** button of the **Address** section, only the **Address** input text will be processed and the **Name** input will be left intact. Since the **Address** input is a required field, we will get that field drawn in red for the error in the following image, but only that one since a descendant command button of the second fragment invokes the action.

The PrimeFaces Cookbook Showcase application

This recipe is available in the demo web application on GitHub (`https://github.com/ova2/primefaces-cookbook/tree/second-edition`). Clone the project if you have not done it yet, explore the project structure, and build and deploy the WAR file on application servers compatible with Servlet 3.x compatible application server, such as *JBoss WildFly* and *Apache TomEE*.

The showcase for the recipe is available at `http://localhost:8080/pf-cookbook/views/chapter1/fragment.jsf`.

Partial view submit

One other cool feature of the enhanced AJAX provided by PrimeFaces is the `partialSubmit` attribute that can be applied to action components and `<p:ajax>`, where only partially processed components are added to the AJAX requests with their ID's. By default, the JSF and PrimeFaces implementation serializes the whole form to send it via AJAX requests, and eventually, with large views, this will increase the size of the network data traffic that will be posted to the server. To overcome this problem, partial submit can be used to reduce the size of the post data when actions take place on views that have quite a lot of input fields. With this approach, only the ID's of the partially processed fields will be sent to the server.

How to do it...

Partial submit is disabled by default; it can be enabled globally with a context parameter in `web.xml`, as follows:

```
<context-param>
  <param-name>primefaces.SUBMIT</param-name>
  <param-value>partial</param-value>
</context-param>
```

Or, it can be declared with the `partialSubmit` attribute explicitly on the command action, as follows:

```
<h:outputLabel for="name" value="Name:"
  style="font-weight:bold" />
<p:inputText id="name" />
<p:commandButton value="Partial Submit (False)"
  partialSubmit="false" process="name" />
<p:commandButton value="Partial Submit (True)"
  partialSubmit="true" process="name" />
<p:inputText /> <p:inputText /> <p:inputText /><br\>
<p:inputText /> <p:inputText /> <p:inputText /><br\>
<p:inputText /> <p:inputText /> <p:inputText /><br\>
```

How it works...

The visual output of the given code snippet will be as follows. So, here we have two buttons, one with the `partialSubmit` attribute set to `false` and another one set to `true`:

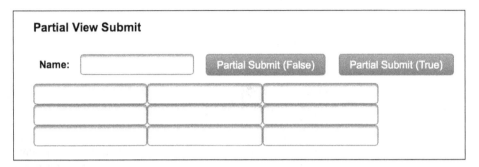

When the button with the **Partial Submit (False)** label is clicked, the AJAX request that will be sent to the server will contain all the ID's of the input text fields that exist on the page. An example output for the AJAX request is extracted from the `<p:log>` component (a visual console to display internal logs of PrimeFaces) and given here:

```
Data:javax.faces.partial.ajax=true&javax.faces.source=j_idt19&jav
ax.faces.partial.execute=name&j_idt19=j_idt19&mainForm=mainForm&bo
okTree_selection=0_6&name=mert&j_idt21=&j_idt22=&j_idt23=&j_id
t24=&j_idt25=&j_idt26=&j_idt27=&j_idt28=&j_idt29=&javax.fac
es.ViewState=-6151865609302284540%3A502720797990996178
```

The ID's that are highlighted belong to the input text fields that exist in the page. If we click on the button with the **Partial Submit (True)** label, we should get an AJAX request with no chained ID list in the data list:

```
Data:javax.faces.partial.ajax=true&javax.faces.source=j_idt20&jav
ax.faces.partial.execute=name&j_idt20=j_idt20&name=&javax.faces.Vi
ewState=-6151865609302284540%3A502720797990996178
```

 The partial submit feature does not exist within the core JSF features; it's a feature provided by PrimeFaces.

There's more...

With version 5.2, PrimeFaces introduced *partial submit filtering*, which allows customization on the AJAX data sent to the server. This comes in handy when you have multiple input fields within a data table, for instance, and try to prevent sending the ID list of those input fields to the server while doing paging, sorting, or row selection. The filter can be defined as a selector and its default value is `:input`. The example AJAX component in the following code will filter on all the input fields and will not send any data to the server:

```
<p:ajax event="page" partialSubmit="true"
    partialSubmitFilter=":not(:input)" />
```

The PrimeFaces Cookbook Showcase application

This recipe is available in the demo web application on GitHub (`https://github.com/ova2/primefaces-cookbook/tree/second-edition`). Clone the project if you have not done it yet, explore the project structure, and build and deploy the WAR file on application servers compatible with Servlet 3.x, such as *JBoss WildFly* and *Apache TomEE*.

The showcase for the recipe is available at `http://localhost:8080/pf-cookbook/views/chapter1/partialSubmit.jsf`.

Internationalization (i18n) and Localization (L10n)

Internationalization (**i18n**) and **Localization** (**L10n**) are two important features that should be provided in the web application's world to make it accessible globally.

With Internationalization, we are emphasizing that the web application should support multiple languages, and with Localization, we are stating that the text, date, or other fields should be presented in a form specific to a region.

 PrimeFaces only provides English translations. Translations for other languages should be provided explicitly. In the following sections, you will find details on how to achieve this.

Getting ready

For internationalization, first we need to specify the resource bundle definition under the `application` tag in `faces-config.xml`, as follows:

```
<application>
  <locale-config>
    <default-locale>en</default-locale>
    <supported-locale>tr_TR</supported-locale>
  </locale-config>
  <resource-bundle>
    <base-name>messages</base-name>
    <var>msg</var>
  </resource-bundle>
</application>
```

A resource bundle is a text file with the `.properties` suffix that would contain locale-specific messages. So, the preceding definition states that the resource bundle `messages_{localekey}.properties` file will reside under classpath, and the default value of `localekey` is en, which stands for English, and the supported locale is `tr_TR`, which stands for Turkish. For projects structured by Maven, the `messages_{localekey}.properties` file can be created under the `src/main/resources` project path. The following image was made in the IntelliJ IDEA:

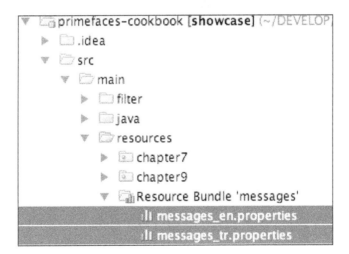

How to do it...

To showcase Internationalization, we will broadcast an information message via the `FacesMessage` mechanism that will be displayed in PrimeFaces' growl component. We need two components—growl itself and a command button—to broadcast the message:

```
<p:growl id="growl" />
<p:commandButton action="#{localizationBean.addMessage}"
  value="Display Message" update="growl" />
```

The `addMessage` method of `localizationBean` is as follows:

```
public String addMessage() {
  addInfoMessage("broadcast.message");
  return null;
}
```

The preceding code uses the `addInfoMessage` method, which is defined in the static `MessageUtil` class as follows:

```
public static void addInfoMessage(String str) {
  FacesContext context = FacesContext.getCurrentInstance();
  ResourceBundle bundle =
    context.getApplication().getResourceBundle(context, "msg");
  String message = bundle.getString(str);
  FacesContext.getCurrentInstance().addMessage(null,
    new FacesMessage(FacesMessage.SEVERITY_INFO, message, ""));
}
```

Localization of components, such as `calendar` and `schedule`, can be achieved by providing the `locale` attribute. By default, locale information is retrieved from the view's locale, and it can be overridden by a string locale key or with a `java.util.Locale` instance.

Components such as `calendar` and `schedule` use a shared `PrimeFaces.locales` property to display labels. As stated before, PrimeFaces only provides English translations, so in order to localize the calendar, we need to put the corresponding locales into a JavaScript file and include the scripting file to the page.

The content for the German locale of the `Primefaces.locales` property for `calendar` would be as shown in the following code snippet. For the sake of the recipe, only the German locale definition is given and the Turkish locale definition is omitted; you can find it in the showcase application Here's the code snippet we talked about:

```
PrimeFaces.locales['de'] = {
  closeText: 'Schließen',
  prevText: 'Zurück',
  nextText: 'Weiter',
  monthNames: ['Januar', 'Februar', 'März', 'April', 'Mai',
    'Juni', 'Juli', 'August', 'September', 'Oktober', 'November',
    'Dezember'],
  monthNamesShort: ['Jan', 'Feb', 'Mär', 'Apr', 'Mai', 'Jun',
    'Jul', 'Aug', 'Sep', 'Okt', 'Nov', 'Dez'],
  dayNames: ['Sonntag', 'Montag', 'Dienstag', 'Mittwoch',
    'Donnerstag', 'Freitag', 'Samstag'],
  dayNamesShort: ['Son', 'Mon', 'Die', 'Mit', 'Don', 'Fre',
    'Sam'],
  dayNamesMin: ['S', 'M', 'D', 'M ', 'D', 'F ', 'S'],
  weekHeader: 'Woche',
  FirstDay: 1,
  isRTL: false,
  showMonthAfterYear: false,
  yearSuffix: '',
  timeOnlyTitle: 'Nur Zeit',
  timeText: 'Zeit',
  hourText: 'Stunde',
  minuteText: 'Minute',
  secondText: 'Sekunde',
  currentText: 'Aktuelles Datum',
  ampm: false,
  month: 'Monat',
  week: 'Woche',
  day: 'Tag',
  allDayText: 'Ganzer Tag'
};
```

The definition of the `calendar` components both with and without the `locale` attribute would be as follows:

```
<p:calendar showButtonPanel="true" navigator="true" mode="inline"
  id="enCal"/>
```

```
<p:calendar locale="tr" showButtonPanel="true" navigator="true"
  mode="inline" id="trCal"/>

<p:calendar locale="de" showButtonPanel="true" navigator="true"
  mode="inline" id="deCal"/>
```

They will be rendered as follows:

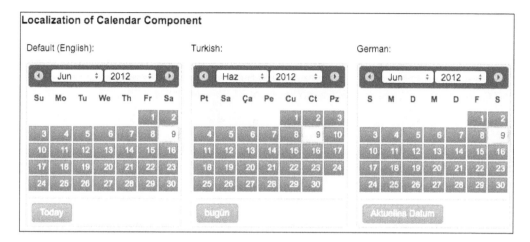

How it works...

For Internationalization of the PrimeFaces message, the `addInfoMessage` method retrieves the message bundle via the defined `msg` variable. It then gets the string from the bundle with the given key by invoking the `bundle.getString(str)` method. Finally, the message is added by creating a new PrimeFaces message with the `FacesMessage.SEVERITY_INFO` severity level.

There's more...

For some components, localization could be accomplished by providing labels to the components via attributes, such as with `p:selectBooleanButton`:

```
<p:selectBooleanButton
  value="#{localizationBean.selectedValue}"
  onLabel="#{msg['booleanButton.onLabel']}"
  offLabel="#{msg['booleanButton.offLabel']}" />
```

The `msg` variable is the resource bundle variable that is defined in the resource bundle definition in the PrimeFaces configuration file. The English version of the bundle key definitions in the `messages_en.properties` file that resides under the classpath would be as follows:

```
booleanButton.onLabel=Yes
booleanButton.offLabel=No
```

The PrimeFaces Cookbook Showcase application

This recipe is available in the demo web application on GitHub (`https://github.com/ova2/primefaces-cookbook/tree/second-edition`). Clone the project if you have not done it yet, explore the project structure, and build and deploy the WAR file on application servers compatible with Servlet 3.x, such as *JBoss WildFly* and *Apache TomEE*.

For the demos of this recipe, refer to the following:

▶ *Internationalization* is available at `http://localhost:8080/pf-cookbook/views/chapter1/internationalization.jsf`

▶ *Localization of the calendar component* is available at `http://localhost:8080/pf-cookbook/views/chapter1/localization.jsf`

▶ *Localization with resources* is available at `http://localhost:8080/pf-cookbook/views/chapter1/localizationWithResources.jsf`

For already translated locales of the calendar, see `http://code.google.com/p/primefaces/wiki/PrimeFacesLocales`.

Right to left language support

In PrimeFaces, components such as `accordionpanel`, `datatable`, `dialog`, `fileupload`, `schedule`, `tabview`, and `tree` offer right-to-left text direction support for languages such as Arabic, Hebrew, and so on. These components possess the `dir` attribute that can either get the value `ltr` (which is the default behavior with left-to-right text direction) or `rtl`.

How to do it...

We are going to create a dialog box that contains Arabic characters, as given here:

```
<p:commandButton value="Show Dialog"
  onclick="PF('arabicDlg').show();" type="button" />
<p:dialog widgetVar="arabicDlg" dir="rtl">
  <h:outputText value="PrimeFaces وهو مصدر للاسم همة في المشروع المكنون
    جناح مفتوح مع الملحقات المختلفة." />
</p:dialog>
```

When you click on the **Show Dialog** button, you will get the following output:

How it works...

Within the example, we're setting the `dir` attribute of the `<p:dialog>` component to `rtl`, stating that the text direction will be *right to left*.

There's more...

The direction of text can also be changed globally by setting `primefaces.DIR` in the `web.xml` file:

```
<context-param>
  <param-name>primefaces.DIR</param-name>
  <param-value>rtl</param-value>
</context-param>
```

A parameter value can either be `ltr` or `rtl`. It can also be an EL expression to provide dynamic values.

The PrimeFaces Cookbook Showcase application

This recipe is available in the demo web application on GitHub (`https://github.com/ova2/primefaces-cookbook/tree/second-edition`). Clone the project if you have not done it yet, explore the project structure, and build and deploy the WAR file on application servers compatible with Servlet 3.x, such as *JBoss WildFly* and *Apache TomEE*.

The showcase for the recipe is available at `http://localhost:8080/pf-cookbook/views/chapter1/rightToLeft.jsf`.

Improved resource ordering

PrimeFaces provides improved resource ordering to support customization of content. This ability could be used when Internet Explorer demands special meta tags to be placed first or for scenarios where the styling for PrimeFaces components needs to be overridden by custom styling.

How to do it...

Define `<h:head>` using facet definitions where necessary:

```
<h:head title="PrimeFaces Cookbook - ShowCase">
<f:facet name="first">
</f:facet>
...
<f:facet name="middle">
</f:facet>
...
<f:facet name="last">
</f:facet>
...
</h:head>
```

> The `<h:head>` tag is used by JSF components to add their resources to pages; thus, it's a must-have tag throughout your JSF-based applications. One of the commonly made mistakes among developers is forgetting to put in the `head` tag.

For instance, if a stylesheet gets declared in multiple CSS files, which would be linked in the middle and last facets respectively, the stylesheet definition referred to in the `middle` facet will be overridden by the one defined in the `last` facet.

How it works...

With PrimeFaces' own `HeadRenderer` implementation, the resources are handled in the following order:

1. If defined, first facet.
2. PF-JSF registered CSS.
3. Theme CSS.
4. If defined, middle facet.

5. PF-JSF registered JS.

6. Head content.

7. If defined, last facet.

There's more...

Internet Explorer introduced a special tag named `meta`, which can be used as `<meta http-equiv="X-UA-Compatible" content="..." />`. The `<meta>` tag is X-UA-Compatible and its content helps to control document compatibility, such as specifying the rendering engine to render the related pages in the browser. For example, inserting the following statement into the head of a document would force IE 8 to render the page using the new standards mode:

```
<meta http-equiv="X-UA-Compatible" content="IE=8" />
```

X-UA-Compatible must be the first child of the `head` component. Internet Explorer won't accept this `<meta>` tag if it's placed after the `<link>` or `<script>` tag. Therefore, it needs to be placed within the `first` facet. This is a good demonstration of resource ordering with the use of the `first` facet.

The PrimeFaces Cookbook Showcase application

This recipe is available in the demo web application on GitHub (`https://github.com/ova2/primefaces-cookbook/tree/second-edition`). Clone the project if you have not done it yet, explore the project structure, and build and deploy the WAR file on application servers compatible with Servlet 3.x, such as *JBoss WildFly* and *Apache TomEE*.

The showcase for the recipe is available at `http://localhost:8080/pf-cookbook/views/chapter1/resourceOrdering.jsf`.

2
Theming Concepts

In this chapter, we will cover the following topics:

- ▸ Understanding structural and skinning CSS
- ▸ Installing themes
- ▸ Customizing default theme styles
- ▸ Adjusting the font and size throughout the web application
- ▸ Simple ways to create a new theme
- ▸ Stateless and stateful theme switchers
- ▸ Integrating Font Awesome with PrimeFaces

Introduction

In this chapter, readers will be introduced to PrimeFaces themes and the concepts involved. Later on, we will build on these concepts to learn theming of the PrimeFaces components. The theming concept used in PrimeFaces is similar to the jQuery ThemeRoller CSS Framework (`http://jqueryui.com/themeroller`). All PrimeFaces components are designed to allow a developer to integrate them seamlessly into the look and feel of an entire web application. At the time of writing, there are 38 plus ready-to-use themes, which you can preview and download from the PrimeFaces Theme Gallery (`http://primefaces.org/themes`). There are two kinds of themes: *ELITE themes* that are available to ELITE & PRO users exclusively or as a standalone purchase, and *Community themes* that are free to use under Apache License. Community themes include the ones available in ThemeRoller and custom themes such as Twitter Bootstrap.

Powered by ThemeRoller, PrimeFaces separates structural CSS from skinning CSS. The difference between the two CSS concepts is the topic of the first recipe. Installation and customization of PrimeFaces themes, along with creation of new themes, will be detailed. We will also see how to adjust the font family and font size throughout the PrimeFaces components. Adapted font settings provide a consistent look and feel in a multi-theme web application. Two variants of theme switcher will demonstrate how to switch PrimeFaces themes with and without page refresh. Discussion about integrating the Font Awesome CSS toolkit for scalable vector icons will finish this chapter.

Understanding structural and skinning CSS

Each component is styled with CSS and contains two layers of style information—structural or component-specific and skinning or component-independent styles.

In this recipe, you will understand the difference between these two types of CSS, learn some useful selectors, and see an exemplary styling of the `pickList` component in the generated HTML.

Getting ready

To learn about different layers of style information, you can go to the PrimeFaces Showcase (`http://primefaces.org/showcase`) and look at it in the Firefox browser with an installed Firebug add-on (`http://getfirebug.com`). Firebug allows live editing, debugging, and monitoring CSS, HTML, and JavaScript in any web page. Another useful tool is the built-in Developer Tools for the Google Chrome browser, which is similar to the Firebug. Both these tools can be opened by pressing the *F12* key.

How to do it...

Go to the PrimeFaces Showcase and choose the **PickList** component from the left sidebar (the **PickList** menu item belongs to the **Data** menu). Open the Firebug now. It has a toolbar with tabs and a small icon having the tooltip **Click an element in the page to inspect**. Select the **HTML** tab and then click on that small icon. After that, click on the left (source) area in the displayed **Basic PickList** box. You will see the **HTML** code that belongs to the selected area as seen in the following screenshot:

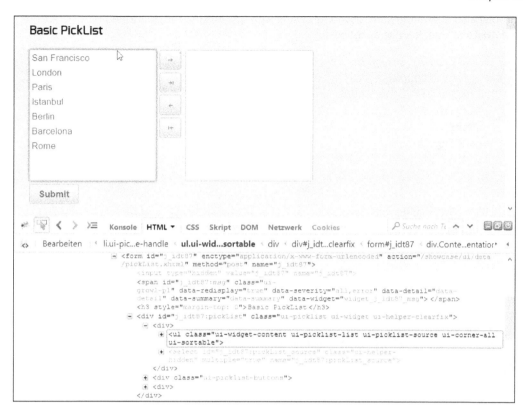

In the highlighted line in the preceding screenshot, the source area of `pickList` is presented as an HTML `ul` element with the following style classes:

- `ui-picklist-list`
- `ui-picklist-source`
- `ui-widget-content`
- `ui-corner-all`
- `ui-sortable`

Firebug also shows the corresponding styling with CSS next to the generated HTML code. For the **Aristo** theme, it looks as follows:

```
.ui-picklist .ui-picklist-list {
   height: 200px;
   list-style-type: none;
   margin: 0;
   overflow: auto;
   padding: 0;
   width: 200px;
}

.ui-widget-content {
   background: none repeat scroll 0 0 #ffffff;
   border: 1px solid #a8a8a8;
   color: #4f4f4f;
}

.ui-corner-all {
   border-radius: 3px;
}
```

How it works...

The first two style classes `ui-picklist-list` and `ui-picklist-source` are generated by PrimeFaces and provide a semantic presentation to indicate the role of an element within a component. In this case, it is a list of the `pickList` items. Other examples are `ui-datatable` for a table and `ui-button` for a button. These are structural style classes. In general, structural style classes define the skeleton of the components and include CSS properties such as margin, padding, display type, overflow behavior, dimensions, and positioning.

As already said, PrimeFaces leverages the jQuery ThemeRoller CSS Framework. The `ui-widget-content` and `ui-corner-all` classes in the preceding code are defined by ThemeRoller and affect the look and feel of the underlying HTML element and component. These are skinning style classes, which define CSS properties such as text colors, border colors, and background images.

Selector	Applies
`.ui-widget`	This is the class applied to all PrimeFaces components. It applies, for example, font family and font size to any component.
`.ui-widget-header`	This is the class applied to the header section(s) of a component.
`.ui-widget-content`	This is the class applied to the content section(s) of a component.

Selector	Applies
`.ui-state-default`	This is the default class applied to clickable, button-like components or their elements.
`.ui-state-hover`	This is the class applied on a mouseover event to clickable, button-like components or their elements.
`.ui-state-active`	This is the class applied on a mousedown event to clickable, button-like components or their elements.
`.ui-state-disabled`	This is the class applied to components or their elements when they are disabled.
`.ui-state-highlight`	This is the class applied to components or their elements when they are highlighted or selected.
`.ui-state-error`	This is the class applied to error messaging container elements.
`.ui-icon`	This is the class applied to elements representing an icon. It sets dimensions and hides inner text and the background image.
`.ui-corner-all`	This is the class that applies corner-radius to all four corners of a component.
`.ui-corner-top`	This is the class that applies corner-radius to both top corners of a component.
`.ui-corner-bottom`	This is the class that applies corner-radius to both bottom corners of a component.

These styles are applied consistently across all PrimeFaces components, so a clickable button and accordion tab have the same `ui-state-default` class applied to indicate that they are clickable. When a user moves the mouse over one of these elements, this class gets changed to `ui-state-hover`, and then to `ui-state-active` when these elements are selected. This approach makes it easy to ensure that all elements with a similar interaction state will look identical across all components.

The main advantage of the presented PrimeFaces selectors is a great flexibility in theming because you don't need to know each and every skinning selector to change the styles of all available components in your web application consistently.

There's more...

Some style classes are not generated by PrimeFaces explicitly and not defined by the ThemeRoller. There is, for instance, the structural class `ui-sortable` (listed in the *How to do it...* section of this recipe). This class defines a sortable behavior and tells us that `pickList` items can be sorted by a drag-and-drop action. The PrimeFaces library utilizes the jQuery Sortable plugin (`http://jqueryui.com/demos/sortable`) for the underlying JavaScript widget used in `pickList` to enable a group of DOM elements to be sortable. The plugin adds the structural style class `ui-sortable` automatically, on the fly, while the component gets rendered.

It is also important to say that the prefix of both types of style classes is `ui`. Most jQuery-based plugins typically have this prefix too. This fact might lead to a CSS collision when you use a jQuery plugin, which overrides PrimeFaces styles. An example is the jQuery UI (native) and PrimeFaces dialogs. Both use the style class `ui-dialog`. Manage this case properly with a CSS selector's specificity to avoid CSS collisions. Selector's specificity is the weight of the selector applied when multiple selectors affect the same element (`http://w3.org/TR/CSS21/cascade.html#specificity`).

 More information on the ThemeRoller selectors can be found in the official documentation at `http://api.jqueryui.com/theming/css-framework`

 Almost every component description in the PrimeFaces User's Guide (`http://primefaces.org/documentation.html`) contains a *Skinning* section with the component's structural style classes.

Installing themes

PrimeFaces themes are bundled as JAR files. Community themes are free and available for download at the PrimeFaces repository (`http://repository.primefaces.org/org/primefaces/themes`). Each theme can be quickly previewed before download at PrimeFaces Theme Gallery (`http://primefaces.org/themes`) or tested in the PrimeFaces Showcase with an integrated theme switcher.

In this recipe, we will install and configure themes to use them in an JSF application. The steps to accomplish this task are straightforward.

Getting ready

If you are a Maven (`http://maven.apache.org`) user, ensure that you have Maven installed. Maven is a build and project management tool, which manages installation of all dependencies in an easy way. PrimeFaces is a Maven-based project and offers all artifacts, including themes, as Maven dependencies.

How to do it...

Maven users should define any desired theme artifact in their project's `pom.xml` as follows:

```
<dependency>
  <groupId>org.primefaces.themes</groupId>
  <artifactId>cupertino</artifactId>
  <version>1.0.10</version>
</dependency>
```

`artifactId` is the name of the theme as defined at the Theme Gallery page. Also, make sure that you have the PrimeFaces repository in your `pom.xml`:

```
<repository>
  <id>prime-repo</id>
  <name>PrimeFaces Maven Repository</name>
  <url>http://repository.primefaces.org</url>
  <layout>default</layout>
</repository>
```

Non-Maven users should download the theme manually from the PrimeFaces repository and place it in the classpath of your application. You can repeat this step for all the themes you need.

Once you have included one or multiple themes, configure PrimeFaces to use them. Set the `primefaces.THEME` context parameter in `web.xml` (deployment descriptor) with its value as the name of the theme that you would like to use as default. Assuming you would like to use **Home** theme, then, the configuration is:

```
<context-param>
  <param-name>primefaces.THEME</param-name>
  <param-value>home</param-value>
</context-param>
```

That's all. You don't need to manually include any CSS files on your pages or anything else. PrimeFaces will handle everything for you. In case you would like to make the theme dynamic, define an EL expression as the `param` value. Assume that you have managed bean `UserSettings` keeping the current theme name in a `theme` variable. A proper configuration is as follows:

```
<context-param>
  <param-name>primefaces.THEME</param-name>
  <param-value>#{userSettings.theme}</param-value>
</context-param>
```

This is a case where you have installed multiple themes and let users switch them as per a theme switcher. All community themes are also available in an "all-in-one" bundled JAR file that can be included with just one dependency:

```
<dependency>
    <groupId>org.primefaces.themes</groupId>
    <artifactId>all-themes</artifactId>
    <version>1.0.10</version>
</dependency>
```

How it works...

The PrimeFaces component library has a special implementation for the JSF standard `head` component. PrimeFaces provides the `HeadRenderer` class, which is responsible for rendering of the `<h:head>` tag. `HeadRenderer` automatically detects the current configured theme in `web.xml` regardless of whether it is static or dynamic, via the managed bean and renders theme-related resources on the page. After that the page contains a link to `theme.css`:

```
<link type="text/css" rel="stylesheet"
  href="/showcase/javax.faces.resource/theme.css.jsf
  ?ln=primefaces-home"/>
```

There's more...

Aristo is the built-in default theme of PrimeFaces. There is no separate JAR file for it; the theme is delivered with the core PrimeFaces JAR file itself. Therefore, you don't need to install it via Maven or have it extra in the classpath.

If you are using Apache Trinidad (`http://myfaces.apache.org/trinidad`) or JBoss RichFaces (`http://jboss.org/richfaces`), PrimeFaces Theme Gallery includes Trinidad's **Casablanca** and RichFaces' **BlueSky** themes. You can use them to make the PrimeFaces components look like the Trinidad or RichFaces themes during migration.

- ▶ You may also want to check the *Themes* section in *PrimeFaces User's Guide* (`http://primefaces.org/documentation`)
- ▶ See the use of dynamic themes in the *Stateless and stateful theme switchers* recipe

Customizing default theme styles

How to customize theme styles is one of the most asked questions by the PrimeFaces users. There are simple rules to be followed to overwrite bundled theme styles with custom CSS. There is no need to edit bundled themes and repackage theme JAR files.

In this recipe, we will present two examples for theme customization—one for `selectOneMenu` and another for the `tree` component. We will see how to change styles for a particular component or for all components of the same type. The reason to do that could be a company style guide with the need to maintain corporate identity throughout all applications. Furthermore, we will learn tips for customizing default styles on input components.

How to do it...

Let's set a fixed width for `p:selectOneMenu` and remove the background and border for `p:tree`. The default width of `p:selectOneMenu` is calculated at runtime. That means, the width of `p:selectOneMenu` is dynamic and depends on its content (select items). Large select items cause large `p:selectOneMenu`. A fixed width would sometimes show a better `p:selectOneMenu` for items with a short text. `p:tree` without background and border could better fit a custom design in certain circumstances. This is demonstrated in the following screenshot:

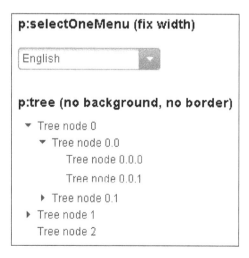

The corresponding XHTML part looks as follows:

```
<h:panelGrid styleClass="customStyles">
  <h3>p:selectOneMenu (fix width)</h3>

  <p:selectOneMenu value="dummy">
    <f:selectItem itemLabel="English" itemValue="en"/>
    <f:selectItem itemLabel="German" itemValue="de"/>
    <f:selectItem itemLabel="Russian" itemValue="ru"/>
  </p:selectOneMenu>

  <h3 style="margin:20px 0 0 0;">
    p:tree (no background, no border)
  </h3>

  <p:tree value="#{treeController.root}" var="node">
    <p:treeNode>
      <h:outputText value="#{node}"/>
    </p:treeNode>
  </p:tree>
</h:panelGrid>
```

The most interesting part is CSS. Our aim is to customize styles for only two particular components which are placed below a h:panelGrid with style class customStyles. Use namespacing to do this. Simply prepend the .customStyles style class to the PrimeFaces styles:

```
.customStyles .ui-selectonemenu {
  width: 157px !important;
}

.customStyles .ui-selectonemenu .ui-selectonemenu-label {
  width: 130px !important;
}

.customStyles .ui-tree {
  border: none;
  background: none;
}
```

 PrimeFaces styles can be inspected by the Firefox add-on Firebug or Google Chrome built-in Developer Tools.

Any other CSS selector can be used for namespacing too, but the use of ID is not recommended. ID in CSS is a component's client ID—an ID in the generated HTML. This is normally not the ID used in facelets (XHTML files). JSF prepends IDs of parent components that extend `NamingContainer` (for example, `h:form` or `p:dataTable`) while generating client IDs. It has disadvantages such as:

- The default separator for `NamingContainer` is a colon which should always be escaped in CSS by a backslash
- A style class can be used several times, while an ID can only be used once
- IDs can be changed accidentally while refactoring and developers have to change the client IDs in CSS too

Namespacing is not needed if you want to change styles for all components of the same type. In this case, `.customStyles` should be omitted.

Use `h:outputStylesheet` to add custom CSS files to your JSF application. An example:

```
<h:outputStylesheet library="css" name="customStyles.css"/>
```

How it works...

Custom styles will be rendered after the PrimeFaces theme (skinning) and component (structural) styles. The correct output is ensured by the PrimeFaces resource ordering. Therefore, custom styles, being rendered after PrimeFaces ones, overwrite the default settings.

We used the `!important` keyword to set a fixed width for the container and the label of `selectOneMenu`. This was necessary because `selectOneMenu` renders the width as an inline style in HTML markup, for example, `style="width:76px"`. Inline styles always have the highest specificity and win against IDs and other CSS selectors. The different weight of selectors is usually the reason why your CSS rules are not applied to some elements, although you think they should have.

 You can learn about CSS specificity (weight of selectors) at **World Wide Web Consortium (W3C)** `http://w3.org/TR/CSS21/cascade.html#specificity`.

To remove the default border and background settings for `Tree`, we applied the `none` keyword on the `border` and `background` properties.

There's more...

Generally, to distinguish between input and non-input elements, there is a style class `ui-inputfield` assigned to every input element. Examples of components with `ui-inputfield` are `p:inputText`, `p:inputTextarea`, `p:calendar` and `p:spinner`. There are also additional CSS selectors on those elements such as `ui-state-disabled`. They affect the look and feel for various states. To modify default styles on input components, we should overwrite the style classes `ui-inputfield`, `ui-state-disabled`, `ui-state-error`, `ui-state-default`, `ui-state-focus`, and so on. In the following code snippet, we have removed the border, background and shadow on input components. Furthermore, we have changed the styling of disabled inputs and assigned a custom background to the `ui-state-error` style class, which is applied to inputs when the validation fails:

```css
.ui-inputfield {
  background: #ffffff;
  -moz-box-shadow: none;
  -webkit-box-shadow: none;
  box-shadow: none;
  color: #000000;
}

.ui-inputfield.ui-state-focus {
  -moz-box-shadow: none;
  -webkit-box-shadow: none;
  box-shadow: none;
}

.ui-inputfield.ui-state-default {
  background: none;
  border: 1px inset;
}

.ui-inputfield.ui-state-disabled,
.ui-state-disabled .ui-inputfield {
  background-color: #8F8F8F;
  border: solid 1px gray;
}

.ui-inputfield.ui-state-error,
.ui-state-error .ui-inputfield {
  background-color: #F43939;
}
```

We write `.ui-inputfield` concatenated with `.ui-state-default`, `.ui-state-disabled`, `.ui-state-error`, `.ui-state-focus`, and so on. because these style classes are defined on the same HTML elements.

The order of resource rendering may be broken when you use dynamic includes (the `ui:include` tag with the dynamic `src` attribute bound to a bean). CSS resources for dynamic included component tags, which were not presented on the page before including, are being added to the head as the last elements. That means that the existing custom styles will be rendered before, and not after, the newly added PrimeFaces styles.

PrimeFaces Cookbook Showcase application

This recipe is available in the demo web application on GitHub (`https://github.com/ova2/primefaces-cookbook/tree/second-edition`). Clone the project if you have not done it yet, explore the project structure, build, and deploy the WAR file on every Servlet 3.x compatible application server such as *JBoss WildFly* or *Apache TomEE*.

The showcase for the recipe is available at `http://localhost:8080/pf-cookbook/views/chapter2/customThemeStyles.jsf`.

See also

> ► Refer to the *Improved resource ordering* recipe from *Chapter 1, Getting Started with PrimeFaces*, for better understanding of PrimeFaces resource ordering

Adjusting the font and size throughout the web application

Each PrimeFaces theme has a specific font family and font size, which can differ from theme to theme. This may have a disadvantage in a multi-theme application because switching from one theme to another would cause a broken layout. Furthermore, default font sizes of themes might be bigger than expected. Hence, it is important to know how to change font properties of the PrimeFaces components globally.

In this recipe, we will learn how to adjust the font family and font size throughout the web application.

How to do it...

A simple way to change fonts globally can be accomplished by using the `.ui-widget` style class. An example of smaller font is as follows:

```
.ui-widget, .ui-widget .ui-widget {
  font-size: 90% !important;
}
```

Using !important in CSS can sometimes be useful to force a rule, so that you can place your CSS in any order in HTML.

This might not be enough in some cases, especially when you mix PrimeFaces and JSF standard components based on native HTML pendants. In this case, more CSS selectors are required to be listed in order to adjust fonts globally. Assume that we have decided to use the font **Arial** with size as 12 pixel. CSS selectors working for all known components would be as in the following code:

```
body,
input,
select,
textarea,
button,
.ui-widget,
.ui-widget input,
.ui-widget select,
.ui-widget textarea,
.ui-widget button,
.ui-widget-header,
.ui-widget-content,
.ui-widget-header .ui-widget-header,
.ui-widget-content .ui-widget-content {
    font-family: Arial, Verdana, sans-serif;
    font-size: 12px !important;
}
```

 The universal selector * is much shorter, but it has no CSS specificity. Its specificity is 0,0,0,0. That means, it cannot overwrite, for example, an inline style with a specified font size.

How it works...

All PrimeFaces components are styled by the ui-widget style class. It is a skinning style specified by jQuery ThemeRoller and applied to HTML elements rendered by PrimeFaces. An input element has it, for instance:

```
<input type="text" class="ui-inputfield ui-inputtext ui-widget ui-
    state-default ui-corner-all" name="..." id="..." role="textbox">
```

In rare cases, when some component parts have been assigned font properties, but are not styled by .ui-widget or you use non-PrimeFaces components, more CSS selectors are needed for changing font properties throughout the web application.

See also

▸ More explanation for CSS selectors in the PrimeFaces-based applications can be found in the *Understanding structural and skinning CSS* and *Customizing default theme styles* recipes

Simple ways to create a new theme

We sometimes need to create our own themes instead of using the predefined ones. Web applications should often feature a company-specific look and feel, which is constant and preset by company-wide style guides. Creating new themes is easy with PrimeFaces because it is powered by the ThemeRoller CSS Framework (`http://jqueryui.com/themeroller`). ThemeRoller provides a powerful and easy-to-use online visual tool.

In this recipe, we will systematically show all the required steps to create a new theme.

Getting ready

To gain first-hand experience of the ThemeRoller online visual tool, go to the ThemeRoller home page, explore the available theme's **Gallery**, and play with the CSS properties to see changes for jQuery widgets embedded on the page. All CSS changes will be applied on the fly.

How to do it...

The simplest way to make our own theme is to modify one of the existing PrimeFaces themes. Choose one from the PrimeFaces Theme Gallery (`http://primefaces.org/themes`), which is close to your needs. All the themes are downloadable JAR files. The JAR structure is listed here (example for the **Home** theme):

```
- jar
  - META-INF
    - resources
      - primefaces-home
        - theme.css
          - images
            - ...
```

Assume that our new theme has the name `funny`. We can now create the following structure in a web project below the `resources` folder:

```
- war
  - resources
    - primefaces-funny
      - theme.css
        - images
          - ...
```

Or create quite a new JAR project for the new theme as follows:

```
- jar
  - META-INF
    - resources
      - primefaces-funny
        - theme.css
          - images
            - ...
```

The second way is preferred because it would be conforming to the PrimeFaces theme convention. JAR files can be shared across multiple web applications by adding them to the classpath. The last step consists of modifying `theme.css` according to our needs. Knowledge of CSS selectors is necessary.

If no predefined theme matches our requirements, we should use the ThemeRoller online tool. We have to select one of the existing themes (the **Gallery** tab) and edit it (the **Roll Your Own** tab). A click on the **Download theme** button accomplishes the work.

We should choose the **Deselect all components** option on the **Download** page so that our new theme only includes the skinning styles.

Next, we need to migrate the downloaded theme files from ThemeRoller to the PrimeFaces theme infrastructure. The migration steps are straightforward.

1. The theme package that we have downloaded will have a CSS file `jquery-ui-{version}.custom.css` and a folder `images`. Extract the package and rename the CSS file as `theme.css`.

2. Image references in the `theme.css` file must be converted to JSF expressions, which can be understood by the JSF resource loading mechanism. An example for the original CSS file would be as follows:

   ```
   url("images/ui-bg_highlight-hard_100_f9f9f9.png")
   ```

   This should be converted to the following:

   ```
   url("#{resource['primefaces-funny:images/ui-bg_highlight-
     hard_100_f9f9f9.png']}")
   ```

3. Create a JAR theme project with the structure shown in this section.

4. Once the JAR file is in the classpath, we can use it as per the configuration in `web.xml`.

   ```
   <context-param>
     <param-name>primefaces.THEME</param-name>
     <param-value>funny</param-value>
   </context-param>
   ```

How it works...

JSF 2 has a built-in facility for serving resources. The JSF implementation looks for resources in two locations and in the following order:

- `/resources`: This location represents resources in the web application itself
- `/META-INF/resources`: This location represents resources on the classpath

The syntax for image references in CSS files is `#{resource[...]}`; it activates this facility and allows to load resources from JAR files.

The PrimeFaces' renderer implementation for the `<h:head>` tag automatically detects the current configured theme in `web.xml` and renders theme-related resources on the page.

There's more...

There is also a third-party *Theme Converter* application where you can upload your custom theme (zip file) created with ThemeRoller (`https://themeroller.osnode.com/themeroller`). The application will generate a JAR file for you. This is the easiest way to create your custom themes without requiring knowledge of CSS.

Stateless and stateful theme switchers

Multi-theme web applications require a theme switcher component. The default PrimeFaces' theme switcher is a component which enables switching themes on the fly, without sending an AJAX or a full-page request. We speak about a stateless theme switcher because the current selected theme is only known on the client side. Users also often need a stateful theme switcher to save the chosen theme on the server side in user preferences or settings.

In this recipe, we will show the usage of a stateless theme switcher and implement a stateful theme switcher, which is able to save the current selected theme on the server side.

How to do it...

The theme switcher usage is very similar to the usage of `p:selectOneMenu`. The component is represented by the `p:themeSwitcher` tag and accepts `f:selectItem` or `f:selectItems`. The code snippet for a stateless theme switcher is as follows:

```
<p:themeSwitcher style="width:165px" effect="fade">
  <f:selectItem itemLabel="Choose Theme" itemValue=""/>
  <f:selectItems value="#{userSettingsBean.themes}"/>
</p:themeSwitcher>
```

Themes are prepared in a CDI bean `UserSettingsBean`:

```
@Named
@SessionScoped
public class UserSettingsBean implements Serializable {

  private Map<String, String> themes;

  public Map<String, String> getThemes() {
    return themes;
  }

  @PostConstruct
  public void init() {
    themes = new TreeMap<String, String>();
```

```
    themes.put("Afterdark", "afterdark");

    ...
    themes.put("Vader", "vader");
    }
}
```

The next code snippet demonstrates a stateful theme switcher:

```
<p:themeSwitcher value="#{userSettingsBean.theme}" var="t"
  style="width:170px" effect="fade"
  converter="#{themeConverter}"
  onchange="$('#mainForm').submit()">
  <f:selectItems value="#{userSettingsBean.availableThemes}"
    var="theme"
    itemLabel="#{theme.displayName}"
    itemValue="#{theme}"/>
  <p:column>
    <h:graphicImage library="images"
      name="themes/#{t.name}.png"/>
  </p:column>
  <p:column>
    #{t.displayName}
  </p:column>
</p:themeSwitcher>
```

It supports the display of theme previews in the form of small images.

The implementation requires `p:column`. This theme switcher sends full-page requests when the user changes themes. `UserSettingsBean` is a bean class providing getters / setters for the current selected theme and a public method `List<Theme> getAvailableThemes()`. This method returns all available themes as a list of instances of type `Theme`. The model class `Theme` consists of two attributes, `displayName` and `name`:

```
public class Theme implements Serializable {

  private String displayName;
  private String name;

  public Theme(String displayName, String name) {
    this.displayName = displayName;
    this.name = name;
  }

  // getters
  ...
}
```

How it works...

The resource URL to `theme.css` contains a current theme name. The stateless theme switcher changes the theme name in the resource URL by JavaScript. The changed resource link streams down a new `theme.css` to the page dependent on the user selection.

In the second example for the stateful theme switcher, we defined a JavaScript `onchange` callback to submit the closest form with a current selected theme. It results in a regular HTTP request. The `p:column` tag is needed to display table-like custom content. The model class `Theme` encapsulates the displayed name and the name of the picture for every single theme and exposes this information on the page via the `var` attribute.

In case you would like to be notified when a user changes the theme (for example, to update user preferences), you can use an attached `p:ajax`:

```
<p:themeSwitcher value="#{userSettingsBean.theme}">
  <f:selectItems value="#{userSettingsBean.themes}"/>
  <p:ajax listener="#{userSettingsBean.saveTheme}"/>
</p:themeSwitcher>
```

There's more...

We used a JSF converter for the stateful theme switcher, which was developed as a CDI bean. The converter as bean allows to inject another bean into the converter instance. In our case, we injected an instance of `UserSettingsBean`:

```
@Named
@SessionScoped
public class ThemeConverter implements Serializable, Converter {

  @Inject
  private UserSettingsBean userSettingsBean;

  public Object getAsObject(FacesContext context, UIComponent
    component, String value) {
    List<Theme> themes = userSettingsBean.getAvailableThemes();
    for (Theme theme : themes) {
      if (theme.getName().equals(value)) {
        return theme;
      }
    }

    return null;
  }

  public String getAsString(FacesContext context, UIComponent
    component, Object value) {
    return ((Theme) value).getName();
  }
}
```

PrimeFaces Cookbook Showcase application

This recipe is available in the demo web application on GitHub (https://github.com/ova2/primefaces-cookbook/tree/second-edition). Clone the project if you have not done it yet, explore the project structure, build and deploy the WAR file on every Servlet 3.x compatible application server such as *JBoss WildFly* or *Apache TomEE*.

The showcase for the recipe is available at http://localhost:8080/pf-cookbook/views/chapter2/statelessThemeSwitcher.jsf and http://localhost:8080/pf-cookbook/views/chapter2/statefulThemeSwitcher.jsf.

Integrating Font Awesome with PrimeFaces

The jQuery ThemeRoller provides various icons and corresponding style classes, but the number of icons is limited. If you need more icons, check out the *Font Awesome* project. (`http://fortawesome.github.io/Font-Awesome`). *Font Awesome* gives you hundreds of scalable vector icons that can be customized—size, color, drop shadow, and anything that can be done with the power of CSS. With a little effort, you are able to use many new icons in your JSF application in the same way that you use predefined icons from ThemeRoller.

In this recipe, we will learn step- by- step how to integrate additional icons from *Font Awesome* with PrimeFaces themes. We will develop an example with custom icons for buttons and links.

How to do it...

First of all, we need two dependencies in the `pom.xml` (two JAR files in the classpath)—one for the premade Font Awesome JAR created by the *WebJars* project (`http://webjars.org`) and one for the *OmniFaces* (`http://omnifaces.org`):

```
<dependency>
    <groupId>org.webjars</groupId>
    <artifactId>font-awesome</artifactId>
    <version>4.2.0</version>
</dependency>
<dependency>
    <groupId>org.omnifaces</groupId>
    <artifactId>omnifaces</artifactId>
    <version>1.8.1</version>
</dependency>
```

The next steps are straightforward. Register *OmniFacess'* `UnmappedResourceHandler` in `faces-config.xml`:

```
<application>
    ...
    <resource-handler>
      org.omnifaces.resourcehandler.UnmappedResourceHandler
    </resource-handler>
</application>
```

In `web.xml`, add `/javax.faces.resource/*` to `FacesServlet` URL-mapping:

```
<servlet>
  <servlet-name>Faces Servlet</servlet-name>
  <servlet-class>javax.faces.webapp.FacesServlet</servlet-class>
  <load-on-startup>1</load-on-startup>
```

```
  </servlet>
  <servlet-mapping>
    <servlet-name>Faces Servlet</servlet-name>
    <url-pattern>/javax.faces.resource/*</url-pattern>
    <url-pattern>*.jsf</url-pattern>
  </servlet-mapping>
```

And the following `mime-type` mappings:

```
<mime-mapping>
  <extension>eot</extension>
  <mime-type>application/vnd.ms-fontobject</mime-type>
</mime-mapping>
<mime-mapping>
  <extension>otf</extension>
  <mime-type>font/opentype</mime-type>
</mime-mapping>
<mime-mapping>
  <extension>ttf</extension>
  <mime-type>application/x-font-ttf</mime-type>
</mime-mapping>
<mime-mapping>
  <extension>woff</extension>
  <mime-type>application/x-font-woff</mime-type>
</mime-mapping>
<mime-mapping>
  <extension>svg</extension>
  <mime-type>image/svg+xml</mime-type>
</mime-mapping>
<mime-mapping>
  <extension>ico</extension>
  <mime-type>image/x-icon</mime-type>
</mime-mapping>
```

The last step is including `font-awesome.css` from the *Font Awesome* JAR file, which is available via the Maven dependency:

```
<h:outputStylesheet name="webjars/font-awesome/4.2.0/css/font-
  awesome.css"/>
```

Let us now develop PrimeFaces buttons and links with some custom icons. All available icons can be viewed on the *Font Awesome* site at `http://fontawesome.io/icons`. The pattern for the icons' style class is always the same—`fa fa-*` where * is an icon name:

```
<p:commandButton value="Area Chart" icon="fa fa-area-chart"
  style="margin-right:10px;"/>
```

```
<p:commandButton value="Bar Chart" icon="fa fa-bar-chart"/>

<p/>

<p:commandLink style="margin-right:15px;">
  <i class="fa fa-linux"/>
  <h:outputText value="Linux" style="margin-left:5px;"/>
</p:commandLink>
<p:commandLink>
  <i class="fa fa-windows"/>
  <h:outputText value="Windows" style="margin-left:5px;"/>
</p:commandLink>

<p/>

<p:selectBooleanButton onLabel="Bus" offLabel="Taxi"
  onIcon="fa fa-bus" offIcon="fa fa-taxi"
  style="width:80px"/>

<style type="text/css">
  .ui-icon.fa {
    text-indent: 0;
    margin-top: -6px;
  }
</style>
```

The result looks as follows:

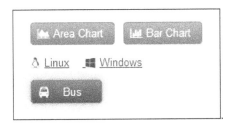

How it works...

WebJars are client-side web libraries packaged into JAR files. The project structure inside a JAR file is compatible with the JSF resource identifier format. *OmniFaces'* `UnmappedResourceHandler` is typically needed to manage the JSF resource handling in third-party CSS files, such as `font-awesome.css`. Third-party files normally contain relative URLs to images and don't have `#{resource[...]}` to activate the JSF 2 facility for resources loading from JAR files. The `UnmappedResourceHandler` helps to load images by relative URLs in CSS files.

Setting `text-indent` to 0 pixels is required for overriding the PrimeFaces own `ui-icon` style `{text-indent: -99999px}`:

```
.ui-icon.fa {
  text-indent: 0;
}
```

There's more...

PrimeFaces 5.1.1 (and upwards) bundles *Font Awesome* and provides the CSS tuning of components for the icons. Any component that provides an icon attribute such as a button or menu item can accept an icon from the *Font Awesome* project. In order to enable this feature, a context parameter in `web.xml` is required:

```
<context-param>
  <param-name>primefaces.FONT_AWESOME</param-name>
  <param-value>true</param-value>
</context-param>
```

See also

▸   Some inside information for the JSF 2 built-in facility for serving resources is available in the *Simple ways to create a new theme* recipe

PrimeFaces Cookbook Showcase application

This recipe is available in the demo web application on GitHub (`https://github.com/ova2/primefaces-cookbook/tree/second-edition`). Clone the project if you have not done it yet, explore the project structure, build and deploy the WAR file on every Servlet 3.x compatible application server such as *JBoss WildFly* or *Apache TomEE*.

The showcase for the recipe is available at `http://localhost:8080/pf-cookbook/views/chapter2/fontAwesome.jsf`.

3
Enhanced Inputs and Selects

In this chapter, we will cover the following topics:

- ▸ Formatted input with inputMask
- ▸ Auto suggestion with autoComplete
- ▸ Usable features of inputTextArea
- ▸ Discovering selectBooleanCheckbox and selectManyCheckbox
- ▸ Choosing a single item with selectOneMenu
- ▸ Basic and advanced calendar scenarios
- ▸ Spinner – different ways to provide input
- ▸ Slider – different ways to provide input
- ▸ Rich text editing with the editor
- ▸ Advanced editing with an in-place editor
- ▸ Enhanced password input
- ▸ Star-based rating input

Introduction

In this chapter, we will learn how to work with the input and select components available in PrimeFaces. PrimeFaces provides over 25 components for data input, which extend standard corresponding JSF components with skinning capabilities and useful features such as user-friendly interface, validation, and so on.

Formatted input with inputMask

`inputMask` minimizes the chances for the user to input incorrect data. It applies client-side validation with the provided masking template.

How to do it...

A basic example of an input mask for a phone number input would be as follows:

```
<p:inputMask value="#{inputMaskBean.phone}"
  mask="(999) 999-9999"/>
```

As can be seen with the mask `(999) 999-9999`, it is stated that only numbers can be input along with the parenthesis and dashed structure. The initial visual of the input will be as seen in the following screenshot:

The fields that are filled up with number `9` in the mask will be empty and the rest will be rendered with the initial phase. The character `9` is used to depict only numeric characters that could be input for the field. By providing the alphabetic character `a`, input could also be restricted to alphabetic characters only. An example would be the input of a product key, as follows:

```
<p:inputMask value="#{inputMaskBean.productKey}" mask="a999-a9"/>
```

This will restrict the input of the first characters of the two sections that are separated by the dash, only to the alphabetic characters.

How it works...

The `inputMask` component decorates the input text component with JavaScript to provide the masking feature. With each `keypress` event, the value is checked against the mask provided for the validation on the client-side. The component will unmask itself when the `readonly` attribute is set to `true`. PrimeFaces wraps *masked input plugin* of jQuery for the `inputMask` component.

There's more...

There is also the `slotChar` attribute, which renders the character(s) given in the template. The default value of the `slotChar` is the _ character. For instance, we can change the `slotChar` value for the phone input with the definition X; the component would be defined as follows:

```
<p:inputMask value="#{inputMaskBean.phone}"
  mask="(999) 999-9999" slotChar="X" />
```

The component will be rendered as shown in the following screenshot:

 The `placeHolder` attribute for the `inputMask` component is deprecated with PrimeFaces version 5.1 since `placeHolder` conflicts with the HTML5 placeholder attribute. Please use the `slotChar` attribute instead if you are upgrading from a version prior to 5.1.

Using the asterisk (*) character

With the asterisk character, we can represent an alphanumeric character to be input by the user, which could be A to Z, a to z, or 0 to 9.

```
<p:inputMask value="#{inputMaskBean.productKey}"
  mask="a*-999-a999" />
```

With the preceding `inputMask` definition, inputs such as `ac-223-a481` or `a2-223-a481` will be validated as `true`.

Making a part of the mask optional

It is also possible to make a part of the mask optional with the use of a question mark character. Anything listed after ? within the mask definition will be considered as an optional user input. A common example for this is a phone number with an optional extension:

```
<p:inputMask value="#{inputMaskBean.phoneExt}"
  mask="(999) 999-9999? x99999" />
```

When the user finishes the input by reaching the ? character and un-focusing the component, the rest of the validation will be skipped, and the input up to that section will not be erased. Input values such as `(555) 204-2551` or `(555) 204-2551 x1980` will be valid for this optional input.

Dynamically changing the mask value

With the help of some JavaScript, it's also possible to change the mask value of the component dynamically. In the screenshot given next, we define two masks, one is (99) 9999-9999, which is the default value, and the other one is (99) 9-9999-9999, which is enabled when checkbox gets clicked:

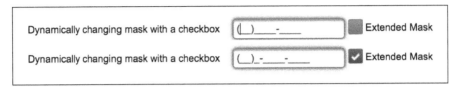

The JavaScript and component definition would be as follows:

```
<script type="text/javascript">
  function setMask() {
    var c = PF('cbxMask');
    var i = PF('phoneMask');
    if (c.isChecked()) {
      i.jq.mask('(99)9-9999-9999');
      i.jq.focus();
    } else {
      i.jq.mask('(99)9999-9999');
      i.jq.focus();
    }

  }
</script>

<p:inputMask id="phone" widgetVar="phoneMask"
  value="#{inputMaskBean.phone2}" mask="(99)9999-9999"/>
<p:selectBooleanCheckbox itemLabel="Extended Mask"
  onchange="setMask()" widgetVar="cbxMask"/>
```

PrimeFaces Cookbook Showcase application

This recipe is available in the demo web application on GitHub (https://github.com/ova2/primefaces-cookbook/tree/second-edition). Clone the project if you have not done it yet, explore the project structure, and build and deploy the WAR file on every Servlet 3.x compatible application server, such as *JBoss WildFly* or *Apache TomEE*.

The showcase for the recipe is available under http://localhost:8080/pf-cookbook/views/chapter3/inputMask.jsf.

Auto suggestion with autoComplete

The autoComplete component provides suggestions while you type into the input field. This enables users to quickly find and select from the list of looked-up values as they type, which leverages the searching and filtering abilities.

How to do it...

For simple usage of the autoComplete component, all we need to do is to define the complete method that will be invoked with the user input, as follows:

```
<p:autoComplete id="simple" value="#{autoCompleteBean.txt1}"
    completeMethod="#{autoCompleteBean.complete}" />
```

This will be rendered as shown in the following screenshot:

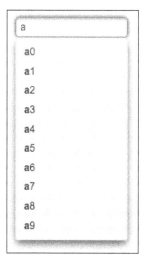

As the user types characters into the input text (as shown in the preceding screenshot) the component will assist 10 selections by appending numbers from 0 to 9. The completeMethod implemented for this in the autoCompleteBean backing bean is shown in the following code snippet. The user input is passed as the parameter to the method:

```
public List<String> complete(String input) {
  List<String> result = new ArrayList<String>();
  for (int i = 0; i < 10; i++) {
    result.add(input + i);
  }
  return result;
}
```

There are several attributes that could be used with the `autoComplete` component. With the `minQueryLength` attribute, we can specify the number of characters to be typed before starting query; its default value is `1`. This minimizes the unnecessary lookups that could be done to the server since the input provided by the user, a couple of characters probably, is often not enough for meaningful prediction most of the time.

With the `queryDelay` attribute, we can specify the delay in milliseconds before sending each query to the server; its default value is 300 ms. This minimizes the round trips that are done to the server to reduce the load on the execution of `completeMethod`.

With the `forceSelection` attribute, a component only accepts input from the selection list; so the typed characters will be transient if no selection is made. This forces the user to select the proper content that could be validated properly via the assistance of the component. The user can also leave the component intact with no selection. Its default value is `false`.

When set to `true`, the `dropdown` attribute provides the `autoComplete` component to be used as a dropdown by rendering the drop-down icon. This will enable the selection of any of the `autoComplete` items by the user without inputting any character.

Starting with version 4.0, when the `cache` attribute is set to `true`, the `autoComplete` component caches previous server side suggestions on the client side if the same query is provided by the user. A time out value can also be set in milliseconds with the `cacheTimeout` attribute.

By default, `autoComplete` does not provide any feedback to the user when no records are found for the suggestion. To achieve this, the `emptyMessage` attribute can be used to display a custom message to the user.

There's more...

Instead of working with primitive types, most of the time we would be using the `autoComplete` component with domain objects. The basic definition of the component for listing the cars for a given brand, for example, would be as follows:

```
<p:autoComplete id="carPOJO"
  value="#{autoCompleteBean.selectedCar}"
  completeMethod="#{autoCompleteBean.completeCar}"
  var="car" itemLabel="#{car.name}" itemValue="#{car}"
  forceSelection="true">
<f:converter
  converterId="org.primefaces.cookbook.converter.CarConverter"
  />
<p:column>
  <p:graphicImage
    value="/resources/images/autocomplete/#{car.name}.png"/>
```

```
      </p:column>
      <p:column>#{car.name}</p:column>
    </p:autoComplete>
```

Here, the component contains column definitions along with a converter declaration. The converter is responsible for converting the submitted value for each car, and with the help of the columns, we render images along with the name of each car. This will enhance the autocompletion for the user, and will ease the selection. The visual of the component definition will be as seen in this screenshot:

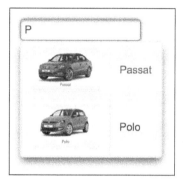

Instant AJAX selection

It's also possible to invoke a server-side method instantly when an item from `autoComplete` is selected. The `autoComplete` component provides the `itemSelect` AJAX behavior event that will be fired instantly when an item is selected:

```
    <p:autoComplete value="#{autoCompleteBean.txt1}"
      completeMethod="#{autoCompleteBean.complete}">
      <p:ajax event="itemSelect"
        listener="#{autoCompleteBean.handleSelect}"
        update="messages" />
    </p:autoComplete>
```

The `itemSelect` method will be invoked with `org.primefaces.event.SelectEvent`. The current value of the selected item can be retrieved with `event.getObject()`, and a Faces message could be added with the current item, as in the following code snippet:

```
    public void handleSelect(SelectEvent event) {
      Object selectedObject = event.getObject();
      MessageUtil.addInfoMessage("selected.object", selectedObject);
    }
```

Multiple selection

With `autoComplete`, it is also possible to select multiple items by setting the `multiple` attribute to `true`:

```
<p:autoComplete id="multipleSelect"
  value="#{autoCompleteBean.selectedTexts}"
  completeMethod="#{autoCompleteBean.complete}"
  multiple="true" />
```

With the help of multiple select, the selected texts can be retrieved as a list in `autoCompleteBean.selectedTexts`, which maps to the property `List<String> selectedTexts`.

Adding item tip

The `autoComplete` component offers an advanced built-in tooltip that gets visible when the mouse is hovered over the suggested items. The following is the screenshot of the tooltip that is rendered for the `Car` domain objects:

The content of the tooltip can be defined within a facet named `itemtip` as follows:

```
<p:autoComplete id="itemTip"
  value="#{autoCompleteBean.selectedCar2}"
  completeMethod="#{autoCompleteBean.completeCar}"
  var="car" itemLabel="#{car.name}" itemValue="#{car}">
  <f:converter
    converterId="org.primefaces.cookbook.converter.CarConverter"
    />
  <f:facet name="itemtip">
    <h:panelGrid columns="2" cellpadding="5">
      <p:graphicImage
        value="/resources/images/autocomplete/#{car.name}.png"
        width="80" height="50"/>
```

```
            <h:outputText value="#{car.name} &lt;br/&gt;
               #{car.year}" escape="false" />
         </h:panelGrid>
      </f:facet>
   </p:autoComplete>
```

Grouping on items

With the value provided to the `groupBy` attribute, it's possible to create groups for the suggested items list. The following screenshot groups a list of cars whose names contain the query string:

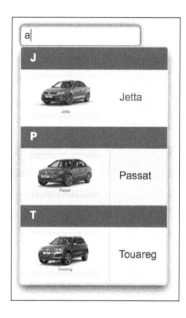

The names of the groups are created from the first character of each car's name. The component declaration and method definition for this grouping is given here:

```
<p:autoComplete id="grouped"
   value="#{autoCompleteBean.selectedCar}"
      completeMethod="#{autoCompleteBean.completeCarContains}
      var="car" itemLabel="#{car.name}" itemValue="#{car}"
      forceSelection="true"
      groupBy="#{autoCompleteBean.getGroup(car)}">
   <f:converter
      converterId="org.primefaces.cookbook.converter.CarConverter"
      />
```

```
    <p:column>
      <p:graphicImage
        value="/resources/images/autocomplete/#{car.name}.png"/>
    </p:column>
    <p:column>#{car.name}</p:column>
  </p:autoComplete>

  public char getGroup(Car car) {
    return car.getName().charAt(0);
  }
```

PrimeFaces Cookbook Showcase application

This recipe is available in the demo web application on GitHub (`https://github.com/ova2/primefaces-cookbook/tree/second-edition`). Clone the project if you have not done it yet, explore the project structure, and build and deploy the WAR file on every Servlet 3.x compatible application server, such as *JBoss WildFly* or *Apache TomEE*.

The showcase for the recipe is available under `http://localhost:8080/pf-cookbook/views/chapter3/autoComplete.jsf`.

Usable features of inputTextArea

The `inputTextArea` component is an extension to the HTML `<textarea>` component with special capabilities, such as auto-growing, auto-resizing, and remaining-character count.

How to do it...

A basic definition for the input text area would be as follows:

```
<p:inputTextarea value="#{inputTextAreaBean.value}" />
```

This will render an input text area with the default values `rows='3'` and `cols='20'` as shown in the following screenshot:

The component also provides auto-resizing with the `autoResize` attribute that allows us to expand the height automatically when the text input overflows. The default value is `true`. If you want to get the vertical scrollbar, you need to set the `autoResize` to `false`.

Like the HTML `<textarea>` component, we can also specify the `rows` and `cols` attributes to specify the size of the text area component in rows and columns.

How it works...

The JavaScript plugin for the `inputTextArea` component is solely implemented by PrimeFaces with jQuery. Auto-resizing is executed on the `keyup`, `focus`, and `blur` JavaScript events and it increases the number of rows that the component owns. Remaining character count is executed on the `keyup` event, and the content gets trimmed if `maxlength` is exceeded. We will get to this trimming feature in the next section.

There's more...

With the `maxlength` attribute, we can limit the maximum allowed characters to be input to the component. There are two more attributes, `counter` and `counterTemplate`, which will dynamically output the number of characters left to be input to the component easily:

```
<p:inputTextarea value="#{bean.propertyName}" counter="display"
  maxlength="20" counterTemplate="{0} characters remaining" />
<h:outputText id="display" />
```

The `counter` attribute should refer to the ID of the label component to display the remaining characters; `counterTemplate` will contain the template text to display in `counter`, with the default value `{0}`. Either `<h:outputText>` or `<p:outputLabel>` can be used as the label component.

Since the maximum length constraint is being triggered by keyboard inputs, it's not possible to control the length of the input if the user right clicks to the text area canvas and pastes his own text content that will exceed the maximum length. To disable pasting, use pass through attributes of JSF 2.2, as given here:

```
<p:inputTextarea value="#{inputTextAreaBean.value}"
  counter="display2" maxlength="20"
  counterTemplate="{0} characters remaining">
<f:passThroughAttribute name="onpaste"
  value="return false;" />
</p:inputTextarea>
```

Autocomplete on content

By defining the `completeMethod` attribute, the `inputTextarea` component also offers autocomplete functionality. The following definition will try to complete input queries at a minimum of 4 characters length:

```
<p:inputTextarea completeMethod="#{inputTextAreaBean.complete}"
   queryDelay="500" minQueryLength="4" cols="40" />
```

```
public List<String> complete(String query) {
   List<String> results = new ArrayList<String>();

   if(query.equals("PrimeFaces")) {
      results.add("PrimeFaces Rocks!!!");
      results.add("PrimeFaces has 100+ components.");
      results.add("PrimeFaces is lightweight.");
      results.add("PrimeFaces Cookbook
        is the best source for PrimeFaces!");
   }
   else {
      for(int i = 0; i < 10; i++) {
         results.add(query + i);
      }
   }

   return results;
}
```

PrimeFaces Cookbook Showcase application

This recipe is available in the demo web application on GitHub (`https://github.com/ova2/primefaces-cookbook/tree/second-edition`). Clone the project if you have not done it yet, explore the project structure, and build and deploy the WAR file on every Servlet 3.x compatible application server, such as *JBoss WildFly* or *Apache TomEE*.

The showcase for the recipe is available under `http://localhost:8080/pf-cookbook/views/chapter3/inputTextArea.jsf`.

Discovering selectBooleanCheckbox and selectManyCheckbox

To provide skinning, `selectBooleanCheckbox` and `selectManyCheckbox` extend the default JSF components `<h:selectBooleanCheckbox>` and `<h:selectManyCheckbox>`, respectively.

How to do it...

Basic definitions for `selectBooleanCheckbox` and `selectManyCheckbox` would be as follows:

```
<p:selectBooleanCheckbox
  value="#{selectCheckboxBean.selectedValue}" />

<p:selectManyCheckbox
  value="#{selectCheckboxBean.selectedCountries}">
  <f:selectItem itemLabel="Turkey" itemValue="Turkey" />
  <f:selectItem itemLabel="Germany" itemValue="Germany" />
  <f:selectItem itemLabel="Switzerland" itemValue="Switzerland" />
</p:selectManyCheckbox>
```

Adding labels to the checkbox is easy with the `itemLabel` attribute. The `itemLabel` attribute displays a label next to the checkbox:

```
<p:selectBooleanCheckbox
  value="#{selectCheckboxBean.selectedValue}"
  itemLabel="#{msg['selectBooleanCheckbox.label']}" />
```

The text that will be rendered right next to the `checkbox` component with the `itemLabel` attribute can also be clicked to select/deselect the checkbox. The `msg` resource bundle variable given in the example is defined in `faces-config.xml`.

The direction of contents of the `selectManyCheckbox` component can be changed from the default horizontal rendering to vertical by setting the `layout` attribute with the `pageDirection` value. The output for both horizontal and vertical rendering of the example given in the basic definition is shown in the following screenshot:

There's more...

The layout of `selectManyCheckbox` can be customized with its `columns` attribute, which would specify the maximum number of allowed columns. When it's exceeded the number of `SelectItem` elements given, a new row will be created automatically.

It's also possible to get the state of the checkbox at the client-side via JavaScript. To achieve this, the `widgetVar` attribute needs to be specified to the component. The `widgetVar` attribute defines the client-side variable, which has various responsibilities, such as progressive enhancement of the markup and communication with the server-side via AJAX. It can also be used directly from the JavaScript code as follows:

```
<p:selectBooleanCheckbox
  value="#{selectCheckboxBean.selectedValue}"
  widgetVar="mySelection" />

<p:commandLink value="Alert Selection"
  onclick="alert(PF('mySelection').isChecked());" />
```

Within the `alert` method of the `onclick` event of `commandLink` (a client-side JavaScript call), the state will be retrieved by the `mySelection.isChecked()` code section. The `checkbox` component is being accessed by `mySelection`, which is the name of the client-side widget variable of the checkbox.

Selection with AJAX behavior on selectBooleanCheckbox

We can also invoke server-side code when the checkbox is checked/unchecked. The definition will update the `growl` message component when it's clicked:

```
<p:selectBooleanCheckbox
  value="#{selectCheckboxBean.selectedValue}">
  <p:ajax update="growl"
    listener="#{selectCheckboxBean.addMessage}" />
</p:selectBooleanCheckbox>
```

The server-side `addMessage` method that is called for adding the actual message is as follows:

```
public void addMessage() {
  String summaryKey =
    selectedValue ? "checkbox.checked" : "checkbox.unchecked";
  MessageUtil.addInfoMessage(summaryKey);

}
```

This will add a Faces message that corresponds to the given key from the defined resource bundle.

PrimeFaces Cookbook Showcase application

This recipe is available in the demo web application on GitHub (`https://github.com/ova2/primefaces-cookbook/tree/second-edition`). Clone the project if you have not done it yet, explore the project structure, and build and deploy the WAR file on every Servlet 3.x compatible application server, such as *JBoss WildFly* or *Apache TomEE*.

The showcase for the recipe is available under `http://localhost:8080/pf-cookbook/views/chapter3/selectBooleanCheckboxSelectManyCheckbox.jsf`.

See also

For details about the `MessageUtil` class, see the *Internationalization (i18n) and Localization (L10n)* recipe in *Chapter 1, Getting Started with PrimeFaces*.

Choosing a single item with selectOneMenu

The `selectOneMenu` component is an extended version of JSF `selectOneMenu`. It provides custom content display along with skinning capabilities.

How to do it...

The simplest component declaration would be as follows:

```
<p:selectOneMenu>
  <f:selectItem itemLabel="English" itemValue="en"/>
  <f:selectItem itemLabel="Turkish" itemValue="tr"/>
</p:selectOneMenu>
```

The output visual will be as follows:

There's more...

Instead of working with primitive types or just string literals, most of the time we would be using the `selectOneMenu` component with domain objects. The basic definition of the component for listing the cars for a given brand would be as follows:

```
<p:selectOneMenu id="carPOJO"
  value="#{selectOneMenuBean.selectedCar}" var="car">
  <f:converter
    converterId="org.primefaces.cookbook.converter.CarConverter"
    />
  <f:selectItems value="#{selectOneMenuBean.cars}" var="c"
    itemLabel="#{c.name}" itemValue="#{c}" />
  <p:column>
    <p:graphicImage
      value="/resources/images/autocomplete/#{car.name}.png"
      width="80" height="50"/>
  </p:column>
  <p:column>#{car.name}</p:column>
</p:selectOneMenu>
```

Here, the component contains column definitions along with a converter declaration. The converter is responsible for converting the submitted value for each car, and with the help of the columns, we render images along with the name of each car.

 You can find the source code of the `Car` converter class available at `http://bit.ly/CarConverter`.

Also, with the `editable` attribute set to `true`, it becomes possible to choose from a given list or to input your own value.

Filtering on items

The `selectOneMenu` component offers filtering of its contents when the `filter` attribute is set to `true`. When enabled, an input field gets rendered on the drop-down list as overlay and filtering is triggered on the `onkeyup` event of the input. The `filterMatchMode` attribute defines the matching mode for filtering the content. Its values could either be `startsWith`, which is the default value, `contains`, `endsWith`, and `custom`.

When set to `custom`, a JavaScript method name should be provided with the `filterFunction` attribute. The visual of the component, when filtering is enabled, will be similar to the following screenshot:

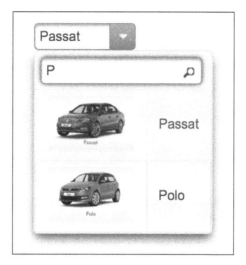

PrimeFaces Cookbook Showcase application

This recipe is available in the demo web application on GitHub (`https://github.com/ova2/primefaces-cookbook/tree/second-edition`). Clone the project if you have not done it yet, explore the project structure, and build and deploy the WAR file on every Servlet 3.x compatible application server, such as *JBoss WildFly* or *Apache TomEE*.

The showcase for the recipe is available under `http://localhost:8080/pf-cookbook/views/chapter3/selectOneMenu.jsf`.

Basic and advanced calendar scenarios

The `calendar` component is used to provide date input with customizable features, such as localization, paging of months, and restriction mechanisms on the date selection.

How to do it...

The simplest component declaration for a basic date selection would be as follows:

```
<p:calendar value="#{calendarBean.date}" />
```

This renders an input text that opens a pop-up date selection dialog when clicked, as shown in the following screenshot:

The pop-up visual of the `calendar` can also be configured to render as an inline visual on the page with the `mode` attribute, as follows:

```
<p:calendar value="#{calendarBean.date}" mode="inline" />
```

The default value of `mode` is `popup`. It is also possible to render multiple months side by side on the page with the `pages` attribute:

```
<p:calendar value="#{calendarBean.date}" pages="3"
  mode="inline" />
```

Paging will start with the month that the given date exists in, and will continue with the number of months specified by the `pages` attribute. The `inline` attribute can also be used along with the paging to display, for instance, three months in a row, as in the preceding example.

The attribute `showOn` defines a client-side event that displays the pop-up calendar. The value `button` can be specified with the `showOn` attribute to render a button right next to the input text field to show the pop-up calendar when clicked. The default value for the `showOn` attribute is `focus`, which will render the popup when the input field gets the focus.

The `mindate` and `maxdate` attributes set the calendar's minimum visible and maximum visible dates. With the following example, the calendar will be rendered with three days available for selection, which are yesterday, today, and tomorrow.

```
<p:calendar id="restrictedDates" value="#{calendarBean.date}"
  mode="inline"
  mindate="#{calendarBean.yesterday}"
  maxdate="#{calendarBean.tomorrow}" />
```

It's also possible to disable the manual input on the input text of a pop-up calendar by setting the `readonlyInput` attribute to `true`.

There's more...

The `pattern` attribute defines the date format that will be applied for localization. A pattern given as `dd.MM.yyyy` will result in a value like `07.01.2015`. A pattern given as `EEE, dd MM, yyyy` will result in the value `Wed, 07 Jan, 2015` for the same date.

It's also possible to invoke a server-side method instantly when a date is selected. The `calendar` component provides the `dateSelect` AJAX behavior event that will be fired instantly when a date is selected:

```
<p:calendar value="#{calendarBean.date}" mode="inline">
  <p:ajax event="dateSelect"
    listener="#{calendarBean.onDateSelect}" update="growl" />
</p:calendar>
```

The `onDateSelect` method will be invoked with `org.primefaces.event.DateSelectEvent`. The current value of the calendar can be retrieved with `event.getDate()`, and a Faces message could be added with the current date, as in the following code snippet:

```
public void onDateSelect(DateSelectEvent event) {
  Date date = event.getDate();
  MessageUtil.addInfoMessage("selected.date", date);
}
```

Localization of the calendar

Defining the locale value to the `locale` attribute provides the localization of the calendar. Definition of a calendar in a Turkish locale would be as follows:

```
<p:calendar locale="tr" mode="inline" id="trCal"/>
```

The `calendar` component uses a shared `PrimeFaces.locales` property to display the labels. PrimeFaces only provides English translations, so in order to localize the calendar, we need to put the corresponding locales into a JavaScript file and include the scripting file to the page, as follows:

```
<h:outputScript library="js" name="turkishLocale.js" />
```

For the usage of the `outputScript` tag, refer to `http://www.mkyong.com/jsf2/how-to-include-javascript-file-in-jsf`. For already translated locales of the calendar, visit `http://code.google.com/p/primefaces/wiki/PrimeFacesLocales`.

Effects with the calendar

When the `calendar` component is in the `popup` mode, effects can be applied for the hide/unhide mechanism of the pop-up dialog box:

```
<p:calendar value="#{calendarBean.date}" effect="bounce"
    effectDuration="slow" />
```

The `effectDuration` attribute can also be set with values `slow`, `normal`, and `fast` to define the duration of the effect. The default value for the duration is `normal`. The list of all the effects that could be used is as follows:

- `blind`
- `bounce`
- `clip`
- `drop`
- `fadeIn`
- `fold`
- `show`
- `slide`
- `slideDown`

Picking time with the calendar

By providing a time format to the `pattern` attribute, the `timePicker` functionality can be enabled:

```
<p:calendar value="#{calendarBean.date}"
    pattern="dd/MM/yyyy HH:mm:ss" />
```

The appearance of the calendar with the time-picking ability would appear as shown in the following screenshot:

To select only time with the `calendar` component, the `timeOnly` attribute should be set to `true`, along with the `pattern` value as `"dd/MM/yyyy HH:mm"`. Sliders of the time input section of the calendar should have the step value 1. In order to change this, the `calendar` component provides three attributes: `stepHour`, `stepMinute`, and `stepSecond`. We can also define ranges for the hour, minute, and second inputs, so as to enable the user to input hours between 3 and 5, minutes between 0 and 30, and seconds between 45 and 55. This is shown in the following code snippet:

```
<p:calendar value="#{calendarBean.date}"
  pattern="dd/MM/yyyy HH:mm:ss"
  minHour="3" maxHour="5"
  minMinute="0" maxMinute="30"
  minSecond="45" maxSecond="55" />
```

To disable entering the date with keyboard input or with pasting, use pass through attributes of JSF 2.2 within the definition of the calendar component, as given here:

```
<f:passThroughAttribute name="onkeypress"
  value="return false;" />
<f:passThroughAttribute name="onpaste"
  value="return false;" />
```

PrimeFaces Cookbook Showcase application

This recipe is available in the demo web application on GitHub (`https://github.com/ova2/primefaces-cookbook/tree/second-edition`). Clone the project if you have not done it yet, explore the project structure, and build and deploy the WAR file on every Servlet 3.x compatible application server, such as *JBoss WildFly* or *Apache TomEE*.

The showcase for the recipe is available under `http://localhost:8080/pf-cookbook/views/chapter3/calendar.jsf`.

See also

For details about the localization of the `calendar` component, see the *Internationalization (i18n) and Localization (L10n)* recipe in *Chapter 1, Getting Started with PrimeFaces*.

Spinner – different ways to provide input

The input component `spinner` provides a numerical input via increment and decrement buttons.

How to do it...

A basic definition of the component would be as follows:

```
<p:spinner value="#{spinnerBean.intValue}" />
```

This will render an input textbox on the page, with controls to increase and decrease the value as shown in the following screenshot:

There's more...

The `stepFactor` attribute defines the stepping factor that will be applied for each increment and decrement with the default value 1. The following definition will increase or decrease the value by 0.5:

```
<p:spinner value="#{spinnerBean.doubleValue}" stepFactor="0.5" />
```

Adding prefix and suffix

The `prefix` and `suffix` attributes provide the ability to place fixed strings on the input field as a prefix or suffix to the input respectively. The first definition will render the $ sign as a prefix, and the second one will render the % sign as a suffix with the value of the input field:

```
<p:spinner value="#{spinnerBean.intValue}" prefix="$" />
```

```
<p:spinner value="#{spinnerBean.intValue}" suffix="%" />
```

Applying boundaries to the input

The `spinner` component also provides attributes to set boundary values on the input value. The `min` attribute defines the minimum boundary value with the minimum value of `java.lang.Double` as default. The `max` attribute defines the maximum boundary value with the maximum value of `java.lang.Double` as default.

The minimum and maximum control on the input field will only get applied on the increment and decrement buttons, and not on manual input done with the keyboard. In order to disable manual input, we need to specify JSF 2.2 pass-through attributes with the name `onkeydown`:

```
<p:spinner value="#{spinnerBean.intValue}" suffix="%"
  min="0" max="100">
  <f:passThroughAttribute name="onkeydown"
    value="return false;" />
</p:spinner>
```

This will result in rendering the `spinner` component with the restriction from 0 to 100, suffixed with the % sign, and disabled with the keyboard input.

Adjusting the width of the spinner

One misleading approach towards setting the width of the `spinner` component is defining the `style` attribute with the `width` value. For example, `style="width:50px;"`, will increase the width of the `spinner` component by having a fixed width for the input part. We can easily resize the field with the `size` attribute, which defines the number of characters used to determine the width of the input element:

```
<p:spinner value="#{spinnerBean.intValue}" size="3" />
```

AJAX update with spinner

It is also possible to update an output field for each click on the spinner, with the `<p:ajax>` component:

```
<p:spinner id="ajaxSpinner" value="#{spinnerBean.intValue2}">
  <p:ajax update="output" process="@this" />
</p:spinner>
<h:outputText id="output" value="#{spinnerBean.intValue2}" />
```

Referring the ID of the `outputText` component with the `update` attribute does the actual update.

PrimeFaces Cookbook Showcase application

This recipe is available in the demo web application on GitHub (`https://github.com/ova2/primefaces-cookbook/tree/second-edition`). Clone the project if you have not done it yet, explore the project structure, and build and deploy the WAR file on every Servlet 3.x compatible application server, such as *JBoss WildFly* or *Apache TomEE*.

The showcase for the recipe is available under `http://localhost:8080/pf-cookbook/views/chapter3/spinner.jsf`.

Slider – different ways to provide input

The `slider` component provides the user with the ability to input a value by using a slider bar. This component requires an input component to work properly.

How to do it...

As mentioned earlier, we first need to define an input component that will be used by the `slider` component. The `for` attribute is used to set the ID of the input component whose input will be provided by the `slider` component. The basic definition of a slider would be as follows:

```
<h:inputText id="basicSlider" value="#{sliderBean.intValue}" />
<p:slider for="basicSlider" />
```

This will render an input text along with a horizontal slider bar as follows:

By default, the slider renders a horizontal bar for sliding. With the `type` attribute, the slider can also be set to render a vertical bar with the value set as `vertical`. The `minValue` attribute defines the minimum value of the slider with the default value as `0`. The `maxValue` attribute defines the maximum value of the slider with the default value as `100`.

 It's possible to provide a minus value for `minValue` attribute but it can only be set via the slider bar of the component. Inputting a hyphen for the minus value with a keyboard is not supported.

By default, the slider provides animation when the background of the slider is clicked. This animation can be enabled/disabled with the `animation` attribute by setting its value as `true` or `false`.

There's more...

The `step` attribute defines the amount of fixed pixels which increment the movement of the slider with the default value of `1`. The `step` attribute only supports integer values:

```
<h:inputText id="steppingSlider" value="#{sliderBean.intValue}" />
<p:slider for="steppingSlider" step="10" />
```

Displaying the value of the slider

With the `display` attribute, we can display the output of the slider while getting input from the user by using an `inputHidden` component. The `display` attribute should refer the `output` component while the `for` attribute refers the hidden input field:

```
<h:outputText id="output" value="#{sliderBean.intValue}" />
<h:inputHidden id="displaySlider"
  value="#{sliderBean.intValue}" />
<p:slider for="displaySlider" display="output" />
```

The `slider` component also provides a `displayTemplate` attribute where we can provide a template while updating the display. A sample usage for the template could be as follows:

```
<h:outputText id="output"
  value="The value is: #{sliderBean.intValue}" />
<h:inputHidden id="displaySlider"
  value="#{sliderBean.intValue}" />
<p:slider for="displaySlider" display="output"
  displayTemplate="The value is: {value}" />
```

Here, `{value}` is a placeholder definition that is being set by the number value selected in the `spinner`.

Disabling manual input with the slider

By default, the `slider` component does not disable the manual input. To get input only with the slider bar, without keyboard input, we need to define the `onfocus` attribute as follows:

```
<h:inputText id="minMaxSlider" value="#{sliderBean.intValue}"
  onfocus="this.readOnly=true;" />
<p:slider for="minMaxSlider" step="10"
  minValue="0" maxValue="100" />
```

This will render an input field and a slider bar for which the user can enter values from 0 to 100 with an increment of 10 only by using the slider bar.

Selecting a range with slider

Range selection is also offered with the `slider` where we can select a minimum and a maximum value. The `range` attribute should be set to `true` in order to achieve this and a comma-separated ID pair should be declared with the `for` attribute, whose IDs are defined by the `inputHidden` components.

The code snippet definition for the range selection is given here:

```
<h:outputText id="outputRange" value="The selected range:
  [#{sliderBean.rangeStart}, #{sliderBean.rangeEnd}]" />
<p:slider for="rangeStart,rangeEnd" style="width:200px"
  range="true" display="outputRange"
  displayTemplate="The selected range: [{min}, {max}]" />
<h:inputHidden id="rangeStart" value="#{sliderBean.rangeStart}" />
<h:inputHidden id="rangeEnd" value="#{sliderBean.rangeEnd}" />
```

The `displayTemplate` attribute can be used with `{min}` and `{max}` placeholders when range selection is enabled. These placeholders will be updated by `spinner` when the user selects his own range. The visual of the range selection is given in the following screenshot:

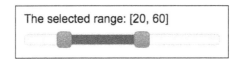

AJAX behavior events on slider

The `slider` provides the `slideEnd` AJAX behavior event that will be fired when the slide gets completed:

```
<h:inputText id="ajaxSliderInput"
  value="#{sliderBean.intValue}" />
<p:slider id="ajaxSlider" for="ajaxSliderInput">
```

```
    <p:ajax event="slideEnd" listener="#{sliderBean.onSlideEnd}"
      update="growl" />
  </p:slider>
```

The `onSlideEnd` method will be invoked with `org.primefaces.event.SlideEndEvent`. The current value of the slider can be retrieved with `event.getValue()`, and a Faces message could be added with the current value, as in the following code snippet:

```
public void onSlideEnd(SlideEndEvent event) {
  int value = event.getValue();
  MessageUtil.addInfoMessage("selected.value", value);
}
```

PrimeFaces Cookbook Showcase application

This recipe is available in the demo web application on GitHub (`https://github.com/ova2/primefaces-cookbook/tree/second-edition`). Clone the project if you have not done it yet, explore the project structure, and build and deploy the WAR file on every Servlet 3.x compatible application server, such as *JBoss WildFly* or *Apache TomEE*.

The showcase for the recipe is available under `http://localhost:8080/pf-cookbook/views/chapter3/slider.jsf`.

See also

For details about the `MessageUtil` class, see the *Internationalization (i18n) and Localization (L10n)* recipe in *Chapter 1, Getting Started with PrimeFaces*.

Rich text editing with the editor

An input component `editor`, provides rich text editing features. It contains a toolbar that can also be configured with custom controls to provide more functionality to the user.

How to do it...

The basic component declaration for `editor`, which renders default controls such as indentation, and font and color selection, would be as follows:

```
<p:editor value="#{editorBean.text}" />
```

The component will be rendered on the page with default controls as shown in the following screenshot:

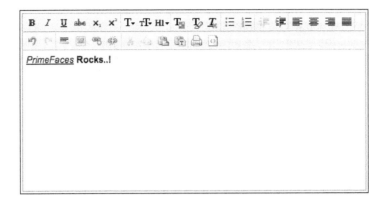

There's more...

The `editor` component offers the `controls` attribute, which can be used to customize the toolbar of the editor. For instance, the following declaration will render only three controls, `bold`, `italic`, and `strikethrough`:

```
<p:editor value="#{editorBean.text}"
  controls="bold italic strikethrough" />
```

The component will be rendered as shown in the following screenshot:

The list of available controls is as follows:

- alignleft
- alignright
- bold
- bullets
- center
- color
- copy
- cut
- font
- highlight
- image
- indent
- italic
- justify
- link
- numbering
- outdent
- paste
- pastetext
- print
- redo
- removeFormat
- rule
- size
- source
- strikethrough
- style
- subscript
- superscript
- underline
- undo
- unlink

Clearing the contents of the editor

The `editor` component also provides a client-side JavaScript API for the execution of methods such as clearing the content of the editor. The `editor` component can be reached within JavaScript with the declaration of the `widgetVar` attribute:

```
<p:editor value="#{editorBean.text}" widgetVar="editor" />
<p:commandButton type="button" value="Clear"
   onclick="PF('editorClear').clear()" icon="ui-icon-close" />
```

Embedding the editor inside a dialog box

We can also embed the `editor` component inside a dialog box to get input from the user in a more user-friendly manner:

```
<p:dialog widgetVar="editorDialog" modal="true">
  <p:editor />
</p:dialog>
<p:commandButton value="Show"
   onclick="PF('editorDialog').show()" />
```

By clicking on the `commandButton`, the dialog box that contains the `editor` component will be rendered on the page as a modal dialog.

The `editor` component is not integrated with ThemeRoller since there is only one icon set for the controls.

 At the time of writing this book, Internationalization is not supported by the `editor` component. All the tool tips for the controls are rendered in English.

PrimeFaces Cookbook Showcase application

This recipe is available in the demo web application on GitHub (`https://github.com/ova2/primefaces-cookbook/tree/second-edition`). Clone the project if you have not done it yet, explore the project structure, and build and deploy the WAR file on every Servlet 3.x compatible application server, such as *JBoss WildFly* or *Apache TomEE*.

The showcase for the recipe is available under `http://localhost:8080/pf-cookbook/views/chapter3/editor.jsf`.

Advanced editing with an in-place editor

The `inplace` component provides easy in-place editing and inline content display. It consists of two members:

▶ The `display` element that is the initial clickable label

▶ The `inline` element, which is the hidden content that'll be displayed when the `display` element is toggled

How it works...

The basic declaration of the component would be as follows:

```
<p:inplace>
  <h:inputText value="Edit Me!" />
</p:inplace>
```

This would render an input text field that could be clicked by the user to go into the edit mode. To go out of the edit mode, the user needs to click on the *Enter* button after typing.

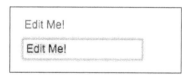

By default, the `inplace` component displays its first child's value as the label; this can also be customized with the `label` attribute. This attribute defines the label that will be shown in the display mode regardless of the text input by the user:

```
<p:inplace label="My Input Field">
  <h:inputText value="Edit Me!" />
</p:inplace>
```

The `emptyLabel` attribute defines the label that will be shown to the user when the value of the input field is empty. The value displayed will change to the one provided if the user, for instance, enters any text into the input field:

```
<p:inplace emptyLabel="My Empty Input Field">
  <h:inputText value="" />
</p:inplace>
```

There's more...

Besides the input text field, other components such as the drop-down list could also be used with the in-place editor, as seen in the following example:

```
<p:inplace label="Countries">
  <h:selectOneMenu>
    <f:selectItem itemLabel="Turkey" itemValue="Turkey" />
    <f:selectItem itemLabel="Germany" itemValue="Germany" />
  </h:selectOneMenu>
</p:inplace>
```

Editing with confirmation buttons

The `editor` attribute specifies the confirmation mode of the editor with the default value `false`. When set to `true`, `approve` and `cancel` buttons will be rendered right next to the editor, as shown in the following screenshot:

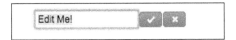

There are two attributes available for introducing i18n to the in-place input when the editor mode is set to `true`. The `saveLabel` attribute sets the tool-tip text of the `save` button with the default value `Save`. The `cancelLabel` attribute sets the tool-tip text of the `cancel` button with the default value `Cancel`.

Giving effects to the in-place input

The `inplace` component also provides ways to customize the effects of editing with the attributes `effect` and `effectSpeed`. The `effect` attribute sets the effect to be used when toggling, with the default value as `fade`. The other option is `slide`. When set to `slide`, the component will slide its content upside down when it's toggled. The `effectSpeed` attribute sets the speed of the effect with the default value `normal`. The other options for the attribute are `slow` and `fast`.

Adding facets

Since version 4.0, the `inplace` component offers `input` and `output` faces, where you can customize what to show as the input and output states of the component. The next example given shows a checkbox for the input and a cross or a thick icon as the output. The names of the icons are set as `false.png` and `true.png` for simplicity:

```
<p:inplace editor="true">
  <f:facet name="output">
    <p:graphicImage
```

```
      value="/resources/images/inplace/#{inplaceBean.value}.png"
      width="30" height="30" />
  </f:facet>
  <f:facet name="input">
    <p:selectBooleanCheckbox value="#{inplaceBean.value}" />
    <h:outputLabel value="PrimeFaces Rocks!" />
  </f:facet>
</p:inplace>
```

The editing process will be as given in the following screenshot:

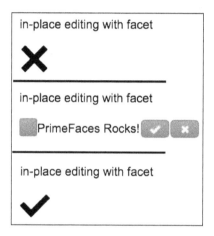

AJAX behavior events

The `inplace` component provides the `save` AJAX behavior event that will be fired when the save button gets clicked:

```
<p:inplace editor="true">
  <p:ajax event="save"
    listener="#{inplaceBean.handleSave}" update="growl" />
  <h:inputText value="Edit Me!" />
</p:inplace>
```

The `handleSave` method will be invoked with `javax.faces.event.AjaxBehaviorEvent`:

```
public void handleSave(AjaxBehaviorEvent event) {
  MessageUtil.addInfoMessageWithoutKey("Input Saved!", null);
}
```

PrimeFaces Cookbook Showcase application

This recipe is available in the demo web application on GitHub (`https://github.com/ova2/primefaces-cookbook/tree/second-edition`). Clone the project if you have not done it yet, explore the project structure, and build and deploy the WAR file on every Servlet 3.x compatible application server, such as *JBoss WildFly* or *Apache TomEE*.

The showcase for the recipe is available under `http://localhost:8080/pf-cookbook/views/chapter3/inPlaceEditor.jsf`.

Enhanced password input

The `password` component is an extended version of the JSF `<h:inputSecret>` component, which also provides a strength indicator and the match mode.

How to do it...

The basic declaration for the component will provide no feedback on the input password and will just render a simple input component:

```
<p:password value="#{passwordBean.password}" />
```

To enable the strength indicator, the `feedback` attribute should be set to `true`. By default, the indicator will be rendered right next to the component when it is hovered:

When `feedback` is enabled, it's also possible to set the prompt label and the strength label with the `promptLabel`, `weakLabel`, `goodLabel`, and `strongLabel` attributes. This will help to localize the password input component according to the need:

```
<p:password value="#{passwordBean.password}" feedback="true"
    promptLabel="#{msg['password.promptLabel']}"
    weakLabel="#{msg['password.weakLabel']}"
    goodLabel="#{msg['password.goodLabel']}"
    strongLabel="#{msg['password.strongLabel']}" />
```

To render the indicator in the inline mode without hovering, the `inline` attribute should be set to `true`.

How it works...

Strength testing is done by differently weighing the characters in the ranges `[0-9]`, `[a-zA-Z]`, and `[!@#$%^&*?_~.,;=]`.

There's more...

It is also possible to check a password match by providing the `match` attribute, which identifies another `password` component with its ID to match the value against. The following panel grid definition contains a message component, along with two `password` components and a `commandButton` component, to invoke the validation:

```
<h:panelGrid id="passwords" columns="1">
  <p:messages id="messages" showDetail="true" />
  <p:password id="passwordMatch1"
    value="#{passwordBean.password}" match="passwordMatch2" />
  <p:password id="passwordMatch2"
    value="#{passwordBean.password}" />
  <p:commandButton update="passwords" value="Save" />
</h:panelGrid>
```

When the input password does not match the actual password, the validation error will be thrown, as shown in the following screenshot:

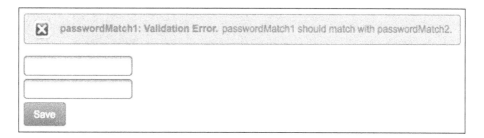

 You can set the `autocomplete` attribute to `off` for the password field, but beware that nearly all major browsers are now ignoring this attribute for the password fields.

PrimeFaces Cookbook Showcase application

This recipe is available in the demo web application on GitHub (`https://github.com/ova2/primefaces-cookbook/tree/second-edition`). Clone the project if you have not done it yet, explore the project structure, and build and deploy the WAR file on every Servlet 3.x compatible application server, such as *JBoss WildFly* or *Apache TomEE*.

The showcase for the recipe is available under `http://localhost:8080/pf-cookbook/views/chapter3/password.jsf`.

Star-based rating input

The `rating` component provides star-based rating with the ability to select and cancel.

How to do it...

The basic declaration for the component would be as follows:

```
<p:rating value="#{ratingBean.rate}" />
```

Here, the `rate` value binding is a `java.lang.Integer` definition. The default visual of the component will be as shown in the following screenshot:

The `stars` attribute sets the number of stars to display with a default value `5`.

There's more...

With the `readonly` attribute, it's possible to only display the value output of the component by disabling user interaction. When set to `true`, the cancellation button will also not be rendered on the left-hand side of the component.

When the `disabled` attribute is set to `true`, the `rating` component will act the same as when the `readonly` attribute is set to `true`, but the color of the stars will get faint, as seen in this screenshot:

 Currently, the rating component does not support half or quarter values.

AJAX behavior events

It is also possible to invoke a server-side method instantly when the user rates or cancels the rating. The `rating` component provides two AJAX behavior events for this, `rate` and `cancel`.

A sample definition that updates the growl component with AJAX behavior would be as follows:

```
<p:rating id="instantRating" value="#{ratingBean.rate}">
  <p:ajax event="rate" listener="#{ratingBean.handleRate}"
    update="growl" />
  <p:ajax event="cancel" listener="#{ratingBean.cancelRate}"
    update="growl" />
</p:rating>
```

The `handleRate` method gets `org.primefaces.event.RateEvent`, as shown in the following code snippet, despite the `cancelRate` method that has no arguments. The rating is contained in `rateEvent` and can be retrieved as an object with the `getRating()` method:

```
public void handleRate(RateEvent rateEvent) {
  Integer rate = (Integer) rateEvent.getRating();
  MessageUtil.addInfoMessage("rating.selected", rate);
}
public void cancelRate() {
  MessageUtil.addInfoMessage("rating.cancelled");
}
```

PrimeFaces Cookbook Showcase application

This recipe is available in the demo web application on GitHub (`https://github.com/ova2/primefaces-cookbook/tree/second-edition`). Clone the project if you have not done it yet, explore the project structure, and build and deploy the WAR file on every Servlet 3.x compatible application server, such as *JBoss WildFly* or *Apache TomEE*.

The showcase for the recipe is available under `http://localhost:8080/pf-cookbook/views/chapter3/rating.jsf`.

See also

For details about the `MessageUtil` class, see the *Internationalization (i18n) and Localization (L10n)* recipe in *Chapter 1, Getting Started with PrimeFaces*.

4

Grouping Content with Panels

In this chapter, we will cover the following topics:

- ▸ Grouping content with a standard panel
- ▸ PanelGrid with colspan and rowspan support
- ▸ Vertical stacked panels with accordion
- ▸ Displaying overflowed content with scrollPanel
- ▸ Working with a tabbed panel
- ▸ Grouping of buttons and more with toolbar
- ▸ The multipurpose output panel
- ▸ Simulating the portal environment with dashboard
- ▸ Creating complex layouts
- ▸ Responsive layout with Grid CSS

Introduction

In this chapter, we will cover various container components, such as panel, accordion, scroll panel, output panel, and tabbed panel, which allow grouping of JSF components.

Grouping content with a standard panel

A generic grouping component for JSF components, `panel` has features such as toggling, closing, a built-in pop-up menu, and AJAX event listeners. In this recipe, we will create panels that can be closed and toggled, with custom action menus and AJAX behaviors added.

How to do it...

A basic definition of the panel would be as follows:

```
<p:panel id="simple" header="PrimeFaces" footer="The Cookbook">
  <h:outputText value="Open Source Primefaces is the leading JSF
     Component Suite in the industry, which is adopted widely and
     being used in production ready projects around the globe." />
</p:panel>
```

The preceding definition of the panel will be rendered as shown in the following image:

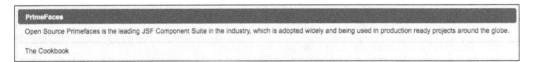

There's more...

The `header` and `footer` attributes can be used to render text at the top of the panel as the header and at the bottom of the panel as the footer. The values defined for the attributes are escaped by default, so the HTML content can be easily provided. With the facets, `header` and `footer`, also offered by `panel`, you can define elements other than texts. The facet definitions override the attributes defined.

In order to enable closing and toggling of the panel, the `closeable` and `toggleable` attributes should be set to `true`. Once the panel gets closed, the page should be refreshed, or the panel should be re-rendered to see the panel back. The toggling speed can also be adjusted using the `toggleSpeed` attribute, which has the default value of `1000` milliseconds. The title values for the buttons can be localized with the `closeTitle` and `toggleTitle` attributes, if needed.

The `options` facet is present in `panel` to provide a built-in menu that would be given within the facet. The definition of a menu with two menu items would be as follows:

```
<p:panel id="panelWithMenu" header="PrimeFaces"
  footer="The Cookbook" widgetVar="panel" closable="true"
  toggleable="true">
  <h:outputText value="Open Source Primefaces is the leading
    JSF Component Suite in the industry, which is adopted widely
    and being used in production ready projects around the
    globe." />
  <f:facet name="options">
    <p:menu>
      <p:submenu label="Settings">
        <p:menuitem value="Toggle" url="#" icon="ui-icon-newwin"
          onclick="PF('panel').toggle()" />
        <p:menuitem value="Remove" url="#" icon="ui-icon-close"
          onclick="PF('panel').close()" />
      </p:submenu>
    </p:menu>
  </f:facet>
</p:panel>
```

The menu will render with the **Settings** icon as shown in the following image. The widget variable `panel` is being used by the menu item's `onclick` events to close and toggle the panel.

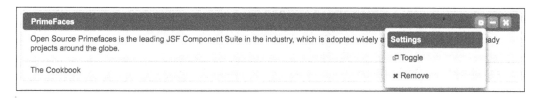

With the `toggleOrientation` attribute, it's possible to toggle the panels horizontally, from right-to-left, instead of the default vertical toggling. The value for the attribute could be either of the values `vertical` and `horizontal`.

Custom actions

The `actions` facet enables you to add custom actions to the title bar of the panel with specified icons. The definition here puts a help icon on the right-hand side of the title bar:

```
<p:panel id="customActions" header="PrimeFaces"
    footer="The Cookbook">
    <f:facet name="actions">
        <h:commandLink styleClass="ui-panel-titlebar-icon
            ui-corner-all ui-state-default"
            onclick="alert('action!')">
            <h:outputText styleClass="ui-icon ui-icon-help" />
        </h:commandLink>
    </f:facet>
    <h:outputText value="Open Source Primefaces is the leading JSF
        Component Suite in the industry, which is adopted widely and
        being used in production ready projects around the globe." />
</p:panel>
```

The `ui-icon-help` used in the preceding example is one of the elements of the *jQuery UI*. It provides an extensive set of icons that can be applied through CSS classes. The complete list can be found at `http://api.jqueryui.com/theming/icons`.

AJAX behavior events on panel

The `panel` component supports the `close` and `toggle` AJAX behavior events that will be fired when the panel is closed or toggled. The definition of the panel with AJAX behavior events will be as follows:

```
<p:panel id="ajaxPanel" header="PrimeFaces" footer="The Cookbook"
    closable="true" toggleable="true">
    <p:ajax event="close" listener="#{panelBean.handleClose}"
        update="growl" />
    <p:ajax event="toggle" listener="#{panelBean.handleToggle}"
        update="growl" />
    <h:outputText value="Open Source PrimeFaces is the leading
        JSF Component Suite in the industry, which is adopted widely
        and being used in production ready projects around the globe."/>
</p:panel>
```

The listener methods, `handleClose` and `handleToggle`, receive an instance of `org.primefaces.event.CloseEvent` and `org.primefaces.event.ToggleEvent`, respectively, as parameters:

```
public void handleClose(CloseEvent event) {
  MessageUtil.addInfoMessage("panel.closed",
    "Closed panel id:'" + event.getComponent().getId());
}

public void handleToggle(ToggleEvent event) {
  MessageUtil.addInfoMessage("panel.toggled",
    "Status:" + event.getVisibility().name());
}
```

To get the `id` parameter of the closed panel, `event.getComponent().getId()` is used, and to retrieve the status of toggling, the visibility enumeration can be retrieved using `event.getVisibility().name()`, which would be either `VISIBLE` or `HIDDEN`.

PrimeFaces Cookbook Showcase application

This recipe is available in the demo web application on GitHub (`https://github.com/ova2/primefaces-cookbook/tree/second-edition`). Clone the project if you have not done it yet, explore the project structure, and build and deploy the WAR file on application servers compatible with Servlet 3.x, such as *JBoss WildFly* and *Apache TomEE*.

The showcase for the recipe is available at `http://localhost:8080/pf-cookbook/views/chapter4/panel.jsf`.

See also

For details about the `MessageUtil` class, see the *Internationalization (i18n) and Localization (L10n)* recipe in *Chapter 1, Getting Started with PrimeFaces*.

PanelGrid with colspan and rowspan support

The `panelGrid` component extends the JSF's `<h:panelGrid>` component with the support of `colspan`, that is, the number of columns a cell should span, and `rowspan`, which is the number of rows a cell should span, and the theming ability. In this recipe, we will create panels with row and column span abilities.

How to do it...

A basic definition of the panel grid would be as follows:

```
<p:panelGrid columns="2">
    <f:facet name="header">User Information</f:facet>
    <h:outputLabel for="firstname" value="First Name" />
    <p:inputText id="firstname" value="" label="firstname" />
    <h:outputLabel for="lastname" value="Last Name" />
    <p:inputText id="lastname" value="" required="true"
      label="lastname"/>
    <f:facet name="footer">
      <p:commandButton type="button" value="Save"
        icon="ui-icon-check" style="margin:0"/>
    </f:facet>
</p:panelGrid>
```

This will render two columns with header and footer facets, as shown in the following image:

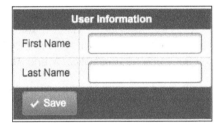

The `panelGrid` component is rendered as an HTML table with borders by default. In order to remove borders, you can specify the custom style, as given here:

```
<p:panelGrid columns="2" styleClass="pGrid">
...
</p:panelGrid>

<style type="text/css">
  .pGrid tr, .pGrid td {
    border: none;
  }
</style>
```

The `style` segment should be placed in the `head` section of the page.

There's more...

The p:row and p:column components can be used to provide column and row spanning on the grid. They could either be used in the header or footer facets or within the content of the panel. Here is a sample with the definition and the visual result:

```
<p:panelGrid style="margin-top:20px">
  <f:facet name="header">
    <p:row>
      <p:column colspan="6">Time Chart</p:column>
    </p:row>
    <p:row>
      <p:column/>
      <p:column>Monday</p:column>
      <p:column>Tuesday</p:column>
      <p:column>Wednesday</p:column>
      <p:column>Thursday</p:column>
      <p:column>Friday</p:column>
    </p:row>
  </f:facet>
  <p:row>
    <p:column rowspan="6">Hours</p:column>
    <p:column>Science</p:column>
    <p:column>Math</p:column>
    <p:column rowspan="2"
      style="text-align:center">Project</p:column>
    <p:column>Math</p:column>
    <p:column>Arts</p:column>
  </p:row>
  <p:row>
    <p:column>Social</p:column>
    <p:column>History</p:column>
    <p:column>Sports</p:column>
    <p:column>Math</p:column>
  </p:row>
  <p:row>
    <p:column colspan="6"
      style="text-align:center">Lunch</p:column>
  </p:row>
  <p:row>
    <p:column>Math</p:column>
    <p:column>History</p:column>
    <p:column>English</p:column>
```

```
      <p:column>Science</p:column>
      <p:column>Arts</p:column>
    </p:row>
    <f:facet name="footer">
      <p:row>
        <p:column colspan="6">Duration: 40 minutes</p:column>
      </p:row>
    </f:facet>
  </p:panelGrid>
```

The preceding sample definition of column and row spanning will be rendered as shown in the following image:

Time Chart					
	Monday	**Tuesday**	**Wednesday**	**Thursday**	**Friday**
Hours	Science	Math	Project	Math	Arts
	Social	History		Sports	Math
			Lunch		
	Math	History	English	Science	Arts
Duration: 40 minutes					

The `panelGrid` component also supports responsive web design with the `layout` attribute, which effectively handles browser resizing. The default value for `layout` is `tabular`, and when the value of the attribute is set to `grid`, the content becomes responsive and promptly responds to the browser resizing, panning, and so on.

 Using `colspan` or `rowspan` is not supported when `layout` is set to `grid`.

PrimeFaces Cookbook Showcase application

This recipe is available in the demo web application on GitHub (`https://github.com/ova2/primefaces-cookbook/tree/second-edition`). Clone the project if you have not done it yet, explore the project structure, and build and deploy the WAR file on application servers compatible with Servlet 3.x, such as *JBoss WildFly* and *Apache TomEE*.

The showcase for the recipe is available at `http://localhost:8080/pf-cookbook/views/chapter4/panelGrid.jsf`.

Vertical stacked panels with accordion

A container component, `accordionPanel` provides the ability to group multiple tabs. In this recipe, we will create accordion panels generated with dynamic content and AJAX behaviors added.

How to do it...

A basic definition of the accordion panel with two panels would be as follows:

```
<p:accordionPanel>
  <p:tab title="Volkswagen CC">
    <h:panelGrid columns="2" cellpadding="10">
      <h:graphicImage library="images"
        name="autocomplete/CC.png" />
      <h:outputText value="The Volkswagen CC (also known as the
        Volkswagen Passat CC) is a four-door coupé version of
        the Volkswagen Passat." />
    </h:panelGrid>
  </p:tab>
  <p:tab title="Volkswagen Golf">
    <h:panelGrid columns="2" cellpadding="10">
      <h:graphicImage library="images"
        name="autocomplete/Golf.png" />
      <h:outputText value="The Volkswagen Golf is a small
        family car manufactured by Volkswagen since 1974 and
        marketed worldwide across six generations, in various
        body configurations and under various nameplates" />
    </h:panelGrid>
  </p:tab>
</p:accordionPanel>
```

The visual output for the panel will be as follows:

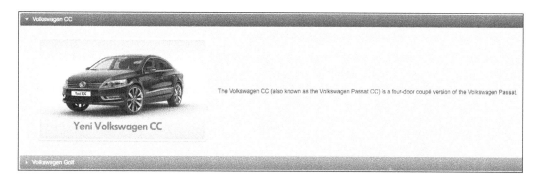

The `multiple` attribute enables the activation of multiple tabs. With the value set as `enabled`, the active tab will not collapse when another tab gets activated. The default value of the attribute is `false`. To disable a tab, just set the `disabled` attribute to `true`.

The `activeIndex` attribute defines the index of the tab that will be expanded by default. Its default value is `0`. If `2` is specified as the value, the third tab will be expanded. When the `multiple` attribute is set to `true`, we can specify the index of the multiple tabs as being separated by commas.

Dynamic content loading

By setting the `dynamic` attribute to `true`, it's also possible to lazily load the content of the tabs with an AJAX request when they get activated in order to save the bandwidth and reduce the size of the page. Also, by setting the `cache` attribute to `true`, consecutive invokes on the same tab will not invoke an AJAX request.

Dynamic tabbing

Dynamic tab loading allows us to load the content of the accordion panel dynamically by providing a data model. We can access the iterator defined by the `var` attribute. The definition of the component for providing a data list on cars to `accordionPanel` would be as follows:

```
<p:accordionPanel value="#{accordionPanelBean.cars}" var="car">
  <p:tab title="#{car.name}">
    <h:panelGrid columns="2" cellpadding="5">
      <p:graphicImage
        value="/resources/images/autocomplete/#{car.name}.png" />
      <h:outputText value="#{car.name}" />
    </h:panelGrid>
  </p:tab>
</p:accordionPanel>
```

The data model here is the list of car objects that will be iterated over, for rendering each panel, along with the image and the name of the car.

AJAX behavior events on accordion

The `accordionPanel` component supports the `tabChange` and `tabClose` AJAX behavior events that will be fired when a tab is changed by clicking on another one or when a tab is closed by clicking on it. The definition of the AJAX behavior events and their method declarations would be as follows:

```
<p:accordionPanel>
  <p:ajax event="tabChange"
```

```
        listener="#{accordionPanelBean.onTabChange}"
        update=":mainForm:growl" />
    <p:ajax event="tabClose"
        listener="#{accordionPanelBean.onTabClose}"
        update=":mainForm:growl" />

    ...
</p:accordionPanel>
```

The listener methods, `onTabChange` and `onTabClose`, receive an instance of `org.primefaces.event.TabChangeEvent` and `org.primefaces.event.TabCloseEvent` respectively, as parameters:

```
public void onTabChange(TabChangeEvent event) {
    MessageUtil.addInfoMessage("tab.changed", "Title: " +
        event.getTab().getTitle());
}

public void onTabClose(TabCloseEvent event) {
    MessageUtil.addInfoMessage("tab.closed", "Closed Tab: " +
        event.getTab().getTitle());
}
```

Since the `accordionPanel` component is an example of *NamingContainer*, the value of the `update` attributes given in the previous example defines the ID of the form that wraps the component, which is `mainForm`.

PrimeFaces Cookbook Showcase application

This recipe is available in the demo web application on GitHub (`https://github.com/ova2/primefaces-cookbook/tree/second-edition`). Clone the project if you have not done it yet, explore the project structure, and build and deploy the WAR file on application servers compatible with Servlet 3.x, such as *JBoss WildFly* and *Apache TomEE*.

The showcase for the recipe is available at `http://localhost:8080/pf-cookbook/views/chapter4/accordionPanel.jsf`.

See also

For details about the `MessageUtil` class, see the *Internationalization (i18n) and Localization (L10n)* recipe in *Chapter 1, Getting Started with PrimeFaces*.

Displaying overflowed content with scrollPanel

The `scrollPanel` component provides customizable scrollbars instead of the browser's scrolls. In this recipe, we will create panels with a fixed viewport and styled scroll bars applied to them.

How to do it...

A basic definition of a scroll panel with a width of 500 pixels and a height of 500 pixels would be as follows:

```
<p:scrollPanel style="width:500px;height:500px">
  <p:dataGrid var="car" value="#{scrollPanelBean.cars}"
    columns="2">
    <p:panel header="#{car.name}" style="text-align:center">
      <p:graphicImage value=
        "/resources/images/autocomplete/#{car.name}.png" />
    </p:panel>
  </p:dataGrid>
</p:scrollPanel>
```

This will render a list of car models within a data grid. The visual size of the grid will be limited to a 500 x 500 pixel view, and the content can be scrollable horizontally and vertically. By default, according to the selected UI theme, customized scrollbars will be rendered on the lines of the following image:

The `mode` attribute with the `scrollbar` value defines whether the component should render customized scroll bars according to a theme or use the browser's default ones with the `native` value.

PrimeFaces Cookbook Showcase application

This recipe is available in the demo web application on GitHub (`https://github.com/ova2/primefaces-cookbook/tree/second-edition`). Clone the project if you have not done it yet, explore the project structure, and build and deploy the WAR file on application servers compatible with Servlet 3.x, such as *JBoss WildFly* and *Apache TomEE*.

The showcase for the recipe is available at `http://localhost:8080/pf-cookbook/views/chapter4/scrollPanel.jsf`.

Working with a tabbed panel

A tabbed panel component, `tabView` has powerful features such as dynamic content loading, orientations, and programmatically managing tabs. In this recipe, we will create tabs with the scrolling ability and with a different tab header orientation, along with the dynamic content generation and AJAX behaviors added.

How to do it...

A basic definition of a tabbed panel with two panels would be as follows:

```
<p:tabView id="tabView">
  <p:tab title="Volkswagen CC">
    <h:panelGrid columns="2" cellpadding="5">
      <h:graphicImage library="images"
        name="autocomplete/CC.png" />
      <h:outputText value="The Volkswagen CC (also known as
        the Volkswagen Passat CC) is a four-door coupé version of
        the Volkswagen Passat." />
    </h:panelGrid>
  </p:tab>
  <p:tab title="Volkswagen Golf">
    <h:panelGrid columns="2" cellpadding="5">
      <h:graphicImage library="images"
        name="autocomplete/Golf.png" />
      <h:outputText value="The Volkswagen Golf is a small
        family car manufactured by Volkswagen since 1974 and
        marketed worldwide across six generations, in various
        body configurations and under various nameplates" />
    </h:panelGrid>
```

```
      </p:tab>
   </p:tabView>
```

This will render two tabs, with the first tab activated by default, as shown in the following image:

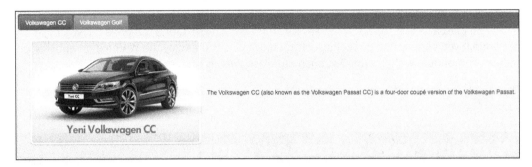

There's more...

We can also enable or disable a tab within the tab view according to a business rule. If we set the `disabled` attribute to `true` in the tab, the tab will have a grayed-out caption that indicates that the tab is disabled, as seen in the image here:

If you have more tabs that could be seen in the title, setting the `scrollable` attribute to `true` will render arrows for navigation in the tab panel header, as shown in the following image.

By setting the `dynamic` attribute to `true`, it's also possible to lazily load the content of the tabs with an AJAX request when they get activated in order to save bandwidth and reduce the size of the page. And by also setting the `cache` attribute to `true`, consecutive invokes on the same tab will not invoke an AJAX request.

Orientation of the tabs

Orientation of the tabs can be set with four positions: `top`, `bottom`, `left`, and `right`. By default, the orientation for the tabs is `top`.

Dynamic tabbing

Dynamic tab loading allows us to load the content of the tab view dynamically by providing a data model. The definition of the component for providing a data list of cars to the `tabView` component would be as follows:

```
<p:tabView value="#{tabViewBean.cars}" var="car">
  <p:tab title="#{car.name}">
    <h:panelGrid columns="2" cellpadding="5">
      <p:graphicImage value=
        "/resources/images/autocomplete/#{car.name}.png" />
    </h:panelGrid>
  </p:tab>
</p:tabView>
```

The data model here is the list of car objects that will be iterated through, to render each tab, along with the image and the name of the car.

Transition effects

With the `effect` attribute, effects can be applied for content transition between the tabs. The possible values are as follows:

- blind
- clip
- drop
- explode
- fade
- fold
- puff
- scale
- slide

The effect duration can also be set with the `effectDuration` attribute. The possible values are `slow`, `normal`, and `fast`.

AJAX behavior events on tabView

The `tabView` component provides the `tabChange` and `tabClose` AJAX behavior events that will be fired when a tab is changed or closed in a tab view. The definition of the event listeners for the `tabView` component would be as follows:

```
<p:ajax event="tabChange" listener="#{tabViewBean.onTabChange}"
  update=":mainForm:growl" />
```

```
<p:ajax event="tabClose" listener="#{tabViewBean.onTabClose}"
    update=":mainForm:growl" />
```

The listener methods, `onTabChange` and `onTabClose`, receive an instance of `org.primefaces.event.TabChangeEvent` and `org.primefaces.event.TabCloseEvent`, respectively, as parameters:

```
public void onTabChange(TabChangeEvent event) {
    MessageUtil.addInfoMessage("tab.changed", "Title: " +
        event.getTab().getTitle());
}

public void onTabClose(TabCloseEvent event) {
    MessageUtil.addInfoMessage("tab.closed", "Closed Tab: " +
        event.getTab().getTitle());
}
```

> Since the `tabView` component is an example of *NamingContainer*, the value of the `update` attributes given in the previous example define the ID of the form that wraps the component, which is `mainForm`.

PrimeFaces Cookbook Showcase application

This recipe is available in the demo web application on GitHub (`https://github.com/ova2/primefaces-cookbook/tree/second-edition`). Clone the project if you have not done it yet, explore the project structure, and build and deploy the WAR file on application servers compatible with Servlet 3.x, such as *JBoss WildFly* and *Apache TomEE*.

The showcase for the recipe is available at `http://localhost:8080/pf-cookbook/views/chapter4/tabView.jsf`.

See also

For details about the `MessageUtil` class, see the *Internationalization (i18n) and Localization (L10n)* recipe in *Chapter 1, Getting Started with PrimeFaces*.

Grouping of buttons and more with toolbar

A horizontal grouping component, `toolbar` can be used to group commands and other components. In this recipe, we will create a toolbar with two groups that bundle buttons and menu items.

How to do it...

A definition of a toolbar with multiple groups would be as follows:

```
<p:toolbar>
  <p:toolbarGroup align="left">
    <p:commandButton type="push" value="New"
      icon="ui-icon-document" />
    <p:commandButton type="push" value="Open"
      icon="ui-icon-folder-open"/>
    <p:separator />
    <p:commandButton type="push" title="Save"
      icon="ui-icon-disk"/>
    <p:commandButton type="push" title="Delete"
      icon="ui-icon-trash"/>
    <p:commandButton type="push" title="Print"
      icon="ui-icon-print"/>
  </p:toolbarGroup>
    <p:toolbarGroup align="right">
      <p:menuButton value="Navigate">
        <p:menuitem value="Home" url="#" />
        <p:menuitem value="Logout" url="#" />
      </p:menuButton>
    </p:toolbarGroup>
  </p:toolbar>
```

This definition will be visualized as shown in the following image:

By default, `toolbar` has two placeholders, `left` and `right`, which can be defined with the `toolbarGroup` component or `facet`. There is no limit on the number of components that can be put inside `toolbarGroup` or `facet`. The `<p:toolbarGroup align="left">` component definition can also be defined as a facet, such as `<f:facet name="left">`. The `separator` component can be used to visually separate the components from each other, such as between the components inside the `toolbarGroup` component, as given in the example.

While using `facet` definitions, the usage of `<p:separator>` is not supported. You can define the separator with `span` as follows:

```
<span class="ui-separator">
  <span class="ui-icon
ui-icon-grip-dotted-vertical" />
</span>
```

PrimeFaces Cookbook Showcase application

This recipe is available in the demo web application on GitHub (`https://github.com/ova2/primefaces-cookbook/tree/second-edition`). Clone the project if you have not done it yet, explore the project structure, and build and deploy the WAR file on application servers compatible with Servlet 3.x, such as *JBoss WildFly* and *Apache TomEE*.

The showcase for the recipe is available at `http://localhost:8080/pf-cookbook/views/chapter4/toolbar.jsf`.

The multipurpose output panel

The `outputPanel` component is a panel component that can be rendered as a div or span HTML component. In this recipe, we will create an output panel that demonstrates deferred loading and placeholder usage for a data table.

How to do it...

A basic definition of an output panel would be as follows:

```
<p:outputPanel layout="block">
  <h3>The Volkswagen CC (also known as the
    Volkswagen Passat CC)</h3>
  <p>is a four-door coupe version of the Volkswagen Passat.</p>
</p:outputPanel>
```

When the `layout` attribute is set to `block`, which is the default value, `outputPanel` renders an HTML div. By setting `layout` as `inline`, we can render an HTML span instead of the div.

There's more...

The `outputPanel` component supports *deferred loading*, where the content of the panel is loaded after the page is loaded. The panel renders a loading animation while loading its contents.

By default, content gets loaded after the page load, but by setting `deferredMode` to `visible`, it's possible to load the contents when the panel becomes visible with a scroll for instance. The default value of `deferredMode` is `load`. The code for this is as follows:

```
<p:outputPanel deferred="true" deferredMode="visible">
  <h3>Loaded after the panel becomes visible
    on page scroll.</h3>
  <p>The Volkswagen CC is a four-door coupe version of
    the Volkswagen Passat.</p>
</p:outputPanel>
```

With `deferred` set to `true`, it's also possible to load the content of the panel with a delay. The `delay` attribute defines this delay in milliseconds.

 When the `autoUpdate` attribute of `outputPanel` is set to `true`, the content of the panel gets updated with each AJAX request.

Using panel as a placeholder component

The PrimeFaces AJAX mechanism is basically based on IDs of the components. When those components get rendered as HTML markups and viewed in the browser with specified IDs, the JavaScript part of PrimeFaces will be responsible for updating the DOM according to the given IDs.

This will work in most cases, but when conditional rendering takes place, such as the `dataTable` component not being rendered on the page when it's empty, there will be no way to update the markup of the table with the AJAX mechanism since its markup won't exist within the content of the page.

To overcome this problem, we can use `outputPanel` as a placeholder component, which wraps the `datatable` component. A sample definition is given here:

```
<p:outputPanel id="wrapper">
  <p:dataTable id="table" rendered="#{tableBean.condition}">
    ...
  </p:dataTable>
</p:outputPanel>
```

The action components should update the panel with the `wrapper` ID instead of the table from now on.

PrimeFaces Cookbook Showcase application

This recipe is available in the demo web application on GitHub (`https://github.com/ova2/primefaces-cookbook/tree/second-edition`). Clone the project if you have not done it yet, explore the project structure, and build and deploy the WAR file on application servers compatible with Servlet 3.x, such as *JBoss WildFly* and *Apache TomEE*.

The showcase for the recipe is available at `http://localhost:8080/pf-cookbook/views/chapter4/outputPanel.jsf`.

Simulating the portal environment with dashboard

A layout component, `dashboard` has the drag-and-drop ability to support reordering of the panels. In this recipe, we will create a dashboard with predefined panels and then add new ones.

How to do it...

A basic definition for a dashboard with six panels would be as follows:

```
<p:dashboard id="board" model="#{dashboardBean.model}">
  <p:ajax event="reorder" listener=
    "#{dashboardBean.handleReorder}" update="growl" />
  <p:panel id="calculator" header="Calculator">
    <h:outputText value="Content for Calculator" />
  </p:panel>
  <p:panel id="calendar" header="Calendar">
    <h:outputText value="Content for Calendar" />
  </p:panel>
  <p:panel id="contact" header="Contacts">
    <h:outputText value="Content for Contacts" />
  </p:panel>
  <p:panel id="dictionary" header="Dictionary">
    <h:outputText value="Weather Content for Dictionary" />
  </p:panel>
  <p:panel id="weather" header="Weather">
    <h:outputText value="Content for Weather" />
  </p:panel>
  <p:panel id="translation" header="Translation">
    <h:outputText value="Content for Translation" />
  </p:panel>
</p:dashboard>
```

A data model needs to be provided in order to preserve the panel order. The data model depends on `org.primefaces.model.DefaultDashboardModel`. The model for the given sample would be as follows:

```
DashboardColumn column1 = new DefaultDashboardColumn();
DashboardColumn column2 = new DefaultDashboardColumn();
DashboardColumn column3 = new DefaultDashboardColumn();

column1.addWidget("calculator");
column1.addWidget("calendar");
column1.addWidget("contact");
column2.addWidget("dictionary");
column3.addWidget("weather");
column3.addWidget("translation");

model.addColumn(column1);
model.addColumn(column2);
model.addColumn(column3);
```

The preceding definition of the dashboard contains three columns and six panels and will look like the following image:

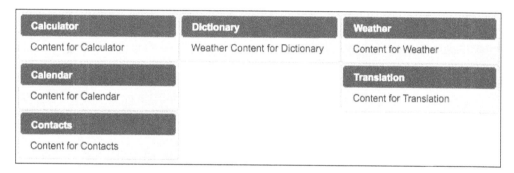

 The `dashboard` component preserves its state whenever a widget is reordered. So, you can easily store the changes made by the user in a persistence layer, such as database management systems.

The `dashboard` component supports the reordering of the AJAX behavior event that will be fired when a panel is dragged and dropped. The `reorder` event definition is given in the previous sample. The `handleReorder` listener method defined next receives `org.primefaces.event.DashboardReorderEvent` as its parameter:

```
public void handleReorder(DashboardReorderEvent event) {
  MessageUtil.addInfoMessageWithoutKey("Reordered: " +
    event.getWidgetId(),
    "Item index: " + event.getItemIndex() +
    ", Column index: " + event.getColumnIndex() +
    ", Sender column index: " +
    event.getSenderColumnIndex());
}
```

As seen in the method, the information about the drag-and-drop action is communicated to the user by adding it as a PrimeFaces message. The order number of the panel can be retrieved from the `event.getItemIndex()` method. The number of the column from which the panel has been dragged can be retrieved by `event.getColumnIndex()`, and the number of the column that the panel will be dragged onto can be retrieved from `event.getSenderColumnIndex()`.

Creating new widgets

To add new panels that reside outside of the `dashboard`, you can use the `draggable` component. The following definition creates a new `panel` component and attaches a `draggable` component that knows the panel and the dashboard, which the panel could be dragged to:

```
<p:panel id="newWidget" style="width: 200px">
  <h:outputText value="Drag me and create a new widget" />
</p:panel>
<p:draggable for="newWidget" helper="clone" dashboard="board" />
```

Having fixed-sized columns

By default, if the user moves panels from one column to another and gets one column empty, it cannot be filled again by dragging panels back. To have columns of a fixed size, the `ui-dashboard-column` style should be defined with the preferred width, as shown in the following code snippet:

```
.ui-dashboard-column {
  width:200px;
}
```

Since `dashboard` contains `panel` components as its widgets, these panels can be defined with the menu or can be stated as closable and toggle-able. See the first recipe, *Grouping content with a standard panel*, in this chapter for detailed usage.

PrimeFaces Cookbook Showcase application

This recipe is available in the demo web application on GitHub (`https://github.com/ova2/primefaces-cookbook/tree/second-edition`). Clone the project if you have not done it yet, explore the project structure, and build and deploy the WAR file on application servers compatible with Servlet 3.x, such as *JBoss WildFly* and *Apache TomEE*.

The showcase for the recipe is available at `http://localhost:8080/pf-cookbook/views/chapter4/dashboard.jsf`.

See also

For details about the `MessageUtil` class, see the *Internationalization (i18n) and Localization (L10n)* recipe in *Chapter 1, Getting Started with PrimeFaces*.

Creating complex layouts

The `layout` component introduces a customizable border layout model that could easily be used to create complex layouts. In this recipe, we will create layouts with five distinct regions and a full-page layout that spans the whole page.

How to do it...

This customizable border layout model can be applied either to a full page or to a specific element. A basic definition of a full-page layout would be as follows:

```
<p:layout fullPage="true">
  <p:layoutUnit position="north" size="100" header=
    "Top" resizable="true" closable="true" collapsible="true">
    <h:outputText value="Layout content for North" />
  </p:layoutUnit>
  <p:layoutUnit position="south" size="100" header="Bottom"
    resizable="true" closable="true" collapsible="true">
    <h:outputText value="Layout content for South" />
  </p:layoutUnit>
  <p:layoutUnit position="west" size="200" header=
    "Left" resizable="true" closable="true" collapsible="true">
```

```
      <h:outputText value="Layout content for West" />
  </p:layoutUnit>
  <p:layoutUnit position="east" size="200" header=
    "Right" resizable="true" closable="true" collapsible="true">
    <h:outputText value="Layout content for Right" />
  </p:layoutUnit>
  <p:layoutUnit position="center">
    <h:outputText value="Layout content for Center" />
  </p:layoutUnit>
</p:layout>
```

This will render five panels in full-page size as shown in the following image:

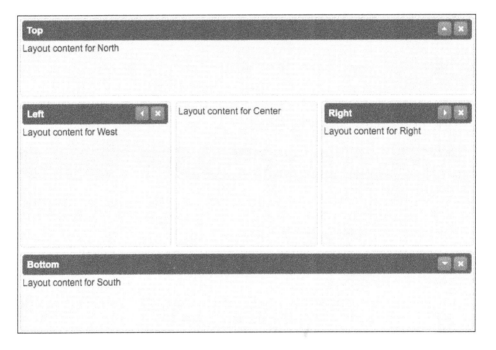

How it works...

The `fullPage` attribute defines whether the layout should span the full page or a specific region. As layout is based on the border layout model, it contains five layout units: top, left, center, right, and bottom. Layout units get placed to the positions respectively, that is, top matches with north, left matches with west, bottom matches with south, right matches with east, and the center unit matches with center, as shown in the following image:

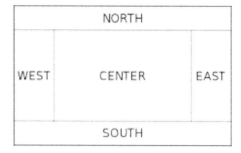

The layout component can contain the `<p:layoutUnit>` components for five different positions according to the border layout. The `position` attribute defines this positioning of the layout unit within the layout. The `layoutUnit` component can have the `resizable`, `closable`, and `collapsible` attributes for interaction.

In addition, the layout state can be preserved with the `stateful` attribute. When enabled by setting its value to `true`, the layout state is saved in a cookie with the name `Layout`. The `header` and `footer` attributes define the text that will be rendered for the layout unit.

There's more...

When working with full-page layouts, using layout units within a `form` component is invalid. Instead of this, a layout unit must have a form owned by itself. Also, instead of updating the layout unit components directly, their content should be updated while doing a partial page rendering. An **invalid** definition of usage of the form component is as follows:

```
<p:layout fullPage="true">
  <h:form>
    <p:layoutUnit position="north">
      <h:outputText value="Layout content for North" />
    </p:layoutUnit>
    <p:layoutUnit position="center">
      <h:outputText value="Layout content for Center" />
    </p:layoutUnit>
  </h:form>
</p:layout>
```

The `gutter` attribute defines the size of the space that will be left between the adjacent units in pixels. The `minSize` and `maxSize` attributes define the minimum and maximum sizes of the layout units that will be set after resizing.

Element-based layouts

By setting the `fullPage` attribute to `false`, which is the default value, the layout can be used as a component within the page, as shown in the following image:

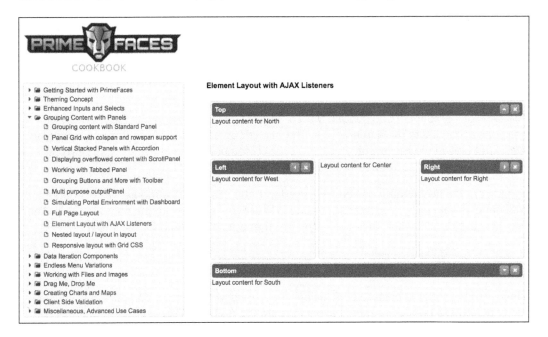

With element-based layouts, CSS should be used for styling the layout component as defined in the following code snippet:

```
<p:layout id="elementLayout" style="min-width:600px;min-
   height:400px;">
   . . .
</p:layout>
```

Nested layouts

The layout unit components can also contain a layout component to provide nested layout abilities:

```
<p:layout id="elementLayout"
   style="min-width:600px;min-height:400px;">
   <p:layoutUnit position="north" size="100"
     header="Top" resizable="true" closable="true"
     collapsible="true">
     <h:outputText value="Layout content for North" />
   </p:layoutUnit>
```

```
  <p:layoutUnit position="south" size="100" header="Bottom"
    resizable="true" closable="true"
    collapsible="true">
    <h:outputText value="Layout content for South" />
  </p:layoutUnit>
  <p:layoutUnit position="center">
    <p:layout>
      <p:layoutUnit position="north" size="100"
        resizable="true" closable="true"
        collapsible="true">
      <h:outputText
        value="Layout content for Top of Center" />
      </p:layoutUnit>
      <p:layoutUnit position="center">
        <h:outputText value="Center of Center" />
      </p:layoutUnit>
    </p:layout>
  </p:layoutUnit>
</p:layout>
```

The visual output of the code will be as shown in the following image:

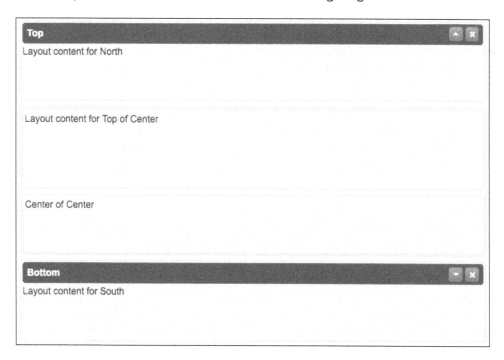

AJAX behavior events on layout

The layout component provides the `toggle`, `close`, and `resize` AJAX behavior events, which will be fired when the layout unit is toggled, closed, or resized. The definition of the event listeners for the layout component would be as follows:

```
<p:ajax event="toggle" listener="#{layoutBean.handleToggle}"
  update="growl" />
<p:ajax event="close" listener="#{layoutBean.handleClose}"
  update="growl" />
<p:ajax event="resize" listener="#{layoutBean.handleResize}"
  update="growl" />
```

The listener methods, `handleToggle`, `handleClose`, and `handleResize`, receive an instance of `org.primefaces.event.ToggleEvent`, `org.primefaces.event.CloseEvent`, and `org.primefaces.event.ResizeEvent`, respectively, as parameters:

```
public void handleClose(CloseEvent event) {
  MessageUtil.addInfoMessageWithoutKey("Unit Closed",
    "Position:'" + ((LayoutUnit)
    event.getComponent()).getPosition());
}

public void handleToggle(ToggleEvent event) {
  MessageUtil.addInfoMessageWithoutKey(((LayoutUnit)event.
    getComponent()).getPosition() + " toggled", "Status:" +
    event.getVisibility().name());
}

public void handleResize(ResizeEvent event) {
  MessageUtil.addInfoMessageWithoutKey(((LayoutUnit)event.
    getComponent()).getPosition() + " resized", "Status:" +
    event.getComponent().getId());
}
```

The visibility of the layout unit can be retrieved from `event.getVisibility().name()`, and the position of the layout unit can be retrieved by casting the component to the layout as `((LayoutUnit) event.getComponent()).getPosition()`.

PrimeFaces Cookbook Showcase application

This recipe is available in the demo web application on GitHub (`https://github.com/ova2/primefaces-cookbook/tree/second-edition`). Clone the project if you have not done it yet, explore the project structure, and build and deploy the WAR file on application servers compatible with Servlet 3.x, such as *JBoss WildFly* and *Apache TomEE*.

When the server is running, the showcase for the recipe is available at the following URLs:

- ► `http://localhost:8080/pf-cookbook/views/chapter4/fullPageLayout.jsf`

- ► `http://localhost:8080/pf-cookbook/views/chapter4/elementLayout.jsf`

- ► `http://localhost:8080/pf-cookbook/views/chapter4/nestedLayout.jsf`

See also

For details about the `MessageUtil` class, see the *Internationalization (i18n) and Localization (L10n)* recipe in *Chapter 1, Getting Started with PrimeFaces*.

Responsive layout with Grid CSS

`Grid CSS` is a lightweight stylesheet bundled with PrimeFaces that offers responsive layout utilities for mobile devices and desktops. In this recipe, we will create a responsive user interface with custom styling and also demonstrate them in a nested version.

How to do it...

A simple definition of a responsive grid is created with the help of HTML `div` components and CSS classes as follows:

```
<div class="ui-grid ui-grid-responsive">
  <div class="ui-grid-row">
    <div class="ui-grid-col-1">1</div>
    <div class="ui-grid-col-1">1</div>
    <div class="ui-grid-col-1">1</div>
    <div class="ui-grid-col-1">1</div>
    <div class="ui-grid-col-1">1</div>
    <div class="ui-grid-col-1">1</div>
    <div class="ui-grid-col-1">1</div>
    <div class="ui-grid-col-1">1</div>
    <div class="ui-grid-col-1">1</div>
    <div class="ui-grid-col-1">1</div>
    <div class="ui-grid-col-1">1</div>
    <div class="ui-grid-col-1">1</div>
  </div>
  <div class="ui-grid-row">
    <div class="ui-grid-col-6">6</div>
    <div class="ui-grid-col-6">6</div>
```

```
    </div>
    <div class="ui-grid-row">
      <div class="ui-grid-col-4">4</div>
      <div class="ui-grid-col-8">8</div>
    </div>
  </div>
```

Grid CSS contains a built-in stylesheet definition for up to 12 columns, matching with ui-grid-col-1 and onward up to ui-grid-col-12. If we have a sum of columns at a fixed number, we can create combinations easily, as seen in the previous sample. But the sum should not exceed 12. The ui-grid-row style class, which defines the style that will be applied per row.

The visual of the sample will be as follows:

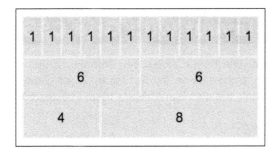

For demonstration purposes, we applied the following style to make the cells more distinct:

```
<style type="text/css">
  .ui-grid .ui-grid-row div {
    background-color: #cccccc;
    border: 1px solid #dddddd;
    padding: 10px 0;
    text-align: center;
  }
</style>
```

There's more...

The `ui-grid-responsive` style class makes the `div` element respond to the screen resizing as seen here:

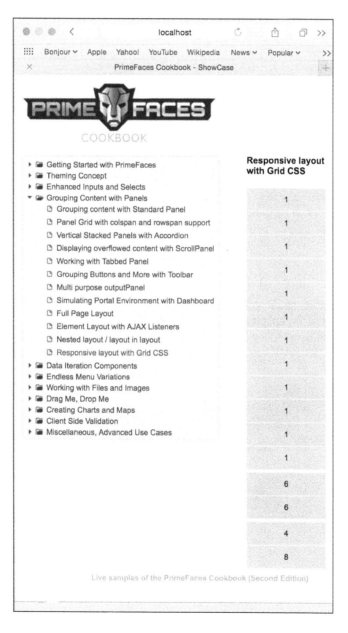

Nesting div elements

It's possible to nest `div` elements that have the `ui-grid-responsive` style. A sample definition is as follows:

```
<div class="ui-grid ui-grid-responsive">
  <div class="ui-grid-row">
    <div class="ui-grid-col-3">3</div>
    <div class="ui-grid-col-9">9
      <div class="ui-grid ui-grid-responsive">
        <div class="ui-grid-row">
          <div class="ui-grid-col-4">4</div>
          <div class="ui-grid-col-4">4</div>
          <div class="ui-grid-col-4">4</div>
        </div>
        <div class="ui-grid-row">
          <div class="ui-grid-col-6">6</div>
          <div class="ui-grid-col-6">6</div>
        </div>
      </div>
    </div>
  </div>
</div>
```

We defined 12 columns separated by 3 to 9, and then within the second section, which consists of 9 columns, we split it into 12, that is, by 4-4-4 and then by 6-6. The visual of the nested definition will be as follows:

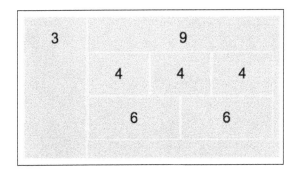

For demonstration purposes, we applied the style as we did in the first example, but here we define it with an immediate children declaration (`>`) as follows:

```
<style type="text/css">
  .ui-grid > .ui-grid-row > div {
    background-color: #cccccc;
    border: 1px solid #dddddd;
    padding: 10px 0;
    text-align: center;
  }
</style>
```

The PrimeFaces Cookbook Showcase application

This recipe is available in the demo web application on GitHub (`https://github.com/ova2/primefaces-cookbook/tree/second-edition`). Clone the project if you have not done it yet, explore the project structure, and build and deploy the WAR file on application servers compatible with Servlet 3.x, such as *JBoss WildFly* and *Apache TomEE*.

When the server is running, the showcase for the recipe is available at the following URLs:

- `http://localhost:8080/pf-cookbook/views/chapter4/gridCSS.jsf`
- `http://localhost:8080/pf-cookbook/views/chapter4/gridCSSNested.jsf`

5
Data Iteration Components

In this chapter, we will cover:

- ▸ Selecting rows in dataTable
- ▸ Sorting and filtering data in dataTable
- ▸ In-cell editing with dataTable
- ▸ Resizing, reordering, and toggling columns in dataTable
- ▸ Making dataTable responsive
- ▸ Using subTable for grouping
- ▸ Handling tons of data – LazyDataModel
- ▸ Listing data with dataList
- ▸ Listing data with pickList
- ▸ Listing data with orderList
- ▸ Visualizing data with tree
- ▸ Visualizing data with treeTable
- ▸ Exporting data in various formats
- ▸ Managing events with schedule by leveraging lazy loading
- ▸ Visualizing data with dataScroller

Introduction

In this chapter, we will cover the basic and advanced features to visualize data with the data iteration components provided by PrimeFaces. We will start with the dataTable component that offers extensive features, such as filtering, sorting, reordering, column resizing, and toggling. We will then focus on various other components, such as dataList that renders data in a listed format and pickList and orderList that provide data selection through listed sets. The tree and treeTable components list data in a tree format, and they are mostly based on the same data model. There is a sophisticated component called schedule to visualize calendar data, and we will demonstrate its usage with its lazy loading feature. Our final recipe for this chapter is based on dataScroller, which lazily loads data according to the page scroll done by the user.

Selecting rows in dataTable

There are several ways to select a row or multiple rows, such as line selection and selection with radio buttons and checkboxes, from the dataTable component. We will cover all the possibilities in this recipe.

How to do it...

To make a single selection possible with a command component, such as commandLink or commandButton, f:setPropertyActionListener can be used to set the selected row as a parameter to the server side:

```
<p:dataTable id="withCommand" var="car"
  value="#{dataTableBean.cars}"
  selection="#{dataTableBean.selectedCar}">
  <p:column>
    <p:commandButton value="Select" update=":mainForm:display"
      oncomplete="carDialog.show()">
      <f:setPropertyActionListener value="#{car}"
        target="#{dataTableBean.selectedCar}" />
    </p:commandButton>
  </p:column>
  ...
</p:dataTable>
```

The selection attribute needs to be bound to an instance of the Car reference in order to get the selected data.

Instead of using `<f:setPropertyActionListener>`, it's also possible to set the selection to the server side by passing a method parameter. The definition of the button and the method is given as follows:

```
<p:commandButton value="Select" update=":mainForm:display"
  oncomplete="PF('carDialog').show()"
  action="#{dataTableBean.selectCar(car)}" />

public String selectCar(Car car) {
  this.selectedCar = car;
  return null;
}
```

The `Car` class is a simple data class that owns two attributes, `year` and `name`.

 To pass the selection as a parameter to the method, you need to use EL 2.2 at least.

There's more...

The `selectionMode` attribute could be used to enable the selection whenever a row is clicked on. Its value should be `single` for the single selection mode. To select multiple items with the modifier key (which is *Ctrl* in Windows and *Command* in Mac OS), `selectionMode` should be set to `multiple` and `selection` needs to be bound to an array of the `Car` reference.

```
<p:dataTable id="multipleSelection" var="car"
  value="#{dataTableBean.cars}" rowKey="#{car.name}"
  selection="#{dataTableBean.selectedCars}"
  selectionMode="multiple">

  . . .
</p:dataTable>
```

 It's also possible to select multiple rows using the *Shift* key.

In multiple-selection mode, whenever a row is clicked on, the previous selection gets cleared. This is the default behavior, and it can be customized by setting the `rowSelectMode` attribute of the `dataTable` component to the `add` value. The default value of the attribute is `new`.

Single selection with a row click

It's possible to select a row with a click and then press `commandButton` to view the details of the selection in a dialog box. This is possible by defining the `rowKey` attribute where its value should point to a unique identifier. The button processes `dataTable` and displays `carDialog` on completion of the event. The definition is given as follows:

```
<p:dataTable id="singleSelection" var="car"
  value="#{dataTableBean.cars}" rowKey="#{car.name}"
  selection="#{dataTableBean.selectedCar}"
  selectionMode="single">
  <p:column headerText="Year">#{car.year}</p:column>
  <p:column headerText="Name">#{car.name}</p:column>
  <f:facet name="footer">
    <p:commandButton id="viewButton1" value="View"
      icon="ui-icon-search" process="singleSelection"
      update=":mainForm:display"
      oncomplete="PF('carDialog').show()" />
  </f:facet>
</p:dataTable>
```

Single selection with radio buttons

The `dataTable` component supports single-row selection with the help of radio buttons out of the box. This can be achieved by defining a column with the `selectionMode` attribute set with the `single` value.

```
<p:dataTable id="withRadioButton" var="car"
  value="#{dataTableBean.cars}" rowKey="#{car.name}"
  selection="#{dataTableBean.selectedCar}">
  <p:column selectionMode="single"/>
  ...
</p:dataTable>
```

The table will be rendered as follows:

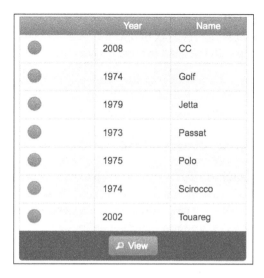

Multiple selection with checkboxes

It's very easy to enable multiple-item selection with `dataTable` by defining a column with the value of the `selectionMode` attribute set to `multiple`, as follows:

```
<p:dataTable id="multipleSelectionCheckbox" var="car"
  value="#{dataTableBean.cars}" rowKey="#{car.name}"
  selection="#{dataTableBean.selectedCars}">
    <p:column selectionMode="multiple" />
  ...
</p:dataTable>
```

For convenience, the component will also provide a checkbox in the header to select all the checkboxes. The appearance of the table with multiple selection will be as follows:

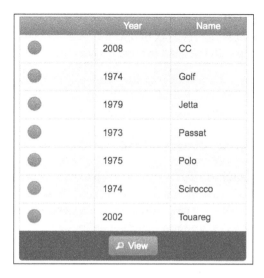

Instant row selection

The `dataTable` component supports AJAX behavior events on row selection/unselection. The definition of the table, along with the AJAX events, is given here:

```
<p:dataTable id="ajaxBehavior" var="car" rowKey="#{car.name}"
  value="#{dataTableBean.cars}"
  selection="#{dataTableBean.selectedCar}"
  selectionMode="single">
  <p:column headerText="Year">#{car.year}</p:column>
  <p:column headerText="Name">#{car.name}</p:column>
  <p:ajax event="rowSelect" update=":mainForm:growl"
    listener="#{dataTableBean.onRowSelect}" />
  <p:ajax event="rowUnselect" update=":mainForm:growl"
    listener="#{dataTableBean.onRowUnselect}" />
</p:dataTable>
```

The `rowSelect` and `rowUnselect` AJAX events invoke the `onRowSelect` and `onRowUnselect` methods respectively. Their implementations are given here:

```
public void onRowSelect(SelectEvent event) {
  MessageUtil.addInfoMessage("car.selected",
    ((Car) event.getObject()).getName());
}

public void onRowUnselect(UnselectEvent event) {
  MessageUtil.addInfoMessage("car.unselected",
    ((Car) event.getObject()).getName());
}
```

Instead of specifying the `rowKey` attribute for instant selection, one other option could be defining a data model that extends `javax.faces.model.DataModel` and implements `org.primefaces.model.SelectableDataModel`. A selectable car data model that meets the requirements is given here:

```
public class CarDataModel extends ListDataModel<Car>
  implements SelectableDataModel<Car> {

  public CarDataModel(List<Car> data) {
    super(data);
  }

  @Override
  public Car getRowData(String rowKey) {
```

```
    List<Car> cars = (List<Car>) getWrappedData();

    for(Car car : cars) {
      if(car.getName().equals(rowKey))
      return car;
    }
    return null;
  }

  @Override
  public Object getRowKey(Car car) {
    return car.getName();
  }
 }
}
```

PrimeFaces Cookbook Showcase application

This recipe is available in the demo web application on GitHub (`https://github.com/ova2/primefaces-cookbook/tree/second-edition`). Clone the project if you have not done it yet, explore the project structure, and build and deploy the WAR file on application servers compatible with Servlet 3.x, such as *JBoss WildFly* and *Apache TomEE*.

The showcase for the recipe is available at `http://localhost:8080/pf-cookbook/views/chapter5/dataTableSelectRow.jsf`.

See also

For details about the `MessageUtil` class, see the *Internationalization (i18n) and Localization (L10n)* recipe in *Chapter 1, Getting Started with PrimeFaces*.

Sorting and filtering data in dataTable

The `dataTable` component provides AJAX-based built-in sorting and filtering based on its columns.

How to do it...

The `dataTable` component provides sorting options based on AJAX by enabling the `sortBy` attribute at the column level. The following is the definition of a table that lists the `Car` data; sorting is enabled on the `name` and `year` attributes:

```
<p:dataTable id="sorting" var="car"
  value="#{dataTableBean.cars}">
```

```
    <p:column headerText="Year" sortBy="#{car.year}">
      <h:outputText value="#{car.year}" />
    </p:column>
    <p:column headerText="Name" sortBy="#{car.name}">
      <h:outputText value="#{car.name}" />
    </p:column>
  </p:dataTable>
```

When sorting is enabled, the headers of those columns will have the sort direction represented with small arrow icons as pointed out in this image:

The `dataTable` component provides filtering based on AJAX by enabling the `filterBy` attribute for the columns. The following is the definition of a table that lists the `Car` data; filtering is enabled on the `name` and `year` attributes:

```
  <p:dataTable id="filtering" var="car"
    value="#{dataTableBean.cars}">
    <p:column headerText="Year" filterBy="#{car.year}">
      <h:outputText value="#{car.year}" />
    </p:column>
    <p:column headerText="Name" filterBy="#{car.name}">
      <h:outputText value="#{car.name}" />
    </p:column>
  </p:dataTable>
```

When filtering is enabled in the headers of those columns, they will contain input text fields in order to retrieve the filtering characters from the user. The appearance of the table will be as follows:

Year	Name
2008	CC
1974	Golf
1979	Jetta
1973	Passat
1975	Polo
1974	Scirocco
2002	Touareg

The `dataTable` component provides the `filteredValue` attribute where you can collect a list of filtered elements through its value.

There's more...

Also, it is possible to set filter matching with custom matchers. The `filterMatchMode` attribute enables this built-in matcher mechanism, which is set to `startsWith` by default. The other possible values are listed as follows:

Attribute Value	Action
`contains`	This applies if the column value contains the filter value
`endsWith`	This applies when the column value ends with the filter value
`equals`	This applies if the column value equals the filter value
`exact`	This applies if the text values of the column and the filter are the same
`gt`	This applies if the column value is greater than the filter value
`gte`	This applies if the column value is greater than or equal to the filter value
`in`	This applies if the column value is in the collection of filter values that are provided
`lt`	This applies if the column value is less than the filter value
`lte`	This applies if the column value is less than or equal to the filter value
`startsWith`	This applies if the column value starts with the filter value

The filter text field can be positioned before or after the header text by setting the `filterPosition` attribute. The values can be either `top` or `bottom` (the latter is the default value).

With the `filterMaxLength` attribute, it is possible to restrict the filter input according to the given number of characters, for example, `filterMaxLength="2"`.

 It is recommended that you use a scope longer than *request scope*, such as *view scope*, to keep the `filteredValue` so that the filtered list is still accessible after filtering.

Custom filtering

When `filterMatchMode` is not enough, it's possible to provide custom filtering with the `filterFunction` attribute. The method signature provided to the `filterFunction` attribute should be stated as follows:

```
public boolean filterMethod(Object value, Object filter,
   Locale locale) {
}
```

Options for filtering

Filtering also supports a drop-down box as the filtering mechanism instead of the input text field. This can be achieved by providing a list with the `filterOptions` attribute. The definition of the column is given here:

```
<p:dataTable id="withFilterOptions" var="car"
  value="#{dataTableBean.cars}" style="width: 300px;">
  <p:column headerText="Year" filterBy="#{car.year}"
    filterMatchMode="startsWith">
    <h:outputText value="#{car.year}" />
  </p:column>
  <p:column headerText="Name" filterBy="#{car.name}"
    filterOptions="#{dataTableBean.carNamesAsOptions}">
    <h:outputText value="#{car.name}" />
  </p:column>
</p:dataTable>
```

Global filtering

The `dataTable` component provides global filtering by invoking the client-side method, `filter()`. The global filter can be positioned at the `header` facet of the table, as shown in the following code snippet:

```
<f:facet name="header">
  <p:outputPanel>
    <h:outputText value="Search all fields:" />
```

```
    <p:inputText id="globalFilter"
      onkeyup="carsTable.filter()" />
  </p:outputPanel>
</f:facet>
```

Filtering will be triggered on the `onkeyup` event by invoking the mentioned `filter()` method of the table, the `widgetVar` attribute of which is set to `carsTable`. The appearance of a table with global filtering will be as follows:

Search all fields:	
Year	**Name**
2008	CC
1974	Golf
1979	Jetta
1973	Passat
1975	Polo
1974	Scirocco
2002	Touareg

Postprocessing events on sorting/filtering

It's possible to execute post-processing events with `<f:event>` that will invoke a method on the backing bean defined with the `listener` attribute. The definition of `dataTable` with postprocessors is given here:

```
<p:dataTable id="withPostEvents" var="car"
  value="#{dataTableBean.cars}">
  <f:event type="org.primefaces.event.data.PostSortEvent"
    listener="#{dataTableBean.postSort}" />
  <f:event type="org.primefaces.event.data.PostFilterEvent"
    listener="#{dataTableBean.postFilter}" />

  <p:column headerText="Year" sortBy="#{car.year}"
    filterBy="#{car.year}">
    <h:outputText value="#{car.year}" />
  </p:column>
  <p:column headerText="Name" sortBy="#{car.name}"
    filterBy="#{car.name}">
    <h:outputText value="#{car.name}" />
  </p:column>
</p:dataTable>
```

The definitions of the listener methods are given as follows:

```
public void postSort(ComponentSystemEvent e) {
  System.out.println(((DataTable)
    e.getComponent()).getSortColumn().getHeaderText());
}

public void postFilter(ComponentSystemEvent e) {
  DataTable dt = (DataTable) e.getComponent();
  for (Iterator it =
    dt.getFilteredValue().iterator(); it.hasNext();) {
    Car car = (Car) it.next();
    System.out.println(car.getName());
  }
}
```

PrimeFaces Cookbook Showcase application

This recipe is available in the demo web application on GitHub (`https://github.com/ova2/primefaces-cookbook/tree/second-edition`). Clone the project if you have not done it yet, explore the project structure, and build and deploy the WAR file on application servers compatible with Servlet 3.x, such as *JBoss WildFly* and *Apache TomEE*.

The showcase for the recipe is available at `http://localhost:8080/pf-cookbook/views/chapter5/dataTableSortFilter.jsf`.

In-cell editing with dataTable

The `dataTable` component supports the in-cell editing feature to update values within the table without navigating to another page.

How to do it...

In order to enable editing, first we need to set the `editable` attribute of the table to `true`. Each column definition that we need to be editable should contain the `<p:cellEditor>` helper component that will contain two facets to render output components—one to visualize the data for the user and the other to get input data from the user. The in-place editor palette, which is the `<p:rowEditor>` component, also needs to be rendered in a column of `dataTable` in order to activate editing with user interaction. Here's the code that encapsulates the discussion in this paragraph:

```
<p:dataTable id="inCellEditing" var="car"
  value="#{dataTableBean.cars}" rowKey="#{car.name}"
  editable="true">
  <p:column headerText="Year">
```

```
    <p:cellEditor>
    <f:facet name="output">
      <h:outputText value="#{car.year}" />
    </f:facet>
    <f:facet name="input">
      <p:inputText value="#{car.year}" />
    </f:facet>
    </p:cellEditor>
  </p:column>
  <p:column headerText="Name">
    <p:cellEditor>
      <f:facet name="output">
        <h:outputText value="#{car.name}" />
      </f:facet>
      <f:facet name="input">
        <h:selectOneMenu value="#{car.name}">
          <f:selectItems value="#{dataTableBean.carNames}"
            var="name" itemLabel="#{name}"
            itemValue="#{name}" />
        </h:selectOneMenu>
      </f:facet>
    </p:cellEditor>
  </p:column>
  <p:column headerText="Actions">
    <p:rowEditor />
  </p:column>
</p:dataTable>
```

The components that reside in the input facet could be an inputText component as well as a selectOneMenu component, which will render a drop-down list for the input. The appearance of a table with output facets will be as follows:

Year	Name	Actions
2008	CC	✎
1974	Golf	✎
1979	Jetta	✎
1973	Passat	✎
1975	Polo	✎
1974	Scirocco	✎
2002	Touareg	✎

When the pencil icon is clicked on, the table will transit into edit mode and the `input` facets will be rendered as follows:

Year	Name	Actions
2008	CC	✎
1974	Golf	✎
1979	Jetta	✎
1973	Passat ⬍	✓ ✗
1975	Polo	✎
1974	Scirocco	✎
2002	Touareg	✎

Clicking on the "tick" icon will save the edited row, and clicking on the "cancel" icon will revert all changes.

There's more...

By default, the edit mode for `dataTable` is `row`, where the whole row on the table gets edited. One other possible approach is editing just a cell instead of a whole row. This can be achieved by setting the `editMode` attribute to `cell` instead of `row`. The cell will switch to edit mode when clicked on, and losing focus on the cell triggers an AJAX event to save the changed value.

> When the `editMode` attribute is set to `cell`, you won't need the extra column that contains the `<p:rowEditor>` component since editing can be easily triggered by clicking on a cell.

Editing rows according to a condition

The `editingRow` attribute defines whether cell editors of a row should be displayed as editable or not. The definition given next will display rows of cars (as brands) that were manufactured before the year 2000 in edit mode:

```
<p:dataTable id="editingRowMode" var="car"
  value="#{dataTableBean.cars}"
  rowKey="#{car.name}" editable="true"
  editingRow="#{car.year > 2000}">
</p:dataTable>
```

AJAX behavior events

The dataTable component supports AJAX behavior events in order to handle the interactions of the user on row editing and cancellation of the editing actions. The definition of the AJAX behavior events should be placed within the table, as shown in the following code snippet:

```
<p:ajax event="rowEdit" listener="#{dataTableBean.onEdit}"
  update=":form:growl" />
<p:ajax event="rowEditCancel" listener="#{dataTableBean.onCancel}"
  update=":form:growl" />
```

The onEdit and onCancel methods retrieve org.primefaces.event.RowEditEvent as the parameter. The object that is edited can be retrieved from the event as event.getObject(). The following is the code for this discussion:

```
public void onEdit(RowEditEvent event) {
  MessageUtil.addInfoMessage("car.edit",
    ((Car) event.getObject()).getName());
}

public void onCancel(RowEditEvent event) {
  MessageUtil.addInfoMessage("car.edit.cancelled",
    ((Car) event. getObject()).getName());
}
```

PrimeFaces Cookbook Showcase application

This recipe is available in the demo web application on GitHub (https://github.com/ova2/primefaces-cookbook/tree/second-edition). Clone the project if you have not done it yet, explore the project structure, and build and deploy the WAR file on application servers compatible with Servlet 3.x, such as *JBoss WildFly* and *Apache TomEE*.

The showcase for the recipe is available at http://localhost:8080/pf-cookbook/views/chapter5/dataTableInCellEdit.jsf.

See also

For details about the MessageUtil class, see the *Internationalization (i18n) and Localization (L10n)* recipe in *Chapter 1, Getting Started with PrimeFaces*.

Resizing, reordering, and toggling columns in dataTable

The `dataTable` component offers enhanced features on its content, such as resizing of columns, reordering of rows and columns via drag and drop, and toggling of columns for visibility.

How to do it...

Resizing should be enabled by setting the `resizableColumns` attribute to `true`, as shown here:

```
<p:dataTable id="resizing" var="car" value="#{dataTableBean.cars}"
  resizableColumns="true">
  <p:column headerText="Year">
    <h:outputText value="#{car.year}" />
  </p:column>
  <p:column headerText="Name">
    <h:outputText value="#{car.name}" />
  </p:column>
</p:dataTable>
```

 After resizing, the state of the columns is preserved on the postback of a page via cookie-based persistence.

Reordering of rows and columns is possible with the `draggableRows` and `draggableColumns` attributes respectively. A sample definition is given here:

```
<p:dataTable value="#{dataTableBean.cars}" var="car"
  draggableRows="true" draggableColumns="true">
  . . .
</p:dataTable>
```

While performing reordering, the user is assisted with placeholders, as seen in this image:

Year	Name
1979	Jetta
2008	CC
1974	Golf
1975	Polo
1973	Passat
1974	Scirocco
2002	Touareg

↓

Name		
	Year	

Year	Year
Golf	1974
Jetta	1979
CC	2008
Polo	1975
Passat	1973
Scirocco	1974
Touareg	2002

Row toggling is supported by `dataTable` with the help of the `<p:rowToggler>` and `<p:rowExpansion>` components. The `rowToggler` component renders an expanding/toggling icon when placed in a column, and `rowExpansion` defines the content that will be displayed beneath the expanded row. An AJAX call is made with the expansion. The definition of the table will be as follows:

```
<p:dataTable id="rowToggle" var="car"
  value="#{dataTableBean.cars}">
  <p:column style="width: 20px">
    <p:rowToggler />
  </p:column>
  <p:column headerText="Year">
    <h:outputText value="#{car.year}" />
  </p:column>
  <p:column headerText="Name">
    <h:outputText value="#{car.name}" />
```

```
    </p:column>

    <p:rowExpansion>
      <h:panelGrid id="display" columns="2" cellpadding="4">
        <f:facet name="header">
          <p:graphicImage
            value="/resources/images/autocomplete/#{car.name}.png"
            width="60" height="40" />
        </f:facet>

        <h:outputText value="Name:" />
        <h:outputText value="#{car.name}" />

        <h:outputText value="Year:" />
        <h:outputText value="#{car.year}" />
      </h:panelGrid>
    </p:rowExpansion>
  </p:dataTable>
```

The visual output of the table with the first row expanded will be as follows:

Year	Name
2008	CC

Name:	CC
Year:	2008

Year	Name
1974	Golf
1979	Jetta
1973	Passat
1975	Polo
1974	Scirocco
2002	Touareg

The expandedRow attribute of dataTable with its value set to true, defines whether all the rows of the table should be expanded by default. The rowExpandMode attribute with the value single defines only whether one row should be expanded at a time. When set to multiple, which is the default value, the expanded row will not be collapsed when a second row gets expanded.

There's more...

By default, while resizing a column by dragging it to the left-hand side or the right-hand side, a helper column line is rendered to state the possible final position of the column's line. If you want to resize the column in live mode without this helper, you can set `liveResize` to `true` to see it in action instantly.

AJAX behavior events on resize

The `dataTable` component provides the `colResize` AJAX behavior event that will be fired when a column is resized:

```
<p:dataTable id="resizingAJAX" var="car"
  value="#{dataTableBean.cars}" resizableColumns="true">
  <p:ajax event="colResize" listener="#{dataTableBean.onResize}"
    update=":mainForm:growl" />
</p:dataTable>
```

The `onResize` method will be invoked with an instance of `org.primefaces.event.ColumnResizeEvent`. The width and height of the resized column can be retrieved from the event instance. The definition for the `onResize` method is given here:

```
public void onResize(ColumnResizeEvent event) {
  MessageUtil.addInfoMessage("column.resized",
    "W:" + event.getWidth() + " - H:" + event.getHeight());
}
```

AJAX behavior events on row and column reordering

The `dataTable` component provides the `rowReorder` AJAX behavior event that will be fired when a row is repositioned by dragging and dropping:

```
<p:dataTable id="reorderingAJAX" var="car"
  value="#{dataTableBean.cars}" draggableRows="true">
  <p:ajax event="rowReorder" update=":mainForm:growl"
    listener="#{dataTableBean.onRowReorder}" />
  ...
</p:dataTable>
```

The `onRowReorder` method will be invoked with an instance of `org.primefaces.event.ReorderEvent`. The start and end indices for the column that is repositioned can be retrieved from the event. The definition for the `onReorder` method is given here:

```
public void onRowReorder(ReorderEvent event) {
    MessageUtil.addInfoMessage("row.reordered", "From:" +
        event.getFromIndex() + " - To:" + event.getToIndex());
}
```

The `dataTable` component also provides the `colReorder` AJAX behavior event that will be fired when a column is repositioned by dragging and dropping. The column reorder doesn't support `ReorderEvent` with the listener method at the moment; `AjaxBehaviorEvent` should be used instead.

Toggling columns

With the `<p:columnToggler>` helper component, it's possible to toggle the visible columns of the table. Here's how column toggling is used:

```
<p:dataTable id="colToggle" var="car"
  value="#{dataTableBean.cars}">
  <f:facet name="header">
    <p:commandButton id="toggler" type="button"
      value="Columns" />
    <p:columnToggler datasource="colToggle"
      trigger="toggler" />
  </f:facet>
  <p:column headerText="Year">
    <h:outputText value="#{car.year}" />
  </p:column>
  <p:column headerText="Name">
    <h:outputText value="#{car.name}" />
  </p:column>
</p:dataTable>
```

The `id` parameter of the table should be provided to the `datasource` attribute of `columnToggler`. With the `trigger` attribute, `columnToggler` attaches itself to a button where a list of all the columns will be rendered, along with a checkbox. By default, all the header text values are rendered in the UI. So, if you do not want a column to be on that list for toggling, you can set the `toggleable` attribute of that column to `false`.

 It's advised that you do not use scrollable feature in a table that uses `columnToggler` since they are not fully compatible.

The visual output of `columnToggler` inside the header of the table is shown here:

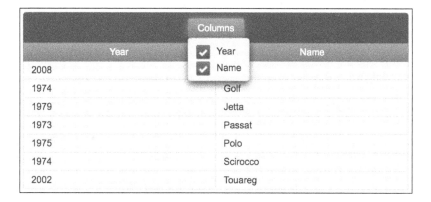

AJAX behavior event on column toggling

The `columnToggler` component offers the `toggle` AJAX behavior event that will be fired when a column is toggled:

```
<p:dataTable id="colToggleAJAX" var="car"
  value="#{dataTableBean.cars}">
  <f:facet name="header">
    <p:commandButton id="togglerAJAX" type="button"
      value="Columns" />
    <p:columnToggler datasource="colToggleAJAX"
      trigger="togglerAJAX">
      <p:ajax event="toggle" update=":mainForm:growl"
        listener="#{dataTableBean.onColumnToggle}" />
    </p:columnToggler>
  </f:facet>
  ...
</p:dataTable>
```

The `onColumnToggle` method will be invoked with an instance of `org.primefaces.event.ToggleEvent`. The visibility of the column can be retrieved from the event as `enum`. The definition for the `onColumnToggle` method is given here:

```
public void onColumnToggle(ToggleEvent e) {
  MessageUtil.addInfoMessage("col.toggled",
    "Visibility:" + e.getVisibility());
}
```

Adding state for column toggling

By default, `columnToggler` is stateless. While doing sorting and filtering on columns of a table where they are toggled, synchronization issues might occur, and this is because those columns will come right back in after filtering or sorting.

To make column toggling with sorting or filtering work, we will set the `visible` attribute of columns by binding them to a list from the backing bean here:

```
<p:dataTable id="colToggleAJAX" var="car"
  value="#{dataTableBean.cars}">
  <f:facet name="header">
    <p:commandButton id="togglerAJAX" type="button"
      value="Columns" />
    <p:columnToggler datasource="colToggleAJAX"
      trigger="togglerAJAX">
      <p:ajax event="toggle" update=":mainForm:growl"
        listener="#{dataTableBean.onColumnToggle}" />
    </p:columnToggler>
  </f:facet>
  <p:column headerText="Year"
    visible="#{dataTableBean.visibleList[0]}">
    <h:outputText value="#{car.year}" />
  </p:column>
  <p:column headerText="Name"
    visible="#{dataTableBean.visibleList[1]}">
    <h:outputText value="#{car.name}" />
  </p:column>
</p:dataTable>
```

The definition of the visible list and the `onColumnToggle` method on the backing bean is shown here:

```
private List<Boolean> visibleList;

public void onColumnToggle(ToggleEvent e) {
  visibleList.set((Integer) e.getData(),
    e.getVisibility() == Visibility.VISIBLE);
}
```

PrimeFaces Cookbook Showcase application

This recipe is available in the demo web application on GitHub (`https://github.com/ova2/primefaces-cookbook/tree/second-edition`). Clone the project if you have not done it yet, explore the project structure, and build and deploy the WAR file on application severs compatible with Servlet 3.x, such as *JBoss WildFly* and *Apache TomEE*.

The showcase for the recipe is available at `http://localhost:8080/pf-cookbook/views/chapter5/dataTableResizeReorderToggle.jsf`.

See also

For details about the `MessageUtil` class, see the *Internationalization (i18n) and Localization (L10n)* recipe in *Chapter 1, Getting Started with PrimeFaces*.

Making dataTable responsive

Starting with PrimeFaces v5.2, it's possible to make the `dataTable` component act responsively according to the resizing of the browser.

How to do it...

The `priority` attribute of `<p:column>` should be set to a value between 1 to 6, from the highest priority to the lowest one. A definition of the `priority` attribute is given here:

```
<p:dataTable id="withPriority" var="car"
  value="#{dataTableBean.detailedCars}">
  <p:column headerText="Name">
    <h:outputText value="#{car.name}" />
  </p:column>
  <p:column headerText="Year" priority="1">
    <h:outputText value="#{car.year}" />
  </p:column>
  <p:column headerText="Color" priority="3">
    <h:outputText value="#{car.color}" />
  </p:column>
  <p:column headerText="Seat Number" priority="2">
    <h:outputText value="#{car.seatNumber}" />
  </p:column>
</p:dataTable>
```

Here, the color column has the lowest priority and will be dropped first when the browser is resized to a smaller size.

There's more...

By setting the `reflow` attribute of `dataTable` to `true`, it's possible to visualize the rows of the table in stacked mode when the browser is resized to a smaller size. A visual output of the table in default mode and in resized mode is given here:

Name	Year	Color	Seat Number
CC	2008	black	4
Golf	1974	white	2
Jetta	1979	blue	5
Passat	1973	magenta	5
Polo	1975	brown	4
Scirocco	1974	red	2
Touareg	2002	silver	7

Name	CC
Year	2008
Color	black
Seat Number	4
Name	Golf
Year	1974
Color	white
Seat Number	2
Name	Jetta
Year	1979
Color	blue
Seat Number	5
Name	Passat
Year	1973
Color	magenta
Seat Number	5
Name	Polo
Year	1975
Color	brown
Seat Number	4
Name	Scirocco
Year	1974
Color	red
Seat Number	2
Name	Touareg
Year	2002
Color	silver
Seat Number	7

PrimeFaces Cookbook Showcase application

This recipe is available in the demo web application on GitHub (`https://github.com/ova2/primefaces-cookbook/tree/second-edition`). Clone the project if you have not done it yet, explore the project structure, and build and deploy the WAR file on application servers compatible with Servlet 3.x, such as *JBoss WildFly* and *Apache TomEE*.

The showcase for the recipe is available at `http://localhost:8080/pf-cookbook/views/chapter5/responsiveDataTable.jsf`.

Using subTable for grouping

A helper component, `subTable` can be used to group row data inside a table.

How to do it...

A basic definition of a table that contains `subTable` is given here:

```
<p:dataTable value="#{dataTableBean.boxers}" var="boxer">
  <f:facet name="header">
    Boxers
  </f:facet>

  <p:columnGroup type="header">
    <p:row>
      <p:column rowspan="2" headerText="Boxer" />
      <p:column colspan="2" headerText="Stats" />
    </p:row>
    <p:row>
      <p:column headerText="Wins" />
      <p:column headerText="Losses" />
    </p:row>
  </p:columnGroup>

  <p:subTable var="stats" value="#{boxer.stats}">
    <f:facet name="header">
      <h:outputText value="#{boxer.name}" />
    </f:facet>
    <p:column>
      <h:outputText value="#{stats.match}" />
    </p:column>
```

```
    <p:column>
      <h:outputText value="#{stats.win}" />
    </p:column>
    <p:column>
      <h:outputText value="#{stats.loss}" />
    </p:column>
    <p:columnGroup type="footer">
      <p:row>
        <p:column footerText="Totals: "
          style="text-align:right"/>
        <p:column footerText="#{boxer.allWins}" />
        <p:column footerText="#{boxer.allLosses}" />
      </p:row>
    </p:columnGroup>
  </p:subTable>
</p:dataTable>
```

The `columnGroup` component is used to combine rows and columns in headers and footers of the table. The model used within the table is briefly described here:

```
public class Boxer {
  private String name;
  private List<Stat> stats = new ArrayList<Stat>();
}

public class Stat {
  private String match;
  private int win;
  private int loss;
}
```

A visual output of the table is given here:

Boxers		
Boxer	Stats	
	Wins	Losses
Muhammad Ali		
2005-2006	7	5
2006-2007	10	5
2007-2008	3	8
2008-2009	10	4
2009-2010	10	5
2010-2011	3	10
Totals:	43	37
George Foreman		
2005-2006	4	10
2006-2007	6	8
2007-2008	10	5
2008-2009	7	6
2009-2010	10	8
2010-2011	7	4
Totals:	44	41

PrimeFaces Cookbook Showcase application

This recipe is available in the demo web application on GitHub (`https://github.com/ova2/primefaces-cookbook/tree/second-edition`). Clone the project if you have not done it yet, explore the project structure, and build and deploy the WAR file on application servers compatible with Servlet 3.x, such as *JBoss WildFly* and *Apache TomEE*.

The showcase for the recipe is available at `http://localhost:8080/pf-cookbook/views/chapter5/subTable.jsf`.

Handling tons of data – LazyDataModel

The `dataTable` component provides support for displaying tons of data by enabling lazy loading. In order to handle large datasets, a data model needs to be implemented based on `org.primefaces.model.LazyDataModel` to support pagination, sorting, filtering, and live scrolling.

How to do it...

First, the `lazy` attribute should be set to `true` for lazy loading to be enabled for the table, and the abstract `load` method should be implemented in `org.primefaces.model.LazyDataModel`. We must also implement the `getRowData` and `getRowKey` methods when selection is enabled in the table. The lazy data model should be constructed with the list of `Car` instances and be bound to the table:

```
List<Car> cars = new ArrayList<Car>(millions_of_cars);
LazyDataModel<Car>lazyModel = new LazyCarDataModel(cars);
```

The table calls the `load` method implementation with the following parameters when paging, sorting, or filtering actions occur:

- ▸ `first`: This is the index of the first data to display
- ▸ `pageSize`: This is the number of data items to load on the page
- ▸ `sortField`: This is the name of the sort field (for example, `"name"` for `sortBy="#{car.name}"`)
- ▸ `sortOrder`: This is the `org.primefaces.model.SortOrder` enumeration; the value could be either `ASCENDING`, `DESCENDING`, or `UNSORTED`
- ▸ `filter`: This filters the map with a field name as the key (for example, `"name"` for `filterBy="#{car.name}"`) and the value

The total row count should also be set to the lazy data model in order to get the pagination work done properly by invoking the `setRowCount` method of the data model.

There's more...

The `field` attribute is provided by `<p:column>`; this is where the name of the field is passed to the `load` method in the `sortField` or `filter` method arguments according to the action taken. If `field` is not provided, the name of the field will be extracted from the values of the `filterBy` or `sortBy` attributes.

 Integrating JPA's Criteria API with `LazyDataModel` is a good approach to generalize the sorting and filtering features of every table.

PrimeFaces Cookbook Showcase application

This recipe is available in the demo web application on GitHub (`https://github.com/ova2/primefaces-cookbook/tree/second-edition`). Clone the project if you have not done it yet, explore the project structure, and build and deploy the WAR file on application servers compatible with Servlet 3.x, such as *JBoss WildFly* and *Apache TomEE*.

The showcase for the recipe is available at `http://localhost:8080/pf-cookbook/views/chapter5/dataTableLazyDataModel.jsf`.

Listing data with dataList

A collection of data in a list layout is presented by `dataList` with several display types and features, such as AJAX pagination.

How to do it...

A basic definition of a data list with a `header` facet for listing the names of countries starting with the letter "A" would be as follows:

```
<p:dataList id="simple" value="#{dataListBean.countriesShort}"
  var="country" itemType="disc">
  <f:facet name="header">
    Countries starting with 'A'
  </f:facet>
  <h:outputText value="#{country}" />
</p:dataList>
```

By default, the `dataList` component renders an unordered list, which corresponds to the `<ul>` HTML tag. The visual output is given here:

Countries starting with 'A'
• Armenia • Australia • Albania • Afghanistan • Andorra • Algeria • Azerbaijan • Argentina • Angola • Austria

The bullet type can be customized with the `itemType` attribute, which has the default value `disc`. For an unordered list, the other possible values are `circle` and `square`.

When `type` is set to `ordered`, `dataList` renders an ordered list, which corresponds to the `<ol>` HTML tag. The visual output is given here:

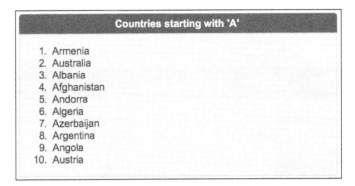

With ordered lists, the default value for the `itemType` is set to `1` to render a numerically ordered list. The other possible values to render alphabetically ordered characters as bullets in lowercase and uppercase are `a` and `A`, respectively. The last alternatives for rendering roman numbers as bullets in lowercase and uppercase are `i` or `I`.

There's more...

The third type of the `dataList` component is `definition`, where an inline description can be visualized for each item. The next definition displays a list of car names along with their small images. The detailed definition should be provided with the facet named `description`. The definition of `definition` is provided here:

```
<p:dataList id="withDescription" value="#{dataListBean.cars}"
  var="car" type="definition">
  Name: #{car.name}
  <f:facet name="description">
    <p:graphicImage
      value="/resources/images/autocomplete/#{car.name}.png"
      width="60" height="40" />
  </f:facet>
</p:dataList>
```

Pagination

The `dataList` component has a built-in AJAX pagination that is enabled by setting the `paginator` attribute to `true`. To support the pagination, the number of rows to display per page should be set with the `rows` attribute. Its default value is `0`, which indicates that all the data available will be displayed. Pagination can be customized using the `paginatorTemplateOption` attribute, which accepts keys to specify the content of the `paginator`:

- `FirstPageLink`
- `LastPageLink`
- `PreviousPageLink`
- `NextPageLink`
- `PageLinks`
- `CurrentPageReport`
- `RowsPerPageDropdown`

The default rendering for the pagination would be as shown here:

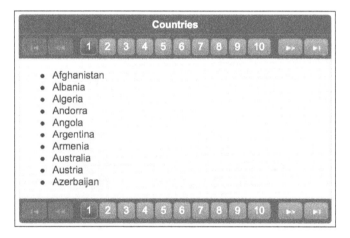

It would be the same as the pagination template, as shown in the following code snippet:

```
{FirstPageLink} {PreviousPageLink} {PageLinks} {NextPageLink}
{LastPageLink}
```

A more complex `paginator` definition is given here:

```
{CurrentPageReport} {FirstPageLink} {PreviousPageLink} {PageLinks}
{NextPageLink} {LastPageLink} {RowsPerPageDropdown}
```

This will be rendered as shown here:

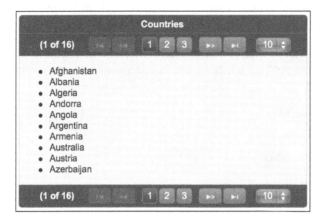

The {RowsPerPageDropdown} attribute has its own mechanism to produce templates, and the mechanism should be provided in order to render the dropdown (for example, rowsPerPageTemplate="5,10,15").

Also, {CurrentPageReport} has its own template defined with the currentPageReportTemplate option.

We can use the {currentPage}, {totalPages}, {totalRecords}, {startRecord}, and {endRecord} keywords within currentPageReportTemplate. The default value is {currentPage} of {totalPages}.

The pageLinks attribute defines the maximum number of page links to display. Its default value is 10. For the complex paginator definition given previously, it's set to 3. The paginator attribute can be positioned in three different locations by setting the paginatorPosition attribute to top, bottom, or both (the last value being the default value). The paginatorAlwaysVisible attribute defines whether the pagination should be hidden or not when the total data count is less than the number of rows per page.

The content of paginator can also be customized with a custom facet definition, as shown here:

```
<p:dataList value="#{dataListBean.countries}" var="country"
  rows="10" paginator="true"
  paginatorTemplate="{CurrentPageReport} {CustomContent}">
  <f:facet name="{CustomContent}">
    ..custom content..
  </f:facet>
  <f:facet name="header">
    Countries
```

```
      </f:facet>
      <h:outputText value="#{country}" />
   </p:dataList>
```

As seen in the example, the name of the facets should match with the name of the token given in the template.

PrimeFaces Cookbook Showcase application

This recipe is available in the demo web application on GitHub (`https://github.com/ova2/primefaces-cookbook/tree/second-edition`). Clone the project if you have not done it yet, explore the project structure, and build and deploy the WAR file on application servers compatible with Servlet 3.x, such as *JBoss WildFly* and *Apache TomEE*.

The showcase for the recipe is available at `http://localhost:8080/pf-cookbook/views/chapter5/dataList.jsf`.

Listing data with pickList

The `pickList` dual list is an input component that is used to transfer data between two different collections with drag-and-drop-based reordering, transition effects, POJO support, client-server callbacks, and more.

How to do it...

The `pickList` component uses a custom data model, which is an instance of `org.primefaces.model DualListModel` that contains two lists—one for the source and one for the target. For a `pickList` implementation that would be used to select countries, the data model could be as follows:

```
   private List<String> countriesSource = new ArrayList<String>();
   private List<String> countriesTarget = new ArrayList<String>();

   countriesSource.add("England");
   countriesSource.add("Germany");
   countriesSource.add("Switzerland");
   countriesSource.add("Turkey");

   private DualListModel<String> countries =
      new DualListModel<String>(countriesSource, countriesTarget);
```

The definition of the component could be as follows:

```
<p:pickList id="simple" value="#{pickListBean.countries}"
    var="country"
    itemLabel="#{country}" itemValue="#{country}" />
```

The visual output (of the previous two code snippets) of the component will be two containers—one for the source list and one for the target list—and will be as follows:

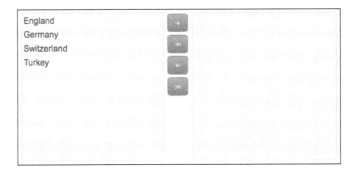

There's more...

The `itemDisabled` attribute specifies whether an item can be picked or not. When it is set to `true`, the source and target list will be rendered as disabled so as to prevent the selection.

It's possible to add captions at the top of the source list and the target list. The captions should be defined with the `sourceCaption` and `targetCaption` facets, as shown here:

```
<p:pickList id="withCaption" value="#{pickListBean.countries}"
        var="country" itemLabel="#{country}" itemValue="#{country}">
    <f:facet name="sourceCaption">Available</f:facet>
    <f:facet name="targetCaption">Selected</f:facet>
</p:pickList>
```

Control buttons visibility

The `showSourceControls` and `showTargetControls` attributes specify the visibility of the reorder buttons of the source list and the target list.

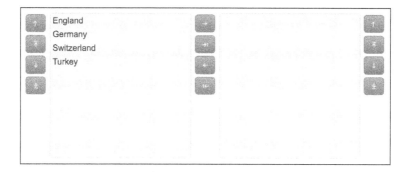

The labels for the control buttons can also be customized with the `addLabel`, `addAllLabel`, `removeLabel`, `removeAllLabel`, `moveUpLabel`, `moveTopLabel`, `moveDownLabel`, and `moveBottomLabel` attributes.

POJO support

The `pickList` component supports dealing with complex POJOs as well. The data model should be based on `org.primefaces.model.DualListModel` as it's defined with the example of strings. A converter for the `Car` class should also be implemented and used as defined next. The following is a definition of a data model that contains a source list and target list for the `Car` class:

```
DualListModel<Car> cars =
    new DualListModel<Car>(carsSource, carsTarget);
```

The `<p:column>` element could be used while visualizing the instances of `Car` within `pickList` to clearly identify the attributes of the `Car` class:

```
<p:pickList id="pojoSupport" value="#{pickListBean.cars}"
  var="car" itemLabel="#{car.name}" itemValue="#{car}">
  <f:converter
    converterId="org.primefaces.cookbook.converter.CarConverter"
    />
  <p:column>
    <p:graphicImage
      value="/resources/images/autocomplete/#{car.name}.png"
      width="100" height="70" />
  </p:column>
  <p:column>
    #{car.name}
  </p:column>
</p:pickList>
```

Transition effects

Effects can be applied with the `effect` attribute for content transition when a selection is moved from the source list to the target list or vice versa. The default value of the `effect` attribute is `fade`. The other possible values for the attribute are given here:

- `blind`
- `bounce`
- `clip`
- `drop`
- `explode`
- `fold`
- `highlight`
- `puff`
- `pulsate`
- `scale`
- `shake`
- `size`
- `slide`

To customize the animation speed, `effectSpeed` can be used. Its default value is `fast`; the other possible values are `slow` and `normal`.

Executing custom JavaScript on transfer

The `pickList` component supports the execution of a client-side callback when an item is transferred from one list to another. This could be achieved by providing a JavaScript method definition for the `onTransfer` attribute, as shown here:

```
<p:pickList id="withCustomJS" onTransfer="handleTransfer(e)"
   value="#{pickListBean.countries}" var="country"
   itemLabel="#{country}" itemValue="#{country}" />
```

The definition of the script method to list the values of the item that is transferred, the definition of from- and to-lists, and so on, is given here:

```
<script type="text/javascript">
  function handleTransfer(e) {
    alert(e.item);
    alert(e.from);
    alert(e.to);
    alert(e.type);
  }
</script>
```

The variable `e` provides access to the item transferred, the source and target unordered lists (named `from` and `to`, as an instance of `HTMLUListElement`), and the type of action taken, such as `command`, `dblclick`, or `dragdrop`.

AJAX behavior events

The `pickList` component provides the `transfer` AJAX behavior event that will be fired when an item is moved from the source list to the target list or vice versa:

```
<p:pickList id="withAJAX" value="#{pickListBean.countries}"
  var="country"
  itemLabel="#{country}" itemValue="#{country}">
  <p:ajax event="transfer" update="growl"
    listener="#{pickListBean.handleTransfer}" />
</p:pickList>
```

The `handleTransfer` method will be invoked with `org.primefaces.event.TransferEvent`. The items selected and the action taken can be identified through the instance of this event. A sample definition for the `handleTransfer` method is given here:

```
public void handleTransfer(TransferEvent event) {
  MessageUtil.addInfoMessage("items.transferred",
    event.getItems());
  MessageUtil.addInfoMessage("is.added", event.isAdd());
  MessageUtil.addInfoMessage("is.removed", event.isRemove());
}
```

Be aware that if large datasets (approximately 1,000 items) are added to the source list of `pickList` on *IE* or *Chrome* browsers, performance drawbacks might arise and affect the user experience of your application.

As it's not a `UIData` component, `pickList` doesn't do server-side processing for action and input handling. So, for example, using checkboxes inside `pickList` will not work.

PrimeFaces Cookbook Showcase application

This recipe is available in the demo web application on GitHub (`https://github.com/ova2/primefaces-cookbook/tree/second-edition`). Clone the project if you have not done it yet, explore the project structure, and build and deploy the WAR file on application servers compatible with Servlet 3.x, such as *JBoss WildFly* and *Apache TomEE*.

The showcase for the recipe is available at `http://localhost:8080/pf-cookbook/views/chapter5/pickList.jsf`.

See also

For details about the `MessageUtil` class, see the *Internationalization (i18n) and Localization (L10n)* recipe in *Chapter 1, Getting Started with PrimeFaces*.

Listing data with orderList

The `orderList` component is used to sort a collection with the support of drag-and-drop reordering, transition effects, and POJO support.

How to do it...

A basic definition for the `orderList` that sorts a collection of strings would be as shown here:

```
<p:orderList id="simple" value="#{orderListBean.countries}"
    var="country" itemLabel="#{country}" itemValue="#{country}" />
```

The visual output of the component will be as shown here:

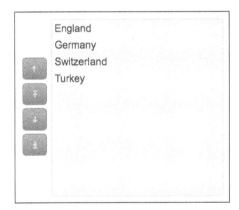

There's more...

To define a header on top of `orderList`, a facet with the name `caption` should be provided as shown here:

```
<p:orderList id="withCaption" value="#{orderListBean.countries}"
    var="country" itemLabel="#{country}" itemValue="#{country}">
```

```
<f:facet name="caption">
   Countries
</f:facet>
</p:orderList>
```

With the `controlsLocation` attribute, we can control the position of the controls. The default value is `left`; the other possible values are `right` and `none`.

Transition effects

Effects can be applied with the `effect` attribute for content transition when a selection is moved upwards or downwards. The default value of the `effect` attribute is `fade`. The other possible values for the effect attribute are as follows:

- blind
- clip
- drop
- explode
- fade
- fold
- puff
- scale
- slide

 As `orderList` is not a `UIData` component, it doesn't do server-side processing for action and input handling. So, for example, using checkboxes inside `orderList` will not work.

PrimeFaces Cookbook Showcase application

This recipe is available in the demo web application on GitHub (`https://github.com/ova2/primefaces-cookbook/tree/second-edition`). Clone the project if you have not done it yet, explore the project structure, and build and deploy the WAR file on application servers compatible with Servlet 3.x, such as *JBoss WildFly* and *Apache TomEE*.

The showcase for the recipe is available at `http://localhost:8080/pf-cookbook/views/chapter5/orderList.jsf`.

Visualizing data with tree

The `tree` component visualizes hierarchical data in the tree format.

How to do it...

The data for `tree` is provided as instances of `org.primefaces.model.TreeNode`, which correspond to the nodes in the tree. A pure client-side tree might be useful to create tree-based navigation menus. A basic data model for a tree could be constructed as follows:

```
TreeNode root = new DefaultTreeNode("Root", null);
TreeNode node1 = new DefaultTreeNode("Node1", root);
TreeNode node2 = new DefaultTreeNode("Node2", root);
TreeNode node11 = new DefaultTreeNode("Node1.1", node1);
TreeNode node12 = new DefaultTreeNode("Node1.2", node1);
TreeNode node21 = new DefaultTreeNode("Node2.1", node2);
TreeNode node211 = new DefaultTreeNode("Node2.1.1", node21);
```

The definition of `tree` for the previously mentioned model will be as shown here:

```
<p:tree id="simple" value-"#{treeDataBean.root}" var="node">
  <p:treeNode>
    <h:outputText value="#{node}" />
  </p:treeNode>
</p:tree>
```

The visual of the tree will be as shown in the following screenshot. By default, the nodes will not be expanded as given in the image; it's done for demonstration purposes.

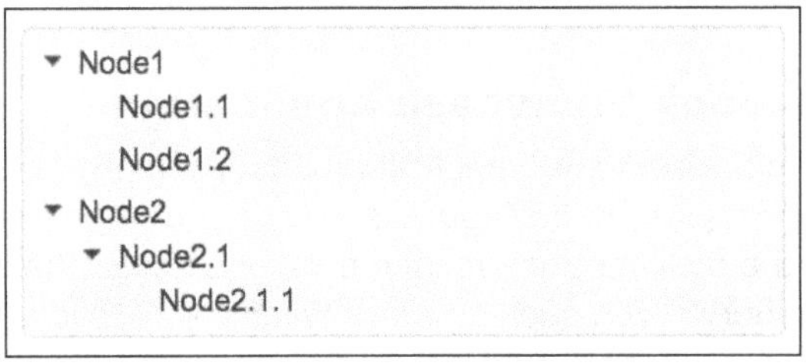

There's more...

If the hierarchical data model of `tree` contains too many nodes, it would be useful to dynamically load the tree by setting the `dynamic` attribute to `true` in order to load a part of tree when requested by expanding a node with a click.

Also, by enabling caching with setting the `cache` attribute to `true`, expanding a previously loaded node will not result in an AJAX request to load its children again. Here's the code that encapsulates this discussion:

```
<p:tree id="dynamic" value="#{treeDataBean.root}" var="node"
  dynamic="true" cache="true">
  <p:treeNode>
    <h:outputText value="#{node}" />
  </p:treeNode>
</p:tree>
```

Node type support

It's possible to provide different visuals for each node with custom node definitions. To achieve this, the `<p:treeNode>` component could be used with defined node types. The following definition contains two node definitions—one for expandable nodes with `type="node"` and one for the leaf nodes with `type="leaf"`. To differentiate the nodes visually, the tree nodes use the `ui-icon-minusthick` icon for leaf nodes and `ui-icon-plusthick` for expandable icons:

```
<p:tree id="customNodes" value="#{treeDataBean.rootWithType}"
  var="node">
  <p:treeNode type="node" icon="ui-icon-plusthick">
    <h:outputText value="#{node}" />
  </p:treeNode>
  <p:treeNode type="leaf" icon="ui-icon-minusthick">
    <h:outputText value="#{node}" />
  </p:treeNode>
</p:tree>
```

The integration is achieved with the `type` attribute where it matches the parameter given to `DefaultTreeNode`. The code to construct the model is given here:

```
rootWithType = new DefaultTreeNode("node", "Root", null);
TreeNode node1_type = new DefaultTreeNode("node", "Node1",
  rootWithType);
```

```
TreeNode node2_type = new DefaultTreeNode("node", "Node2",
   rootWithType);

TreeNode node11_type = new DefaultTreeNode("leaf", "Node1.1",
   node1_type);
TreeNode node12_type = new DefaultTreeNode("leaf", "Node1.2",
   node1_type);

TreeNode node21_type = new DefaultTreeNode("node", "Node2.1",
   node2_type);
TreeNode node211_type = new DefaultTreeNode("leaf", "Node2.1.1",
   node21_type);
```

If you want the node to react to an expand/collapse action by changing its icon, you can use `expandedIcon` and `collapsedIcon` to display the different icons based on the status of the node.

The definition of the `<p:treeNode>` component with `type` set to `node` is given here with the aforementioned attributes:

```
<p:treeNode type="node" expandedIcon="ui-icon-minusthick"
   collapsedIcon="ui-icon-plusthick">
   <h:outputText value="#{node}" />
</p:treeNode>
```

Node selection

The `tree` component provides built-in selection with a single node or multiple nodes or with a checkbox selection on the nodes. The `selectionMode` attribute enables selection with its value set to `single` for the single selection mode, `multiple` for multiple node selection, and `checkbox` to select nodes with checkboxes. The selected nodes are collected in the `selection` attribute as an instance of `TreeNode` or as an array of `TreeNode` instances. Here's the code that encapsulates this discussion:

```
<p:tree id="single" value="#{treeDataBean.root}" var="node"
   selectionMode="single"
   selection="#{treeDataBean.selectedNode}">
   <p:treeNode>
      <h:outputText value="#{node}" />
   </p:treeNode>
</p:tree>

<p:tree id="multiple" value="#{treeDataBean.root}" var="node"
   selectionMode="multiple"
```

```
    selection="#{treeDataBean.selectedNodes}">
  <p:treeNode>
    <h:outputText value="#{node}" />
  </p:treeNode>
</p:tree>
```

PrimeFaces also provides the `CheckboxTreeNode` model class that differs from the `DefaultTreeNode` model class with its `partialSelected` property, where it provides hierarchical selection. In order to modify selection behaviors, you can set the `propagateSelectionUp` and `propagateSelectionDown` attributes of `tree` that propagate upward selection to the root element or downward selection to children, respectively.

It's also possible to select multiple nodes with a modifier key, which would be *Ctrl* in *Windows* and *Command* in *MacOS*.

Drag and drop

Reordering is possible between the nodes of a tree with drag and drop. It's also possible to drag nodes between multiple trees by placing them into a scope. Dragging and dropping within a tree is exemplified here:

```
<p:tree id="dnd" value="#{treeDataBean.root}" var="node"
  draggable="true" droppable="true">
  <p:treeNode>
    <h:outputText value="#{node}" />
  </p:treeNode>
</p:tree>
```

Dragging a node between different trees is exemplified here:

```
<p:tree id="dndSource" value="#{treeDataBean.root}" var="node"
  selectionMode="single"
  selection="#{treeDataBean.selectedNode1}"
  draggable="true" droppable="true"
  dragdropScope="treeScope">
  <p:treeNode>
    <h:outputText value="#{node}" />
  </p:treeNode>
</p:tree>

<p:tree id="dndTarget" value="#{treeDataBean.root2}" var="node"
  selectionMode="single"
  selection="#{treeDataBean.selectedNode2}"
```

```
        draggable="true" droppable="true"
        dragdropScope="treeScope">
      <p:treeNode>
        <h:outputText value="#{node}" />
      </p:treeNode>
  </p:tree>
```

As seen in the code, `dragdropScope` should also be set to the same value for both trees. The `draggable` and `droppable` attributes of both trees could be set to `true` to enable drag and drop between the trees as well as between within the nodes of one tree.

> Using drag and drop between multiple trees inside panel components might lead to problems with the current version of framework. Try to implement the user interface by keeping it simple when drag and drop between trees is a requirement.

AJAX behavior events

The `tree` component supports AJAX behavior events in order to handle node expand/collapse or selection/unselection. The definition of the AJAX behavior events should be placed within the tree, as shown in the following code snippet:

```
<p:tree id="withAJAX" value="#{treeDataBean.root}" var="node"
  selectionMode="single"
  selection="#{treeDataBean.selectedNode}">
  <p:ajax event="expand" update=":mainForm:growl"
    listener="#{treeDataBean.onNodeExpand}" />
  <p:ajax event="collapse" update=":mainForm:growl"
    listener="#{treeDataBean.onNodeCollapse}" />
  <p:ajax event="select" update=":mainForm:growl"
    listener="#{treeDataBean.onNodeSelect}" />
  <p:ajax event="unselect" update=":mainForm:growl"
    listener="#{treeDataBean.onNodeUnselect}" />
  <p:treeNode>
    <h:outputText value="#{node}" />
  </p:treeNode>
</p:tree>
```

The events and their corresponding listener method's parameter types are given in the following table; for all the events, the tree can be accessed with the `event.getNode()` method call.

Action	Event name	Listener method parameter type
When a node is expanded	`expand`	`org.primefaces.event.NodeExpandEvent`
When a node is collapsed	`collapse`	`org.primefaces.event.NodeCollapseEvent`
When a node is selected	`select`	`org.primefaces.event.NodeSelectEvent`
When a node is unselected	`unselect`	`org.primefaces.event.NodeUnselectEvent`

Context menu support

The `tree` component easily integrates with the `contextMenu` component, and the context menu can be assigned to the nodes for a right-click event. It is also possible to assign different context menus with different tree nodes using the `nodeType` attribute.

There are two context menu definitions—one for the nodes of the tree that contain child nodes and the other one for the leaf nodes that have no child nodes. They are given here with the tree definition (the menus differ according to the given `nodeType` attribute):

```
<p:tree id="withContextMenu" var="node" selectionMode="single"
  value="#{treeDataBean.rootWithType}"
  selection="#{treeDataBean.selectedNode}">
  <p:treeNode type="node">
    <h:outputText value="#{node}" />
  </p:treeNode>

  <p:treeNode type="leaf">
    <h:outputText value="#{node}" />
  </p:treeNode>
</p:tree>

<p:contextMenu for="withContextMenu" nodeType="node">
  <p:menuitem value="View" update="dialogPanel"
    icon="ui-icon-search"
    oncomplete="PF('nodeDialog').show()" />
```

```
    </p:contextMenu>

    <p:contextMenu for="withContextMenu" nodeType="leaf">
      <p:menuitem value="View" update="dialogPanel"
        icon="ui-icon-search"
        oncomplete="PF('nodeDialog').show()" />
      <p:menuitem value="Delete"
        actionListener="#{treeDataBean.deleteNode}"
        update="withContextMenu" icon="ui-icon-close" />
    </p:contextMenu>
```

While only displaying the context menu with the view and delete actions for the leaf nodes of the tree, the context menu with just a view action will be displayed for the nodes that contain child nodes.

Horizontal layout

With the `orientation` attribute, it's possible to set the layout of the nodes as horizontal by setting the attribute to `horizontal`. The default value of the attribute is `vertical`. The visual output of the horizontal layout is given here. By default, the nodes will not be expanded as given in the image; it's done for demonstration purposes.

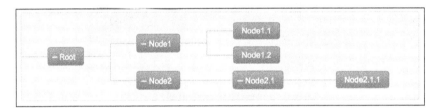

PrimeFaces Cookbook Showcase application

This recipe is available in the demo web application on GitHub (`https://github.com/ova2/primefaces-cookbook/tree/second-edition`). Clone the project if you have not done it yet, explore the project structure, and build and deploy the WAR file on application servers compatible with Servlet 3.x, such as *JBoss WildFly* and *Apache TomEE*.

The showcase for the recipe is available at `http://localhost:8080/pf-cookbook/views/chapter5/tree.jsf`.

Visualizing data with treeTable

The `treeTable` component visualizes tree where each tree item can have some additional fields that could be displayed in a tabular format.

How to do it...

A basic implementation for `treeTable` with three columns would be as follows:

```
<p:treeTable id="simple" value="#{treeTableBean.root}"
  var="element">
  <f:facet name="header">Tree Table</f:facet>
  <p:column>
    <f:facet name="header">Name</f:facet>
    <h:outputText value="#{element.name}" />
  </p:column>
  <p:column>
    <f:facet name="header">Column 1</f:facet>
    <h:outputText value="#{element.column1}" />
  </p:column>
  <p:column>
    <f:facet name="header">Column 2</f:facet>
    <h:outputText value="#{element.column2}" />
  </p:column>
</p:treeTable>
```

The visual output of the table expanded on every node will be as shown here:

Tree Table		
Name	Column 1	Column 2
▾ Node1	N1 1st Column	N1 2nd Column
Node1.1	N11 1st Column	N11 2nd Column
Node1.2	N12 1st Column	N12 2nd Column
▾ Node2	N2 1st Column	N2 2nd Column
▾ Node2.1	N21 1st Column	N21 2nd Column
Node2.1.1	N211 1st Column	N211 2nd Column

The root element of the tree table will be an instance of `org.primefaces.model.TreeNode`. The whole model provided to the tree table would be a collection of `TreeTableElement` components wrapped by `TreeNode` instances. `TreeTableElement` is a simple class created for demonstration purposes and is defined as follows:

```
public class TreeTableElement implements Serializable {
    private String name;
    private String column1;
    private String column2;

    // getters & setters
}
```

The implementation of constructing the table would be as follows:

```
root = new DefaultTreeNode("root", null);
TreeNode node1 = new DefaultTreeNode(new TreeTableElement("Node1",
    "1st Column", "2nd Column"), root);
TreeNode node2 = new DefaultTreeNode(new TreeTableElement("Node2",
    "1st Column", "2nd Column"), root);
TreeNode node11 = new DefaultTreeNode(new TreeTableElement(
    "Node1.1", "1st Column", "2nd Column"), node1);
TreeNode node12 = new DefaultTreeNode(new TreeTableElement(
    "Node1.2", "1st Column", "2nd Column"), node1);
TreeNode node21 = new DefaultTreeNode(new TreeTableElement(
    "Node2.1", "1st Column", "2nd Column"), node2);
TreeNode node211 = new DefaultTreeNode(new TreeTableElement(
    "Node2.1.1", "1st Column", "2nd Column"), node21);
```

There's more...

It's possible to make the table scrollable by setting the `scrollable` attribute to `true`. The `scrollWidth` and `scrollHeight` attributes can be provided to constrain the view of the table to a fixed width and height. Also, the width of the columns must be provided as fixed integer values when the `scrollable` attribute is set to `true` in order to preserve the layout.

Node selection

The `selectionMode` attribute should be used to enable selection whenever a row is clicked on. Its value should be `single` for the single selection mode, and the `selection` attribute should be bound to an instance of `TreeNode`. To select multiple items with the modifier key (for example, *Ctrl* in *Windows/Linux* or *Command* in *MacOS*), the `selectionMode` attribute should be set to `multiple` and the `selection` attribute needs to be bound to an array of the `TreeNode` class.

It's also possible to handle selection with checkboxes by setting `selectionMode` to `checkbox`. As with multiple-selection mode, the `selection` attribute needs to be bound to an array of the `TreeNode` class.

Sorting

It's possible to enable sorting for the columns of a table by setting the `sortBy` attribute:

```
<p:treeTable id="sorted" value="#{treeTableBean.root}"
  var="element" style="width: 400px;">
  <f:facet name="header">Tree Table</f:facet>
  <p:column sortBy="#{element.name}">
    <f:facet name="header">Name</f:facet>
    <h:outputText value="#{element.name}" />
  </p:column>
  ...
<p:treeTable>
```

When sorting is enabled, the headers of those columns will have the sort direction represented with small arrow icons, as shown here:

Tree Table		
Name ⇕	Column 1	Column 2
▸ Node1	N1 1st Column	N1 2nd Column
▸ Node2	N2 1st Column	N2 2nd Column

Context menu support

The `treeTable` component easily integrates with the `contextMenu` component, and the context menu can be assigned to the nodes for a right-click event. Using the `nodeType` attribute, it is also possible to assign different context menus with different nodes.

There are two context menu definitions—one for the nodes of the table that contain child nodes and the other one for the leaf nodes that have no child nodes. The definitions are given as follows with the tree table definition; the menus differ according to the given `nodeType` attribute:

```
<p:treeTable id="withContextMenu" value="#{treeTableBean.root}"
  var="element" selectionMode="single"
  selection="#{treeTableBean.selectedItemForContextMenu}">
  <f:facet name="header">Tree Table</f:facet>
  <p:column>
    <f:facet name="header">Name</f:facet>
```

```
      <h:outputText value="#{element.name}" />
    </p:column>
    <p:column>
      <f:facet name="header">Column 1</f:facet>
      <h:outputText value="#{element.column1}" />
    </p:column>
    <p:column>
      <f:facet name="header">Column 2</f:facet>
      <h:outputText value="#{element.column2}" />
    </p:column>
  </p:treeTable>

  <p:contextMenu for="withContextMenu" nodeType="node">
    <p:menuitem value="View" update="dialogPanel"
      icon="ui-icon-search"
      oncomplete="PF('nodeDialog').show()"/>
  </p:contextMenu>

  <p:contextMenu for="withContextMenu" nodeType="leaf">
    <p:menuitem value="View" update="dialogPanel"
      icon="ui-icon-search"
      oncomplete="PF('nodeDialog').show()"/>
    <p:menuitem value="Delete"
      actionListener="#{treeTableBean.deleteNode}"
      update="withContextMenu" icon="ui-icon-close"/>
  </p:contextMenu>
```

The nodeType attribute is given while constructing the treeTable data model.

```
TreeNode node1 = new DefaultTreeNode("node", new
TreeTableElement("Node1", "1st Column", "2nd Column"), root);
...
TreeNode node11 = new DefaultTreeNode("leaf", new
TreeTableElement("Node1.1", "1st Column", "2nd Column"), node1);
...
```

While only displaying the context menu with view and delete actions for the leaf nodes of the table, the context menu with just the view action will be displayed for the nodes that contain child nodes.

The visual output of the table with the context menu triggered on a leaf is given here:

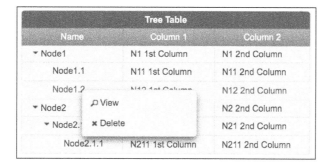

AJAX behavior events

It's possible to invoke server-side methods instantly according to user interactions such as expanding, collapsing, and selecting a node. The declaration for the node's expand event of the table is given here:

```
<p:treeTable id="withAJAX" value="#{treeTableBean.root}"
  var="element">
  <p:ajax event="expand" update=":mainForm:growl"
    listener="#{treeTableBean.onNodeExpand}" />
  <p:ajax event="collapse" update=":mainForm:growl"
    listener="#{treeTableBean.onNodeCollapse}" />
  <p:ajax event="select" update=":mainForm:growl"
    listener="#{treeTableBean.onNodeSelect}" />
  <p:ajax event="unselect" update=":mainForm:growl"
    listener="#{treeTableBean.onNodeUnselect}" />
</p:treeTable>
```

The definition of the `onNodeExpand` method is given here:

```
public void onNodeExpand(NodeExpandEvent event) {
  MessageUtil.addInfoMessageWithoutKey("Expanded",
    event.getTreeNode().getData().toString());
}
```

The list of all possible events with their listener parameters is as follows:

Event name	Parameter of the listener method	When it gets executed
colResize	org.primefaces.event. ColumnResizeEvent	This gets executed when the column is resized
collapse	org.primefaces.event. NodeCollapseEvent	This gets executed when the node is collapsed
expand	org.primefaces.event. NodeExpandEvent	This gets executed when the node is expanded
select	org.primefaces.event. NodeSelectEvent	This gets executed when the node is selected
unselect	org.primefaces.event. NodeUnselectEvent	This gets executed when the node is unselected

PrimeFaces Cookbook Showcase application

This recipe is available in the demo web application on GitHub (`https://github.com/ova2/primefaces-cookbook/tree/second-edition`). Clone the project if you have not done it yet, explore the project structure, and build and deploy the WAR file on application severs compatible with Servlet 3.x, such as *JBoss WildFly* and *Apache TomEE*.

The showcase for the recipe is available at `http://localhost:8080/pf-cookbook/views/chapter5/treeTable.jsf`.

Exporting data in various formats

The `dataExporter` component allows us to export the content of the table into various formats such as XLS, PDF, CSV, and XML. It also supports the exporting of the current data on a page. It also supports only selected data of the table by providing the ability to exclude particular columns and manipulate the exported data with pre- and post-processors.

How to do it...

A basic definition of `dataExporter` is given here:

```
<h:commandLink>
  <p:graphicImage value="/resources/images/export/pdf.png" />
  <p:dataExporter type="pdf" target="countriesTable"
    fileName="countries" />
</h:commandLink>
```

How it works...

The `dataExporter` component should be nested in a `UICommand` component, such as `commandLink` or `commandButton`. In the previous definition, `target` defines the server-side ID of the table, the data of which will be exported. The `type` attribute defines the export type, the values of which could be `xls`, `pdf`, `csv`, or `xml`. The `fileName` attribute defines the filename of the generated export file; by default, the server-side ID of `dataTable` is used as the filename.

 The `target` attribute must point to a PrimeFaces `dataTable` component.

The necessary libraries should be available in the classpath to export to PDF or XLS. See the *Setting up and configuring the PrimeFaces library* recipe in *Chapter 1, Getting Started with PrimeFaces*, for details on dependencies.

There's more...

By default, the export is done for the whole dataset. But, it could also be done for the current page by setting the `pageOnly` attribute to `true` or for only the selected data by setting the `selectionOnly` attribute to `true`.

The `<p:column>` component provides the `exportable` attribute where it defines whether the column should be exported or not.

Character encoding can also be set while exporting by setting the `encoding` attribute to the corresponding encoding value. The default encoding is `UTF-8`.

 While exporting to Excel, `dataExporter` only creates string-based cells. So, exporting numeric data into numeric cells is not currently supported.

Preprocessing and postprocessing of documents

The `dataExporter` component enables preprocessing and postprocessing on the document for customization, such as adding logos, captions, headers/footers, and so on. *Preprocessors* are executed before the data is exported, and *postprocessors* are processed after the data is included in the document. The document object is passed to the processor methods as a Java object so that it can be easily cast to the appropriate class. An example of a preprocessor that adds a footer to page numbers of a PDF document is given here:

```
<p:dataExporter type="pdf" target="countriesTable"
  fileName="countries"
```

```
    preProcessor="#{dataExportBean.preProcessPDF}" />

public void preProcessPDF(Object document) {
  Document pdf = (Document) document;
  HeaderFooter footer =
  new HeaderFooter(new Phrase("This is page:"), true);
  pdf.setFooter(footer);
}
```

Monitoring export status

Data export is a non-AJAX process, so in order to monitor the status, PrimeFaces provides the client-side method `monitorDownload`. The method could be bound to the `onclick` event of a command component that wraps the `dataExporter`, as seen in the following code snippet:

```
<h:commandLink
  onclick="PrimeFaces.monitorDownload(showStatus, hideStatus)">
  <p:graphicImage value="/resources/images/export/csv.png" />
  <p:dataExporter type="csv" target="countriesTable"
    fileName="countries" />
</h:commandLink>
```

While the exporting process occurs, the method will trigger two JavaScript methods, `showStatus` and `hideStatus`, whose names are passed as parameters. These are two simple methods to show and hide a dialog box component and their implementations, along with the dialog, are given here:

```
<script type="text/javascript">
  function showStatus() {
    statusDialog.show();
  }
  function hideStatus() {
    statusDialog.hide();
  }
</script>

<p:dialog modal="true" widgetVar="statusDialog" header="Status"
  draggable="false" closable="false">
  <p:graphicImage value="/resources/images/ajax-loader.gif" />
</p:dialog>
```

While the exporting process occurs, the `dataExporter` component only recognizes values from the `outputText` component.

Data exporting also works collaboratively when sorting and filtering is enabled on columns.

PrimeFaces Cookbook Showcase application

This recipe is available in the demo web application on GitHub (`https://github.com/ova2/primefaces-cookbook/tree/second-edition`). Clone the project if you have not done it yet, explore the project structure, and build and deploy the WAR file on application servers compatible with Servlet 3.x, such as *JBoss WildFly* and *Apache TomEE*.

The showcase for the recipe is available at `http://localhost:8080/pf-cookbook/views/chapter5/dataExport.jsf`.

Managing events with schedule by leveraging lazy loading

The `Schedule` component provides a calendar to manage events, such as *Outlook Calendar* and *iCal*. By default, a whole set of events is eagerly provided via the `ScheduleModel` class. That means all events are loaded at once on page load. The lazy loading feature helps to improve performance if we have a huge dataset of events or if events take too much time to load. In the lazy loading mode, only events that belong to the displayed timeframe are fetched.

In this recipe, we will implement a small example for the `Schedule` component's lazy loading feature.

How to do it...

A basic definition of `schedule` would be as shown here:

```
<p:schedule id="lazySchedule"
  value="#{scheduleBean.lazyScheduleModel}"/>
```

The visual output of the component with two randomly generated events will be as shown here:

By default, the month view is displayed, so the user sees a whole month and can switch between months. Assume that we have to load events for 12 months and every month requires, on average, 1.5 seconds for event loading. The default eager mode would take 18 seconds (12 x 1.5) to load all events. This is too long, so using the lazy loading feature is recommended to improve performance. The `ScheduleBean` bean definition with lazy model construction is given next; for the sake of simplicity, the loading time is simulated with `Thread.sleep(1500)`:

```
@Named
@ViewScoped
public class ScheduleBean implements Serializable {

    private ScheduleModel lazyEventModel;

    @PostConstruct
```

```
public void initialize() {
  lazyEventModel = new LazyScheduleModel() {

    @Override
    public void loadEvents(Date start, Date end) {
      try {
        // simulate a long running task
        Thread.sleep(1500);
      } catch (Exception e) {
      }

      clear();

      Date random = getRandomDate(start);
      addEvent(new DefaultScheduleEvent("Lazy Event 1",
        random, random));

      random = getRandomDate(start);
      addEvent(new DefaultScheduleEvent("Lazy Event 2",
        random, random));
    }
  };
}

public Date getRandomDate(Date base) {
  Calendar date = Calendar.getInstance();
  date.setTime(base);
  date.add(Calendar.DATE, ((int) (Math.random() * 30)) + 1);

  return date.getTime();
}

public ScheduleModel getLazyScheduleModel() {
  return lazyEventModel;
}
}
```

How it works...

To enable lazy loading of the `schedule` component's events, we need to provide an instance of `org.primefaces.model.LazyScheduleModel` and implement the `loadEvents` method. This method is called with new date boundaries every time the displayed timeframe is changed. Events are now loaded on demand on the initial page load or during switching between months. That means the maximum delay for the event's loading is not longer than 1.5 seconds.

There's more...

The `Schedule` component offers five different views, which are `month`, `agendaWeek`, `agendaDay`, `basicWeek`, and `basicDay`. The default view is `month`, and the rest of the modes are given here with their visual outputs:

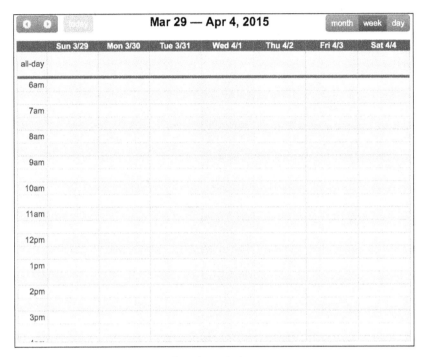

Agenda week view

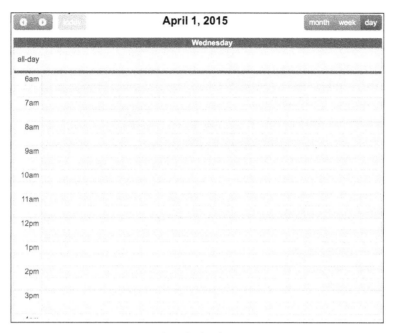

Agenda day view

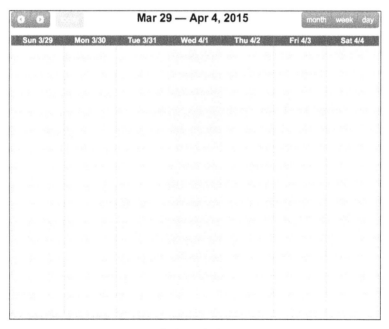

Basic week view

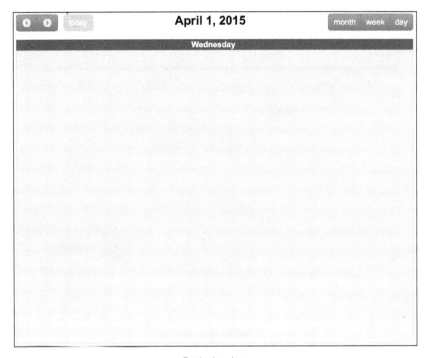

Basic day view

AJAX behavior events

The `schedule` component supports AJAX behavior events in order to handle the interactions of the user by date selection, event selection/deselection, or movement and view change. The definitions of the AJAX behaviors are shown in the following code snippet (they should be defined inside the `schedule` component):

```
<p:ajax event="dateSelect" listener="#{scheduleBean.onDateSelect}"
  update=":mainForm:growl" />
<p:ajax event="eventSelect" update=":mainForm:growl"
  listener="#{scheduleBean.onEventSelect}"/>
<p:ajax event="eventMove" listener="#{scheduleBean.onEventMove}"
  update=":mainForm:growl" />
<p:ajax event="eventResize" update=":mainForm:growl"
  listener="#{scheduleBean.onEventResize}" />
<p:ajax event="viewChange" listener="#{scheduleBean.onViewChange}"
  update=":mainForm:growl" />
```

The method definitions are listed here:

```
public void onDateSelect(SelectEvent event) {
  MessageUtil.addInfoMessage("date.selected", event.getObject());
}

public void onEventSelect(SelectEvent event) {
  MessageUtil.addInfoMessage("event.selected",
    ((DefaultScheduleEvent)event.getObject()).getTitle());
}

public void onEventMove(ScheduleEntryMoveEvent event) {
  MessageUtil.addInfoMessage("event.moved",
    event.getScheduleEvent().getTitle(), event.getDayDelta(),
    event.getMinuteDelta());
}

public void onEventResize(ScheduleEntryResizeEvent event) {
  MessageUtil.addInfoMessage("event.resized",
    event.getScheduleEvent().getTitle(), event.getDayDelta(),
    event. getMinuteDelta());
}

public void onViewChange(SelectEvent event) {
  MessageUtil.addInfoMessage("view.changed", event.getObject());
}
```

Locale support

Defining the locale value to the `locale` attribute provides the localization of `schedule`. The `locale` attribute can either take a `String` or `java.util.Locale` instance as the key. By default, all labels provided by the schedule are in English, so you need to provide the other translations manually. The PrimeFaces community implements the translations, and they are available as JavaScript objects. Please refer to `https://code.google.com/p/primefaces/wiki/PrimeFacesLocales` to access the translations.

PrimeFaces Cookbook Showcase application

This recipe is available in the demo web application on GitHub (`https://github.com/ova2/primefaces-cookbook/tree/second-edition`). Clone the project if you have not done it yet, explore the project structure, and build and deploy the WAR file on application servers compatible with Servlet 3.x, such as *JBoss WildFly* and *Apache TomEE*.

The showcase for the recipe is available at `http://localhost:8080/pf-cookbook/views/chapter5/scheduleLazyLoad.jsf`.

See also

For details about the `MessageUtil` class, see the *Internationalization (i18n) and Localization (L10n)* recipe in *Chapter 1, Getting Started with PrimeFaces*.

Visualizing data with dataScroller

The `dataScroller` component offers lazy loading of a collection via AJAX when the page is scrolled down.

How to do it...

A basic definition of the `dataScroller` component would be as shown here:

```
<p:dataScroller value="#{dataScrollerBean.cars}"
  var="car" chunkSize="10">
  #{car.name}
</p:dataScroller>
```

The data gets loaded with specified chunks where its size is determined with the `chunkSize` attribute, and then the retrieved content will be appended at the bottom of the component.

There's more...

The AJAX loading takes place when the page is scrolled down, and this is achieved by monitoring the vertical scrollbar. This can be modified by the `mode` attribute, which has `document` as its default value. When its value is set to `inline`, the component starts to listen to the scroll event of the `dataScroller` container.

Providing buffer

The `buffer` attribute states the percentage height of the buffer between the bottom of the page and the scroll position to initiate the load for the new chunk. Its value is defined as an integer and the default is `10`, which means that the load would happen after *90 percent* of the viewport is scrolled down.

Loading with a button

Instead of instant loading, a button could be used to trigger the loading. When a button is placed in a facet named `loader`, it will enable the loading. The definition given next uses this facet and also contains columns to display data:

```
<p:dataScroller value="#{dataScrollerBean.cars}" var="car"
  chunkSize="3">
  <p:column>
    <p:graphicImage width="400" height="250"
      value="/resources/images/autocomplete/#{car.name}.png" />
  </p:column>
  <p:column>
    <h:outputText value="#{car.name}" style="font-size: 80px" />
  </p:column>
  <f:facet name="loader">
    <p:commandButton type="button" value="View More" />
  </f:facet>
</p:dataScroller>
```

It's also possible to define a `header` facet that will be rendered as a header to the data list.

Lazy loading

When the `lazy` attribute is set to `true` and a lazy data model is provided, `dataScroller` will list large amounts of data with scrolling. An example is given here:

```
<p:dataScroller value="#{dataScrollerBean.lazyCarModel}"
  var="car" chunkSize="10" lazy="true">
  #{car.name}
</p:dataScroller>
```

For further information about the lazy data model, please refer to the *Handling tons of data – LazyDataModel* recipe in this chapter.

PrimeFaces Cookbook Showcase application

This recipe is available in the demo web application on GitHub (`https://github.com/ova2/primefaces-cookbook/tree/second-edition`). Clone the project if you have not done it yet, explore the project structure, and build and deploy the WAR file on application severs compatible with Servlet 3.x, such as *JBoss WildFly* and *Apache TomEE*.

The showcase for the recipe is available at `http://localhost:8080/pf-cookbook/views/chapter5/dataScroller.jsf`.

6

Endless Menu Variations

In this chapter, we will cover the following topics:

- ▸ Statically and dynamically positioned menus
- ▸ Creating programmatic menus
- ▸ The context menu with nested items
- ▸ Integrating the context menu
- ▸ Breadcrumb – providing contextual information about page hierarchy
- ▸ SlideMenu – menu in the iPod style
- ▸ TieredMenu – submenus in nested overlays
- ▸ MegaMenu – the multicolumn menu
- ▸ PanelMenu – hybrid of accordion and tree
- ▸ MenuButton – multiple items in a popup
- ▸ Accessing commands via menubar
- ▸ Displaying checkboxes in selectCheckboxMenu

Introduction

In this chapter, we will learn about menu components. These days, every website contains menus. Usually, a menu is presented to a user as a list of links to be navigated or commands to be executed. Menus are sometimes organized hierarchically, allowing navigation through different levels of the menu structure. Arranging menu items in logical groups makes it easy for users to quickly locate the related tasks. PrimeFaces' menus fulfill all major requirements. They come with various facets, such as static, dynamic, tiered, iPod-styled, and so on, and leave nothing to be desired.

Several menu variations are covered in the recipes of this chapter. We will see a lot of recipes that will discuss menu structure, configuration options, customizations, and integration with other components. At the end of this chapter, we should know what kind of menu to choose and how to put it on a page for various use cases.

Statically and dynamically positioned menus

A menu can be positioned on a page in two ways: statically and dynamically. A menu is static by default. This means that the menu is in the normal page flow. A dynamic menu, in contrast, is not in the normal page flow and overlays other elements. In terms of CSS, it is absolutely positioned.

In this recipe, we will see how we can develop these two kinds of positioned menus. But first, we will meet submenus and menu items.

How to do it...

A menu is composed of submenus and menu items. Submenus group single menu items. Grouped menu items can be presented in the same page flow or in an overlay over other elements. This behavior depends on the type of menu. The simple p:menu menu shows grouped menu items in the same page flow. Let's define an example structure of a static menu:

```
<p:growl id="growl"/>

<p:menu>
  <p:submenu label="JavaScript Libraries">
    <p:menuitem value="jQuery" url="http://jquery.com"/>
    <p:menuitem value="Yahoo UI" url="http://yuilibrary.com"/>
    <p:menuitem value="Prototype"
      url="http://prototypejs.org"/>
  </p:submenu>
  <p:submenu label="Operations">
    <p:menuitem value="Save"
      actionListener="#{positionedMenuBean.save}"
      update="growl"/>
    <p:menuitem value="Update"
      actionListener="#{positionedMenuBean.update}"
      update="growl"/>
    <p:menuitem value="Delete"
      actionListener="#{positionedMenuBean.delete}"
      update="growl"/>
  </p:submenu>
</p:menu>
```

A dynamic menu is created by setting the `overlay` option to `true` and defining a trigger to show the menu. For example, a command button from the following code snippet acts as such a trigger. It will display a menu, the top-left corner of which is aligned with the bottom-left corner of the button when the user clicks on it. The following code snippet shows this:

```
<p:growl id="growl"/>

<p:menu overlay="true" trigger="btn" my="left top" at="bottom
  left">
  <p:menuitem value="Do something (ajax)"
    action="#{positionedMenuBean.doSomething}"
    update="growl"/>
  <p:menuitem value="Do something (non ajax)"
    action="#{positionedMenuBean.doSomething}"
    ajax="false"/>
  <p:menuitem value="Navigate" url="http://primefaces.org"/>
</p:menu>

<p:commandButton id="btn" value="Show dynamic menu"
  type="button"/>
```

The following screenshot shows both these types of menus. The dynamic menu is opened after the user has clicked on the **Show dynamic menu** button:

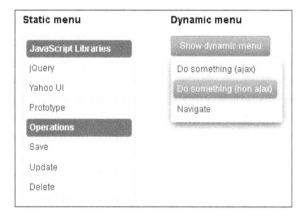

 Place the most frequently used items at the top of the menu. The top of the menu tends to be the most visible part of the menu because users often see it first. Avoid combining semantically different actions/navigations in the same group. Avoid displaying an icon for every menu item. Include them only for menu items for which they add significant value. A menu that includes too many icons can appear cluttered and be hard to read.

How it works...

We saw that `p:menuitem` can be placed either under `p:submenu` or directly under `p:menu`. As the menu uses menu items, it is easy to invoke actions or action listeners with or without AJAX (`ajax="false"`) as well as navigate. Navigation means a GET request that causes a switch to another page. This is always a full page refresh and only works when the `url` attribute on `p:menuitem` is set. In this case, the menu item is rendered as a normal HTML link element. If the `url` attribute is missing, only POST requests (with AJAX or without) can be sent.

The location of the dynamic menu on a page is relative to the trigger and is defined by the `my` and `at` attributes, which take a combination of two values from the following:

- `left`
- `right`
- `bottom`
- `top`

There's more...

We can also specify an icon for the menu item and design attractive menus. There are two ways to specify an icon—either using any predefined jQuery ThemeRoller style class (`http://jqueryui.com/themeroller`) that is a part of PrimeFaces themes or by providing our own style class for the `<p:menuitem icon="home" .../>` icon attribute. The following code shows this:

```
.home {
  background: url("#{resource['images:home.png']}") no-repeat;
  height:16px;
  width:16px;
}
```

You may want to expand and collapse submenus on click. This feature can be achieved by setting toggleable="true" on p:menu.

See also

See the *MenuItem* section in *PrimeFaces User's Guide* (`http://primefaces.org/documentation.html`) to learn more about menu item capabilities.

PrimeFaces Cookbook Showcase application

This recipe is available in the demo web application on GitHub (`https://github.com/ova2/primefaces-cookbook/tree/second-edition`). Clone the project if you have not done it yet, explore the project structure, and build and deploy the WAR file on application servers compatible with Servlet 3.x, such as *JBoss WildFly* and *Apache TomEE*.

The showcase for the recipe is available at `http://localhost:8080/pf-cookbook/views/chapter6/positionedMenus.jsf`.

Creating programmatic menus

Programmatic menus offer a more flexible way in comparison with the declarative approach. The whole menu structure can be created in Java and bound as a model to the `p:menu` tag. Programmatic menu creation is the best choice when we load a menu definition from a database or XML file, and if the menu structure is not known beforehand.

In this recipe, we will learn about the PrimeFaces menu model and create a programmatic menu.

How to do it...

Every programmatically created menu instance should implement the `org.primefaces.model.MenuModel` Java interface. PrimeFaces provides a default implementation, `org.primefaces.model.DefaultMenuModel`, that is sufficient to use in most cases. Your own customized implementations of `MenuModel` are possible as well. Let's create a static menu from the *Statically and dynamically positioned menus* recipe in a programmatic way:

```
@Named
@ViewScoped
public class ProgrammaticMenuBean implements Serializable {

    private MenuModel model;

    @PostConstruct
    protected void initialize() {
        model = new DefaultMenuModel();

        // first submenu
        DefaultSubMenu submenu = new DefaultSubMenu();
        submenu.setLabel("JavaScript Libraries");

        // menu items
        DefaultMenuItem item = new DefaultMenuItem();
```

```
    item.setValue("jQuery");
    item.setUrl("http://jquery.com");
    submenu.addElement(item);

    item = new DefaultMenuItem();
    item.setValue("Yahoo UI");
    item.setUrl("http://yuilibrary.com");
    submenu.addElement(item);

    item = new DefaultMenuItem();
    item.setValue("Prototype");
    item.setUrl("http://prototypejs.org");
    submenu.addElement(item);

    model.addElement(submenu);

    // second submenu
    submenu = new DefaultSubMenu();
    submenu.setLabel("Operations");

    // menu items
    item = new DefaultMenuItem();
    item.setValue("Save");
    item.setCommand("#{positionedMenuBean.save}");
    item.setUpdate("growl");
    submenu.addElement(item);

    item = new DefaultMenuItem();
    item.setValue("Update");
    item.setCommand("#{positionedMenuBean.update}");
    item.setUpdate("growl");
    submenu.addElement(item);

    item = new DefaultMenuItem();
    item.setValue("Delete");
    item.setCommand("#{positionedMenuBean.delete}");
    item.setUpdate("growl");
    submenu.addElement(item);

    model.addElement(submenu);
```

```
    }

    public MenuModel getModel() {
      return model;
    }
  }
```

The created menu can easily be bound to the corresponding component tag by means of the `model` attribute:

```
<p:menu model="#{programmaticMenuBean.model}"/>
```

How it works...

After an instance of the `DefaultMenuModel` class is created, we create the `Submenu` and `MenuItem` instances using `new DefaultSubMenu()` and `new DefaultMenuItem()`, respectively. The `MenuItem` instances are children of `Submenu` and should be added as `submenu.addElement(item)`. `Submenu` itself is added to the model as `model.addElement(submenu)`. URLs are set by `item.setUrl()` as `String` objects. The methods to be invoked are set by `item.setCommand()` as `String` representations of EL expressions.

 For UI components, such as `p:menuitem`, `p:submenu`, and `p:separator`, there exist default implementations in the *MenuModel API* so that the component's counterparts can be created in Java programmatically.

There's more...

If you need to pass parameters in AJAX or non-AJAX commands, use the `setParam(key, value)` method. Parameters can be extracted again from `DefaultMenuItem` in the invoked methods. `DefaultMenuItem` is a property of `MenuActionEvent`. A code sample for a bean named `ParametrizedCommandBean` exemplifies this:

```
@PostConstruct
protected void initialize() {
  model = new DefaultMenuModel();

  DefaultMenuItem item = new DefaultMenuItem();
  item.setValue("Command with parameters");
  item.setCommand("#{parametrizedCommandBean.command}");
  item.setUpdate("growl");
```

```
        item.setIcon("ui-icon-play");
        item.setParam("book", "PrimeFaces Cookbook");
        item.setParam("edition", "Second Edition");

        model.addElement(item);
    }

    public void command(MenuActionEvent event) {
        DefaultMenuItem item = (DefaultMenuItem) event.getMenuItem();
        Map<String, List<String>> params = item.getParams();

        FacesMessage msg = new FacesMessage(
          FacesMessage.SEVERITY_INFO,
          params.get("book").get(0) + ", " +
          params.get("edition").get(0), null);
        FacesContext.getCurrentInstance().addMessage(null, msg);
    }
```

The XHTML snippet is easy and is given here:

```
<p:menu model="#{parametrizedCommandBean.model}"
    style="width:200px"/>
```

The preceding XHTML code results in the following output:

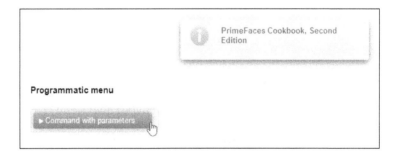

PrimeFaces Cookbook Showcase application

This recipe is available in the demo web application on GitHub (https://github.com/ova2/primefaces-cookbook/tree/second-edition). Clone the project if you have not done it yet, explore the project structure, and build and deploy the WAR file on application servers compatible with Servlet 3.x, such as *JBoss WildFly* and *Apache TomEE*.

The showcase for the recipe is available at http://localhost:8080/pf-cookbook/views/chapter6/programmaticMenu.jsf.

The context menu with nested items

The context menu is displayed when the mouse is right-clicked. It replaces the native context menu in the browser and gives web applications a desktop-like feel and behavior. PrimeFaces' context menu provides an overlay with submenus and menu items.

In this recipe, we will develop a context menu with nested items and see how to attach it to any component. For example, we will attach the context menu to a `panel` component.

How to do it...

The context menu is defined by the `p:contextMenu` tag. We would like to define two submenus—one with menu items having URLs (they send `GET` requests) and one with AJAX-ified menu items (they send `POST` requests). AJAX-ified menu items perform the CRUD operations and update `p:growl`. The context menu is attached to `p:panel`. That means only a right-click on the `panel` component displays the defined context menu. A click anywhere else displays the native web browser's context menu. This is shown in the following code:

```
<p:growl id="growl"/>

<p:panel id="dummyPanel" header="Please click somewhere on panel
  to see a context menu">
  <h:panelGroup layout="block" style="height:100px;"/>
</p:panel>

<p:contextMenu for="dummyPanel">
  <p:submenu label="JavaScript Libraries">
    <p:menuitem value="jQuery" url="http://jquery.com"/>
    <p:menuitem value="Yahoo UI" url="http://yuilibrary.com"/>
    <p:menuitem value="Prototype" url="http://prototypejs.org"/>
  </p:submenu>
  <p:separator/>
  <p:submenu label="Operations">
    <p:menuitem value="Save"
      actionListener="#{contextMenuBean.save}"
      update="growl"/>
    <p:menuitem value="Update"
      actionListener="#{contextMenuBean.update}"
      update="growl"/>
    <p:menuitem value="Delete"
      actionListener="#{contextMenuBean.delete}"
      update="growl"/>
  </p:submenu>
</p:contextMenu>
```

The following screenshot shows the result of the preceding code:

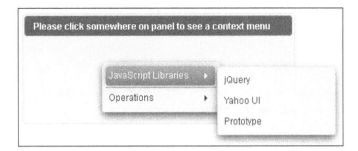

How it works...

By default, `contextMenu` without the defined `for` attribute is attached to the whole page. That means a right-click somewhere on the page will display the menu. The `for` attribute defines a component that `contextMenu` is attached to. The value of `for` specifies a **search expression**, which, in this case, is the ID of `p:panel`.

> *Chapter 1, Getting Started with PrimeFaces, provides more details on search expressions.*

There's more...

Context menus can also be created programmatically and bound to `p:contextMenu` by the `model` attribute. Programmatic menus are discussed in the *Creating programmatic menus* recipe of this chapter.

See also

Data iteration components have an exclusive integration with the context menu. Refer to the *Integrating the context menu* recipe to learn more about such integrations

PrimeFaces Cookbook Showcase application

This recipe is available in the demo web application on GitHub (`https://github.com/ova2/primefaces-cookbook/tree/second-edition`). Clone the project if you have not done it yet, explore the project structure, and build and deploy the WAR file on application servers compatible with Servlet 3.x, such as *JBoss WildFly* and *Apache TomEE*.

The showcase for the recipe is available at `http://localhost:8080/pf-cookbook/views/chapter6/contextMenu.jsf`.

Integrating the context menu

Data iteration components, such as `dataTable`, `tree`, and `treeTable`, have a special integration with the context menu. These components can display a context menu for every right-click of the mouse on any row in `dataTable` or any node in `tree`.

In this recipe, we will integrate a context menu with the `tree` component. Integration with `dataTable` or `treeTable` is similar and described well in the *PrimeFaces User's Guide* documentation (`http://primefaces.org/documentation.html`).

How to do it...

We will develop a context menu with two menu items—**View** and **Delete**. A **View** item shows the currently selected tree node, and the **Delete** item removes it. We would like to implement this behavior for all tree nodes. The following listing demonstrates the integration of `p:contextMenu` with `p:tree`:

```
<p:growl id="growl" showDetail="true"/>

<p:contextMenu for="fileSystem">
  <p:menuitem value="View" update="growl"
    actionListener="#{contextMenuBean.viewNode}"
    icon="ui-icon-search"/>
  <p:menuitem value="Delete" update="fileSystem"
    actionListener="#{contextMenuBean.deleteNode}"
    icon="ui-icon-close"/>
</p:contextMenu>

<p:tree id="fileSystem" value="#{contextMenuBean.root}"
  var="node" dynamic="true"
  cache="false" selectionMode="single"
  selection="#{contextMenuBean.selectedNode}">
  <p:ajax event="select"
    listener="#{contextMenuBean.onNodeSelect}"/>
  <p:ajax event="unselect"
    listener="#{contextMenuBean.onNodeUnselect}"/>
  <p:treeNode>
    <h:outputText value="#{node}"/>
  </p:treeNode>
</p:tree>
```

We can see the context menu over tree nodes in the following screenshot. The **View** item that has been clicked on shows a `growl` notification.

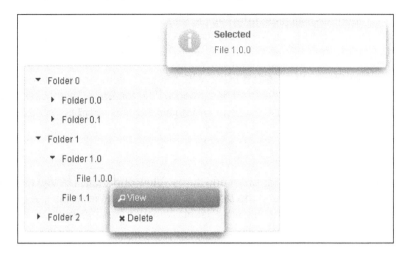

The view-scoped CDI bean, `ContextMenuBean`, creates `tree`. The bean implements all listener methods. This is shown in the following code:

```
@Named
@ViewScoped
public class ContextMenuBean implements Serializable {

    private TreeNode root;
    private TreeNode selectedNode;

    @PostConstruct
    protected void initialize() {
        root = new DefaultTreeNode("Root", null);

        TreeNode node0 = new DefaultTreeNode("Folder 0", root);
        ...
    }

    public TreeNode getRoot() {
        return root;
    }

    public TreeNode getSelectedNode() {
```

```
    return selectedNode;
  }

  public void setSelectedNode(TreeNode selectedNode) {
    this.selectedNode = selectedNode;
  }

  public void onNodeSelect(NodeSelectEvent event) {
    selectedNode = event.getTreeNode();
  }

  public void onNodeUnselect(NodeUnselectEvent event) {
    selectedNode = null;
  }

  public void viewNode() {
    if (selectedNode == null) {
      return;
    }

    FacesMessage msg = new FacesMessage(
      FacesMessage.SEVERITY_INFO,
      "Selected", selectedNode.getData().toString());
      FacesContext.getCurrentInstance().addMessage(null, msg);
  }

  public void deleteNode() {
    if (selectedNode == null) {
      return;
    }

    selectedNode.getChildren().clear();
    selectedNode.getParent().getChildren().
      remove(selectedNode);
    selectedNode.setParent(null);
    selectedNode = null;
  }
}
```

How it works...

When a menu item is clicked on, the whole `tree` component gets processed and the currently selected node is stored in the `ContextMenuBean` bean via the `#{contextMenuBean.selectedNode}` EL expression. After that, an action listener is called and can access the selected node. The `viewNode()` action listener only generates a message with the name of the selected node. The subsequent AJAX response updates `p:growl`. We see a `growl` notification. The `deleteNode()` action listener deletes the selected node from the tree model. The subsequent AJAX response updates `p:tree` (see `<p:menuitem` ... `update="fileSystem"/>`). We see the tree updated without the deleted node.

There's more...

The `nodeType` attribute is featured by `p:contextMenu`. This attribute specifies the type of tree nodes to attach to. It matches the `type` attribute of `p:treeNode`. Hence, different menus can be attached to particular tree nodes by matching the menu's `nodeType` to the tree node's `type`.

 The matching occurs in a manner similar to that for the `for` attribute of a label (`h:outputLabel` or `p:outputLabel`), linking it to an input component.

See also

Explore data iteration components in *Chapter 5, Data Iteration Components*. You will find many tips to use `p:tree`, `p:dataTable`, and `p:treeTable`.

PrimeFaces Cookbook Showcase application

This recipe is available in the demo web application on GitHub (`https://github.com/ova2/primefaces-cookbook/tree/second-edition`). Clone the project if you have not done it yet, explore the project structure, and build and deploy the WAR file on application servers compatible with Servlet 3.x, such as *JBoss WildFly* and *Apache TomEE*.

The showcase for the recipe is available at `http://localhost:8080/pf-cookbook/views/chapter6/contextMenuIntegration.jsf`.

Breadcrumb – providing contextual information about page hierarchy

Breadcrumb is a navigation component that provides contextual information about the page hierarchy. It allows users to keep track of their locations within the workflow.

In this recipe, we will develop a simple breadcrumb with a handy configuration attribute.

How to do it...

The `breadcrumb` component is represented as the `p:breadCrumb` tag with nested menu items. We will use the same CDI bean as in the *Statically and dynamically positioned menus* recipe of this chapter. This is shown in the following code:

```
<p:breadCrumb>
  <p:menuitem value="PrimeFaces" url="http://primefaces.org"/>
  <p:menuitem value="jQuery" url="http://jquery.com"/>
  <p:menuitem value="Yahoo UI" url="http://yuilibrary.com"/>
  <p:menuitem value="Save"
    actionListener="#{positionedMenuBean.save}"
    update="growl"/>
  <p:menuitem value="Update"
    actionListener="#{positionedMenuBean.update}"
    update="growl"/>
</p:breadCrumb>
```

A "home page" icon is shown at the root link, but display of text is possible too. The following code shows this:

```
<p:breadCrumb homeDisplay="text">
  ...
</p:breadCrumb>
```

The next image demonstrates these two cases:

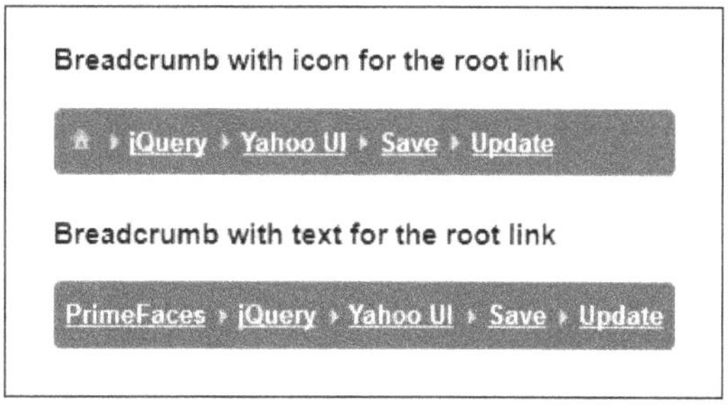

How it works...

Single items within p:breadCrumb are defined as p:menuitem. You can either set the url attribute to navigate to another page or define action/actionListener to invoke a server-side method.

The appearance of the root link is controlled by the homeDisplay attribute. It is set to the icon value by default. Setting homeDisplay="text" will display the text instead of the icon.

There's more...

A breadcrumb can be created programmatically as well. This approach is described in the *Creating programmatic menus* recipe of this chapter.

PrimeFaces Cookbook Showcase application

This recipe is available in the demo web application on GitHub (https://github.com/ova2/primefaces-cookbook/tree/second-edition). Clone the project if you have not done it yet, explore the project structure, and build and deploy the WAR file on application servers compatible with Servlet 3.x, such as *JBoss WildFly* and *Apache TomEE*.

The showcase for the recipe is available at http://localhost:8080/pf-cookbook/views/chapter6/breadcrumb.jsf.

SlideMenu – menu in the iPod style

A slide menu displays nested submenus as slides with animation similar to the iPod menu. A slide menu features the same common behaviors as every PrimeFaces menu. It consists of (nested) submenus and menu items that can be built declaratively or programmatically by the model. The main difference from other menu types is a slide animation when displaying submenus. The positioning of the slide menu is static by default, but it can also be positioned relative to a trigger that shows the menu.

In this recipe, we will develop a slide menu with a button acting as the trigger. When the user pushes the button, the menu will be displayed in an overlay.

How to do it...

We will take `p:commandButton` as the trigger. The `p:slideMenu` tag, representing a slide menu, has a `trigger` attribute that points to the ID of `p:commandButton`. The slide menu consists of submenus (slides) with menu items sending AJAX, non-AJAX (`ajax="false"`), and GET requests (`url` is not null). The following code shows this:

```
<p:commandButton id="btn" value="Show Slide Menu" type="button"/>

<p:slideMenu overlay="true" trigger="btn"
  my="left top" at="left bottom" style="width:190px;">
  <p:submenu label="CRUD Operations" icon="ui-icon-play">
    <p:menuitem value="Save"
      actionListener="#{slideMenuBean.save}"
      icon="ui-icon-disk" update="growl"/>
    <p:menuitem value="Update"
      actionListener="#{slideMenuBean.update}"
      icon="ui-icon-arrowrefresh-1-w" update="growl"/>
    <p:menuitem value="Delete"
      actionListener="#{slideMenuBean.delete}"
      icon="ui-icon-trash" update="growl"/>
  </p:submenu>
  <p:submenu label="Other Operations" icon="ui-icon-play">
    <p:menuitem value="Do something"
      actionListener="#{slideMenuBean.doSomething}"
      ajax="false" icon="ui-icon-check"/>
    <p:menuitem value="Go Home" action="/views/home"
      ajax="false" icon="ui-icon-home"/>
  </p:submenu>

  <p:submenu label="JSF Links" icon="ui-icon-extlink">
    <p:submenu label="JSF Components">
      <p:menuitem value="PrimeFaces" url="http://primefaces.org"/>
      <p:menuitem value="PrimeFaces Extensions"
        url="http://primefaces-extensions.github.io"/>
      <p:menuitem value="RichFaces" url=
        "http://jboss.org/richfaces"/>
    </p:submenu>
    <p:menuitem value="JSF API"
      url="http://javaserverfaces.java.net/nonav/docs/2.2"/>
  </p:submenu>
</p:slideMenu>
```

The following screenshot shows how the slide menu looks when it is open (the left part of the screenshot) and after a click on the **Other Operations** menu item (the right part of the screenshot):

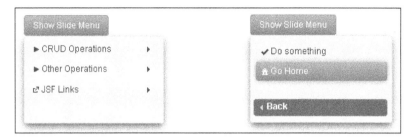

How it works...

By default, the `slideMenu` component is positioned statically in the normal page flow. To position it dynamically, relative to a trigger component, we need to set `overlay="true"`. The preceding sample attaches a `slideMenu` component to the button so that whenever the button is clicked, the menu will display itself in an overlay. The dynamic menu's position can be controlled by the `my` and `at` attributes. The `my` attribute specifies a corner of the menu to align with the trigger element, and the `at` attribute specifies a corner of the trigger to align with the menu element.

There's more...

There is also a `triggerEvent` attribute. It defines an event name for the trigger that will show the dynamically positioned menu. The default value is `click`.

`SlideMenu` can also be opened manually by the client-side API. The menu's widget exposes the `show()` and `hide()` methods to show and hide, respectively, the overlay menu.

See also

See the *Statically and dynamically positioned menus* recipe in this chapter to get some basic knowledge of statically and dynamically positioned menus

PrimeFaces Cookbook Showcase application

This recipe is available in the demo web application on GitHub (`https://github.com/ova2/primefaces-cookbook/tree/second-edition`). Clone the project if you have not done it yet, explore the project structure, and build and deploy the WAR file on application servers compatible with Servlet 3.x, such as *JBoss WildFly* and *Apache TomEE*.

The showcase for the recipe is available at `http://localhost:8080/pf-cookbook/views/chapter6/slideMenu.jsf`.

TieredMenu – submenus in nested overlays

A tiered menu displays nested submenus as overlays. A tiered menu features the same common behaviors as every PrimeFaces menu—it consists of (nested) submenus and menu items that can be built declaratively or programmatically by modeling. The main difference from the default menu described in the *Statically and dynamically positioned menus* recipe of this chapter is the part about displaying with overlays. The positioning of the tiered menu is static by default, but it can also be positioned relative to a trigger that shows the menu.

In this recipe, we will develop static and dynamic tiered menus. A dynamic tiered menu will be shown after a click on a button acting as the trigger. Furthermore, you will learn about the autodisplay feature.

How to do it...

The following code listing demonstrates three tiered menus: static (default), static without the autodisplay feature, and dynamic. As the trigger for the dynamic menu, we will take a p:commandButton tag. The p:tieredMenu tag, representing a tiered menu, has a trigger attribute that points to the ID of p:commandButton. Here's the code that shows this:

```
<p:growl id="growl"/>

<h3>Default TieredMenu</h3>

<p:tieredMenu style="width:190px;">
  <ui:include src="/views/chapter6/tieredMenuStructure.xhtml"/>
</p:tieredMenu>

<h3>TieredMenu without autoDisplay</h3>

<p:tieredMenu autoDisplay="false" style="width:190px;">
  <ui:include src="/views/chapter6/tieredMenuStructure.xhtml"/>
</p:tieredMenu>

<h3>TieredMenu on Overlay</h3>

<p:commandButton id="btn" value="Show Tiered Menu" type="button"/>

<p:tieredMenu overlay="true" trigger="btn"
  my="left top" at="left bottom" style="width:190px;">
  <ui:include src="/views/chapter6/tieredMenuStructure.xhtml"/>
</p:tieredMenu>
```

The tiered menu consists of submenus with menu items sending AJAX, non-AJAX (`ajax="false"`), and GET requests (`url` is not null). The following code shows this:

```
<p:submenu label="CRUD Operations" icon="ui-icon-play">
  <p:menuitem value="Save"
    actionListener="#{tieredMenuBean.save}"
    icon="ui-icon-disk" update="growl"/>
  <p:menuitem value="Update"
    actionListener="#{tieredMenuBean.update}"
    icon="ui-icon-arrowrefresh-1-w" update="growl"/>
  <p:menuitem value="Delete"
    actionListener="#{tieredMenuBean.delete}"
    icon="ui-icon-trash" update="growl"/>
</p:submenu>
<p:submenu label="Other Operations" icon="ui-icon-play">
  <p:menuitem value="Do something"
    actionListener="#{tieredMenuBean.doSomething}"
    ajax="false" icon="ui-icon-check"/>
  <p:menuitem value="Go Home" action="/views/home"
    ajax="false" icon="ui-icon-home"/>
</p:submenu>
<p:submenu label="JSF Links" icon="ui-icon-extlink">
  <p:submenu label="JSF Components">
    <p:menuitem value="PrimeFaces" url="http://primefaces.org"/>
    <p:menuitem value="PrimeFaces Extensions"
      url="http://primefaces-extensions.github.io"/>
    <p:menuitem value="RichFaces"
      url="http://jboss.org/richfaces"/>
  </p:submenu>
  <p:menuitem value="JSF API"
    url="http://javaserverfaces.java.net/nonav/docs/2.2"/>
</p:submenu>
```

The following screenshot shows how the static tiered menu looks when we open nested submenus:

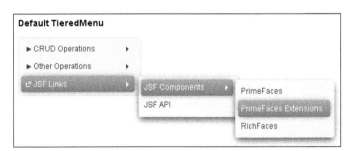

How it works...

By default, the `tieredMenu` component is positioned statically in a normal page flow. There are two modes: with and without the autodisplay feature. If `autoDisplay` is set to `true` (default), the content of the submenu is displayed when the mouse is over it. A menu with `autoDisplay` set to `false` requires a click on a submenu to display its menu items.

A dynamically positioned menu is defined by setting `overlay` to `true`. The preceding sample attaches a `tieredMenu` component to the button so that whenever the button is clicked on, the menu will display itself in an overlay. A dynamic menu position can be controlled by the `my` and `at` attributes, where `my` specifies a corner of the menu to align with the trigger element and `at` specifies a corner of the trigger to align with the menu element.

There's more...

There is also a `triggerEvent` attribute. It defines an event name for the trigger that will show the dynamically positioned menu. The default value is `click`.

A `tieredMenu` can also be opened manually by the client-side API. The menu's widget exposes the `show()` and `hide()` methods to show or hide the overlay menu.

See also

See the *Statically and dynamically positioned menus* recipe in this chapter to get some basic knowledge of statically and dynamically positioned menus

PrimeFaces Cookbook Showcase application

This recipe is available in the demo web application on GitHub (`https://github.com/ova2/primefaces-cookbook/tree/second-edition`). Clone the project if you have not done it yet, explore the project structure, and build and deploy the WAR file on application servers compatible with Servlet 3.x, such as *JBoss WildFly* and *Apache TomEE*.

The showcase for the recipe is available at `http://localhost:8080/pf-cookbook/views/chapter6/tieredMenu.jsf`.

MegaMenu – the multicolumn menu

A mega menu, sometimes also called a mega drop-down menu, is designed to enhance the scannability and categorization of its contents. PrimeFaces' mega menu is a horizontal navigation component that displays menu items grouped in submenus. The main advantage of such a kind of menu is that everything is visible at once—no scrolling is required.

In this recipe, we will design and implement a mega menu for an imaginary online shop selling clothes.

How to do it...

The layout of the `megaMenu` component is grid-based. That means root items require columns as children to define each section in a grid. Root items are direct submenus under `p:megaMenu`.

We will design four root items. The first one will show women's clothing, the second one will show men's clothing, the third one will show a color guide (pictures with available clothing colors), and the last one will show the shopping cart in a dialog. The following code shows this:

```
<p:megaMenu>
  <p:submenu label="Women's Clothing" icon="ui-icon-person">
    <p:column>
      <p:submenu label="Shoes">
        <p:menuitem value="Size UK 3-5" url="#"/>
        ...
      </p:submenu>
      <p:submenu label="Jeans">
        <p:menuitem value="Curve" url="#"/>
        ...
      </p:submenu>
      <p:submenu label="Nightwear">
        <p:menuitem value="Calvin Klein" url="#"/>
        ...
      </p:submenu>
    </p:column>
    <p:column>
      <p:submenu label="Leggings">
        <p:menuitem value="Long Sleeve" url="#"/>
        ...
      </p:submenu>
```

```
        <p:submenu label="Skirts">
          <p:menuitem value="American Apparel" url="#"/>
          ...
        </p:submenu>
      </p:column>
  </p:submenu>

  <p:submenu label="Men's Clothing" icon="ui-icon-person">
    <p:column>
      <p:submenu label="Shoes">
        <p:menuitem value="Size UK 3-5" url="#"/>
        ...
      </p:submenu>
      <p:submenu label="T-Shirts">
        <p:menuitem value="Addict" url="#"/>
        ...
      </p:submenu>
    </p:column>
    <p:column>
      <p:submenu label="Leather Jackets">
        <p:menuitem value="Diesel" url="#"/>
        ...
      </p:submenu>
      <p:submenu label="Jeans">
        <p:menuitem value="Curve" url="#"/>
        ...
      </p:submenu>
      <p:submenu label="Swimwear">
        <p:menuitem value="Boss Black" url="#"/>
        ...
      </p:submenu>
    </p:column>
  </p:submenu>

  <p:submenu label="Color Guide" icon="ui-icon-image">
    <p:column>
      <h:graphicImage library="images" name="colors.gif"/>
    </p:column>
  </p:submenu>

  <p:menuitem value="Shopping Cart"
    onclick="PF('wdgtShoppingCart').show();"
```

```
            update="shoppingCartGrp" icon="ui-icon-cart"/>
    </p:megaMenu>

    <p:dialog id="shoppingCart" header="Shopping Cart"
      widgetVar="wdgtShoppingCart">
      <h:panelGroup id="shoppingCartGrp" layout="block"
        style="padding:20px;">
        <h:outputText value="#{megaMenuBean.items}"/>
      </h:panelGroup>
      <p:commandButton value="Close" type="button"
        onclick="PF('wdgtShoppingCart').hide();"/>
    </p:dialog>
```

The following screenshot shows the designed mega menu:

How it works...

Direct submenus of `p:megaMenu` require `p:column` to be represented in a multicolumn grid. Not only submenus, but also any content can be placed inside columns. In the preceding example, we can see `<h:graphicImage library="images" name="colors.gif"/>` under `p:column`.

Except for `p:column`, the structure of `p:megaMenu` is the same for every PrimeFaces'
menu component—it consists of submenus and menu items. A menu item as a root item is
supported as well. In the designed example, it is the **Shopping Cart** menu item:

There's more...

`MegaMenu` has the autodisplay feature. This feature defines whether submenus will
be displayed on a mouseover event or not. If `autoDisplay` is set to `true` (default),
the content of the submenu is displayed when the mouse is over it. A menu with the
`autoDisplay="false"` setting requires a click on a submenu to display its menu items.

`MegaMenu` is horizontal by default. If you want a vertically oriented menu for root menu items,
change its orientation as `<p:megaMenu orientation="vertical">`. The next screenshot
shows a vertical mega menu:

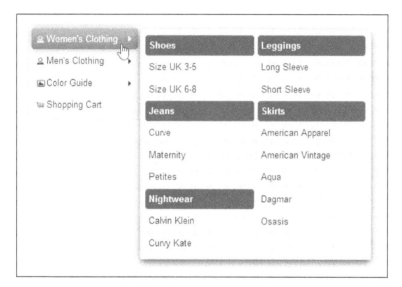

PrimeFaces Cookbook Showcase application

This recipe is available in the demo web application on GitHub (`https://github.com/
ova2/primefaces-cookbook/tree/second-edition`). Clone the project if you have
not done it yet, explore the project structure, and build and deploy the WAR file on application
servers compatible with Servlet 3.x, such as *JBoss WildFly* and *Apache TomEE*.

The showcase for the recipe is available at `http://localhost:8080/pf-cookbook/
views/chapter6/megaMenu.jsf`.

PanelMenu – hybrid of accordion and tree

A panel menu is a hybrid of the accordion and tree components used for navigation and action. It renders a vertical menu structure with support for nested menu items.

In this recipe, we will develop a panel menu with three top submenus acting as accordion tabs and nested menu items with a tree-like look and feel.

How to do it...

A panel menu is rendered by the `p:panelMenu` tag. Top-level submenus define accordion-like tabs. A click on such a tab expands or collapses the subordinated content. The menu structure is similar to every PrimeFaces' menu component—it consists of submenus and menu items. Menu items can call actions, action listeners, or trigger navigations. The following code shows this:

```
<p:panelMenu style="width:200px">
  <p:submenu label="Ajax Operations">
    <p:menuitem value="Save"
      actionListener="#{panelMenuBean.save}"
      icon="ui-icon-disk"/>
    <p:menuitem value="Update"
      actionListener="#{panelMenuBean.update}"
      icon="ui-icon-arrowrefresh-1-w"/>
  </p:submenu>
  <p:submenu label="Non-Ajax Operations">
    <p:menuitem value="Delete"
      actionListener="#{panelMenuBean.delete}"
      ajax="false" icon="ui-icon-close"/>
  </p:submenu>
  <p:separator/>
  <p:submenu label="Navigations">
    <p:submenu label="Links" icon="ui-icon-extlink">
      <p:submenu label="Prime Products">
        <p:menuitem value="Prime UI" icon="ui-icon-home"
          url="http://primefaces.org/primeui"/>
        <p:menuitem value="Prime Mobile" icon="ui-icon-signal"
          url="http://primefaces.org/showcase/mobile/
            index.xhtml"/>
      </p:submenu>
      <p:submenu label="Prime Resources">
        <p:menuitem value="Docs" icon="ui-icon-document"
          url="http://primefaces.org/documentation.html"/>
```

```
        <p:menuitem value="Download" icon="ui-icon-arrowthick-1-s"
          url="http://primefaces.org/downloads.html"/>
      </p:submenu>
    </p:submenu>
  </p:submenu>
</p:panelMenu>
```

The result of the preceding code listing is shown in the following screenshot. This screenshot demonstrates the same menu in two states—completely collapsed on the left-hand side and completely expanded on the right-hand side.

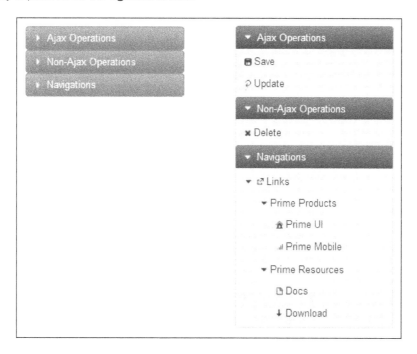

How it works...

We see that direct children of `p:panelMenu` are normally several `p:submenu` tags with labels describing the accordion-like tabs. Tabs can be styled by the `.ui-panelmenu h3` selector. In this recipe, we will use the following definition:

```
.ui-panelmenu h3 {
  font-size: 1em;
}
```

As the menu uses menu items, it is easy to invoke actions or action listeners with or without AJAX (`ajax="false"`) as well as navigate. Navigation means that a GET request causes a switch to another page. This is always a full page refresh and only works when the `url` attribute on `p:menuitem` is set. In this case, the menu item is rendered as a normal HTML link element. If the `url` attribute is missing, only POST requests (with AJAX or without) can be sent.

There's more...

The `panelMenu` component keeps the open or closed state of submenus across web pages. The state is saved in cookies. This means that when the user enters the same page again, `panelMenu` will be displayed in the same state as when he/she had last interacted with it. This feature is pretty useful, but sometimes, it is not desirable, for example, when multiple users with different accounts work on the same PC. In this case, we can either call the widget method `clearState()` (a client-side solution) or clear the cookie on logging out in the response (a server-side solution). The cookie name is `panelMenu-<id>`, where `<id>` is the client ID of `p:panelMenu`.

PrimeFaces Cookbook Showcase application

This recipe is available in the demo web application on GitHub (`https://github.com/ova2/primefaces-cookbook/tree/second-edition`). Clone the project if you have not done it yet, explore the project structure, and build and deploy the WAR file on application servers compatible with Servlet 3.x, such as *JBoss WildFly* and *Apache TomEE*.

The showcase for the recipe is available at `http://localhost:8080/pf-cookbook/views/chapter6/panelMenu.jsf`.

MenuButton – multiple items in a popup

A menu button is a button that displays multiple menu items in a popup when it is clicked on or pressed. A popup is an absolutely positioned element (overlay) in terms of CSS.

In this recipe, we will learn the structure of `p:menuButton`—a JSF tag for the `menuButton` component.

How to do it...

The `p:menuButton` tag incorporates one or more menu items. The following code snippet demonstrates four menu items that send AJAX and GET requests:

```
<p:menuButton value="CRUD Operations" iconPos="right">
  <p:menuitem value="Save"
     actionListener="#{menuButtonBean.save}"
```

```
        icon="ui-icon-disk" update="growl"/>
    <p:menuitem value="Update"
      actionListener="#{menuButtonBean.update}"
      icon="ui-icon-arrowrefresh-1-w" update="growl"/>
    <p:menuitem value="Delete"
      actionListener="#{menuButtonBean.delete}"
      icon="ui-icon-close" update="growl"/>
    <p:separator/>
    <p:menuitem value="PrimeFaces" url="http://primefaces.org"/>
  </p:menuButton>
```

The open menu looks as shown in the screenshot:

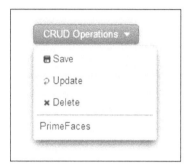

How it works...

Only `p:menuitem` and `p:separator` are allowed as child tags by `p:menuButton`. The `iconPos` attribute defines the position of the displayed icon. The valid values are `left` (default) and `right`. We set the `right` value in the example.

There's more...

There is also the `appendTo` attribute that defines the element that the pop-up menu is appended to. The value of this attribute is a **search expression** in terms of *Search Expression Framework* described in *Chapter 1, Getting Started with PrimeFaces*. A missing value means that the pop-up menu is appended to the document body. The document body is a good place for any kind of overlays when working with layouts such as `p:layout`.

Menus can be created programmatically as well. This approach is described in the *Creating programmatic menus* recipe of this chapter.

PrimeFaces Cookbook Showcase application

This recipe is available in the demo web application on GitHub (`https://github.com/ova2/primefaces-cookbook/tree/second-edition`). Clone the project if you have not done it yet, explore the project structure, and build and deploy the WAR file on application servers compatible with Servlet 3.x, such as *JBoss WildFly* and *Apache TomEE*.

The showcase for the recipe is available at `http://localhost:8080/pf-cookbook/views/chapter6/menuButton.jsf`.

Accessing commands via menubar

`Menubar` is a horizontal navigation component with drop-down menus that are displayed on mouseover or on clicking. `Menubar` features the same common behaviors as every PrimeFaces menu. It consists of (nested) submenus, menu items, and custom content that can be built declaratively or programmatically by modeling.

In this recipe, we will build a declarative menu bar with various commands as nested and direct menu items. The possibility of including any custom content, such as input, select, and button components, will be illustrated as well.

How to do it...

We will create a menu bar as shown in the following screenshot.

In the screenshot, the submenu **Create New** contains three menu items, **Folder**, **Video File**, and **HTML File**. The following complete code listing shows `p:menubar` with submenus `p:submenu` and menu items `p:menuitem` inside. An input component and a button component are included via `f:facet` with `name="options"` as well. The following code shows this:

```
<p:growl id="growl"/>

<p:menubar>
  <p:submenu label="File" icon="ui-icon-document">
```

```
    <p:submenu label="Create New">
      <p:menuitem value="Folder"
        actionListener="#{menubarBean.createFolder}"
        icon="ui-icon-folder-collapsed" update="growl"/>
      <p:menuitem value="Video File"
        actionListener="#{menubarBean.createVideo}"
        icon="ui-icon-video" update="growl"/>
      <p:menuitem value="HTML File"
        actionListener="#{menubarBean.createHTML}"
        icon="ui-icon-script" update="growl"/>
    </p:submenu>
    <p:separator/>
    <p:menuitem value="Quit" url="#"/>
  </p:submenu>
  <p:submenu label="Edit" icon="ui-icon-pencil">
    <p:menuitem value="Cut" actionListener="#{menubarBean.cut}"
      icon="ui-icon-scissors" update="growl"/>
    <p:menuitem value="Copy" actionListener="#{menubarBean.copy}"
      icon="ui-icon-copy" update="growl"/>
    <p:menuitem value="Paste" actionListener="#
      {menubarBean.paste}"
      icon="ui-icon-clipboard" update="growl"/>
  </p:submenu>
  <p:submenu label="View" icon="ui-icon-pencil">
    <p:menuitem value="Zoom In"
      actionListener="#{menubarBean.zoomIn}"
      icon="ui-icon-zoomin" update="growl"/>
    <p:menuitem value="Zoom Out"
      actionListener="#{menubarBean.zoomOut}"
      icon="ui-icon-zoomout" update="growl"/>
    <p:submenu label="View Mode" icon="ui-icon-search">
      <p:menuitem value="View Icons"
        actionListener="#{menubarBean.viewIcons}"
        update="growl"/>
      <p:menuitem value="View Compact"
        actionListener="#{menubarBean.viewCompact}"
        update="growl"/>
      <p:menuitem value="View Details"
        actionListener="#{menubarBean.viewDetails}"
        update="growl"/>
    </p:submenu>
  </p:submenu>
```

```
        <p:menuitem value="Info" action="#{menubarBean.info}"
          ajax="false" icon="ui-icon-help"/>

      <f:facet name="options">
        <p:inputText style="margin:0 10px 0 10px; vertical-
          align:middle;"
          placeholder="Search"/>
        <p:commandButton value="Logout" type="button"
          icon="ui-icon-extlink"/>
      </f:facet>
  </p:menubar>

  <p:dialog visible="#{flash.helpVisible}" header="Info Dialog">
    PrimeFaces Menubar brings desktop menubar to JSF
      applications.<br/>
    Combine submenus and menu items to execute ajax, non-ajax and
      navigations.
  </p:dialog>
```

`Menubar` can also support menu items as root items. In the developed example, this is the **Info** menu item. A click on **Info** shows an information dialog. The following screenshot shows this:

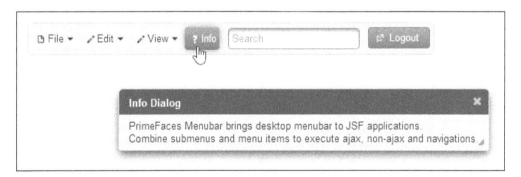

How it works...

Submenus and menu items as child components are required to compose a menu bar. A menu bar with a higher depth consists of nested submenus in parent submenus. Any custom content within a menubar should be placed in `<f:facet name="options">`.

The info dialog is only visible when the `visible="#{flash.helpVisible}"` EL expression returns `true`. The non-AJAX `info` action uses the JSF `FlashScope` variable to pass the value (`true`) of the `helpVisible` variable to the same page with a full-page request. The following code shows this:

```
public String info() {
  FacesContext.getCurrentInstance().getExternalContext().
    getFlash().put("helpVisible", true);

  return "/views/chapter6/menubar.xhtml";
}
```

There's more...

The `autoDisplay` attribute featured by `p:menubar` defines whether the first level of submenus will be displayed on mouseover or on click. When it is set to `false` (default), a click event is required to display the first level of submenus.

The `toggleEvent` attribute specifies the event to toggle the submenus. The valid values are `hover` (mouseover) and `click`. If it is not set, as in this example, the submenus are toggled on hover.

PrimeFaces Cookbook Showcase application

This recipe is available in the demo web application on GitHub (`https://github.com/ova2/primefaces-cookbook/tree/second-edition`). Clone the project if you have not done it yet, explore the project structure, and build and deploy the WAR file on application servers compatible with Servlet 3.x, such as *JBoss WildFly* and *Apache TomEE*.

The showcase for the recipe is available at `http://localhost:8080/pf-cookbook/views/chapter6/menubar.jsf`.

Displaying checkboxes in selectCheckboxMenu

A multiselect input component, `SelectCheckboxMenu` is based on checkboxes in an overlay menu. Although it is an input component, it is presented to users as a menu so that it makes sense to handle `selectCheckboxMenu` in this chapter.

In this recipe, we will implement a `selectCheckboxMenu` component in both simple and advanced forms. In the advanced case, we will learn about the built-in filtering feature. After submitting the selected items, they will be shown in a dialog.

How to do it...

The usage of `p:selectCheckboxMenu` is the same as the usage of
`p:selectManyCheckbox`. Checkbox items can be attached via several `f:selectItem` tags
or one `f:selectItems` tag. In the following simple example, we will use `f:selectItems` to
display colors:

```
<p:selectCheckboxMenu label="Colors"
  value="#{checkboxMenuBean.selectedColors}">
  <f:selectItems value="#{checkboxMenuBean.colors}"/>
</p:selectCheckboxMenu>
```

The `label` attribute defines text shown to the user. The advanced `p:selectCheckboxMenu`
component comes with a filtering feature. The feature is activated by setting `filter` to `true`.
The following code shows this:

```
<p:selectCheckboxMenu label="Languages" filter="true"
  value="#{checkboxMenuBean.selectedLanguages}">
  <f:selectItems value="#{checkboxMenuBean.languages}"/>
  <f:converter
    converterId="org.primefaces.cookbook.converter.
      LocaleConverter"/>
</p:selectCheckboxMenu>

<p:commandButton value="Submit" update="display"
  oncomplete="PF('dlg').show()"
  style="margin-top:20px; display:block;"/>

<p:dialog header="Selected colors and languages" widgetVar="dlg">
  <h:panelGroup id="display">
    <p:dataList value="#{checkboxMenuBean.selectedColors}"
      var="color">
      #{color}
    </p:dataList>
    <p:dataList value="#{checkboxMenuBean.selectedLanguages}"
      var="lang">
      #{lang}
    </p:dataList>
  </h:panelGroup>
</p:dialog>
```

The following screenshot shows the simple and advanced cases as well as a dialog with the selected values:

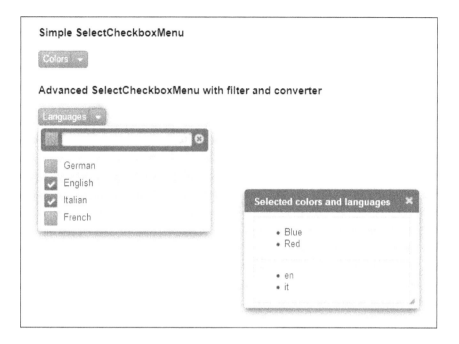

How it works...

The available checkbox items are created in the `CheckboxMenuBean` CDI bean. Items for colors are stored in a `HashMap` class, and items for languages are stored in a list of `SelectItem` objects. The following code shows this:

```
@Named
@ViewScoped
public class CheckboxMenu implements Serializable {

   private List<SelectItem> languages;
   private Map<String, String> color;
   private List<Locale> selectedLanguages;
   private List<String> selectedColors;

   public List<SelectItem> getLanguages() {
     if (languages == null) {
       languages = new ArrayList<SelectItem>();
```

```
        languages.add(
          new SelectItem(new Locale("de"), "German"));
          . . .
      }

    return languages;
  }

  public Map<String, String> getColors() {
    if (color == null) {
      color = new HashMap<String, String>();
      color.put("Red", "Red");
      . . .
    }

    return color;
  }

  // getters / setters
  . . .
}
```

After submitting the form, the selected items get set in the `selectedColors` and `selectedLanguages` variables, respectively. Their values are displayed as lists in the dialog.

There's more...

There are various configuration settings for the filter functionality in `SelectCheckboxMenu`. They are tag attributes described in the following table:

Selector	Applies
filterMatchMode	This is the match mode for filtering. The valid values are `startsWith`, `contains`, `endsWith`, and `custom` (if the value for `filterFunction` exists). The default value is `startsWith`.
filterFunction	This is the client-side function to use in custom filtering.
caseSensitive	This defines whether filtering would be case sensitive. The default value is `false`.

An example of `filterMatchMode="custom"` is a custom JavaScript function that leverages fuzzy matching (`http://dustindiaz.com/autocomplete-fuzzy-matching`). The following code shows this:

```
function customFilter(itemLabel, filterValue) {
  var reg = new RegExp(filterValue.split('').join('\\w*'), 'i');
  if (itemLabel.match(reg)) {
    // return true to accept
    return true;
  }

  // return false to reject
  return false;
}
```

This function can be used by setting `filterFunction="customFilter"`.

In the advanced example, we used `LocaleConverter`—a JSF converter—to convert `java.util.Locale` to `String` and vice versa. The `LocaleConverter` class can be found on GitHub (`https://github.com/ova2/primefaces-cookbook/tree/second-edition`) in the `org.primefaces.cookbook.converter` package.

PrimeFaces Cookbook Showcase application

This recipe is available in the demo web application on GitHub (`https://github.com/ova2/primefaces-cookbook/tree/second-edition`). Clone the project if you have not done it yet, explore the project structure, and build and deploy the WAR file on application servers compatible with Servlet 3.x, such as *JBoss WildFly* and *Apache TomEE*.

The showcase for the recipe is available at `http://localhost:8080/pf-cookbook/views/chapter6/checkboxMenu.jsf`.

7
Working with Files, Images, and Multimedia

In this chapter, we will cover the following topics:

- ▶ Basic, automatic, drag and drop, and multiple file uploading
- ▶ Downloading files
- ▶ Cropping images
- ▶ Creating dynamic image streaming programmatically
- ▶ Displaying a collection of images with galleria
- ▶ Displaying a collection of images with imageSwitch
- ▶ Displaying a collection of images with contentFlow
- ▶ Embedding the multimedia content in JSF pages
- ▶ Capturing images with photoCam

Introduction

In this chapter, we will cover the management of file operations, such as uploading and downloading, and image operations, such as capturing, cropping, and showing a collection of images with various components.

Basic, automatic, drag and drop, and multiple file uploading

The `fileUpload` component provides a file upload mechanism with enhanced features compared to the basic HTML `<input type="file">` file upload definition. The component provides an HTML5-powered UI with capabilities such as drag-and-drop, uploading multiple files, and progress tracking; it also supports legacy browsers (for IE 8+) for compatibility by degrading gracefully.

How to do it...

A basic definition for the file upload would be as follows:

```
<h:form enctype="multipart/form-data">
  <p:fileUpload value="#{fileBean.file}" mode="simple" />
  <p:commandButton value="Upload" ajax="false"/>
</h:form>
```

The `fileUpload` component will be rendered as in the following image with a **Choose File** button and a text button stating **no file selected**:

In the `simple` mode, PrimeFaces renders the `<input type="file">` HTML element. In this case, the **no file selected** label that is seen right next to the file picker button is a browser-centric one, and not applicable for internationalization.

Since the `commandButton` will not work in AJAX mode, the selected file will be uploaded to the server and set to `file` property in the backing bean, which is defined as `org.primefaces.model.UploadedFile`.

How it works...

For the upload mechanism, PrimeFaces offers support for both the *Servlet 3.X* and *Commons Fileupload* implementations. It does the selection seamlessly by detecting the existence of *JSF 2.2* or *Commons FileUpload* APIs respectively on the classpath. We can also force it to use our API selection with a context parameter configuration in `web.xml`.

```
<context-param>
  <param-name>primefaces.UPLOADER</param-name>
  <param-value>auto | native | commons</param-value>
</context-param>
```

The value of the parameter could be as follows:

- `auto`
- `native`
- `commons`

The default value is `auto` and PrimeFaces tries to detect the best method for uploading. If JSF 2.2 runtime gets detected on the classpath, the native uploading mechanism shipping with the Servlet 3.x is used. Otherwise, the commons file-upload mechanism is used.

With `native`, the native uploading mechanism shipping with Servlet 3.x is used. If the version of JSF runtime is below 2.2, an exception gets thrown.

With `commons`, the commons file-upload mechanism is used. This is more appropriate to use with the Servlet 2.5 environments where *Java EE5* is being used. With this configuration, *PrimeFaces FileUpload Filter* needs to be defined in the `web.xml` deployment descriptor file.

```
<filter>
  <filter-name>PrimeFaces FileUpload Filter</filter-name>
  <filter-class>
    org.primefaces.webapp.filter.FileUploadFilter
  </filter-class>
</filter>
<filter-mapping>
  <filter-name>PrimeFaces FileUpload Filter</filter-name>
  <servlet-name>Faces Servlet</servlet-name>
</filter-mapping>
```

The filter definition could either be done by matching `filter-mapping` with the name of the `FacesServlet` name, or by defining its URL pattern. The filter has two default settings which are the threshold size for the uploaded file and the location of the uploaded file.

```
<filter>
  <filter-name>PrimeFaces FileUpload Filter</filter-name>
  <filter-class>
    org.primefaces.webapp.filter.FileUploadFilter
  </filter-class>
  <init-param>
    <param-name>thresholdSize</param-name>
    <param-value>51200</param-value>
  </init-param>
  <init-param>
    <param-name>uploadDirectory</param-name>
    <param-value>/Users/primefaces/temp</param-value>
  </init-param>
</filter>
```

The `thresholdSize` parameter sets the minimum size in bytes for the files that will be written directly to the disk, and the `uploadDirectory` parameter sets the directory used to temporarily store those files. The files will be stored in memory if they are smaller than the `thresholdSize` parameter. If the size is exceeded, they will be stored in the place specified by `uploadDirectory`, which is `System.getProperty("java.io.tmpdir")` by default.

In order to use the commons upload mechanism, dependencies for `commons-fileupload` and `commons-io` should be declared in the project as follows:

```
<dependency>
  <groupId>commons-fileupload</groupId>
  <artifactId>commons-fileupload</artifactId>
  <version>1.3</version>
</dependency>
<dependency>
  <groupId>commons-io</groupId>
  <artifactId>commons-io</artifactId>
  <version>2.2</version>
</dependency>
```

The versions listed above are compatible with PrimeFaces 5.2 that has been officially announced. Please check for possible new releases on the `commons-fileupload` and `commons-io` projects at `http://commons.apache.org/fileupload/download_fileupload.cgi` and `http://commons.apache.org/io/download_io.cgi` respectively.

The `fileUpload` component provides the `mode` attribute, which can be either `simple` or `advanced`; it makes the component work in the simple mode like a normal HTML upload component, or in an advanced mode with HTML5 features. The default mode of the component is `advanced`. A definition and visual for the advanced file upload will be as follows:

```
<p:fileUpload value="#{fileBean.file}"
  fileUploadListener="#{fileBean.handleFileUpload}"
  update="growl" />
```

The visual of the `fileUpload` in `advanced` mode will be as follows:

An image selected for upload will be previewed in the component as given next. The width of the previewed image can be adjusted with the `previewWidth` attribute.

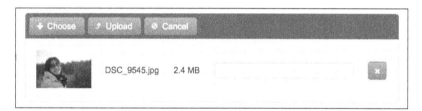

 Starting with the PrimeFaces version 5.2, image preview is also applicable without the case sensitivity of the file extensions.

Accessing files with a listener

Defining a file upload listener is a way to access the uploaded files. The definition of the `handleFileUpload` method is given next. The method receives an instance of `org.primefaces.event.FileUploadEvent` as a parameter.

```
public void handleFileUpload(FileUploadEvent event) {
  UploadedFile file = event.getFile();
  MessageUtil.addInfoMessage("upload.successful",
    file.getFileName() + " is uploaded.");
}
```

Texts for the `upload` and `cancel` buttons can be customized with the `uploadLabel` and `cancelLabel` attributes. The `showButtons` attribute enables/disables the visibility of the `upload` and `cancel` buttons in the button bar of the component. The `auto` attribute enables automatic file upload. A file will be uploaded automatically when it is selected or dragged-and-dropped to the component.

Restricting file upload by type

The `fileUpload` component allows us to restrict the file selection only to the types configured with the `allowTypes` attribute. The `allowTypes` attribute accepts a JavaScript regular expression that will be used to match against the name of the file to be uploaded. The following definition only accepts image files with an extension of `gif`, `jpg`, `jpeg`, or `png`:

```
<p:fileUpload fileUploadListener="#{fileBean.handleFileUpload}"
    allowTypes="/(\.|\/)(gif|jpe?g|png)$/" />
```

When an incorrect type of file is selected or dragged-and-dropped onto the `fileUpload` component, the component renders an error message to alert the user to the wrong file type. The following image shows the error message that occurred when a file with type `flv` was selected for upload:

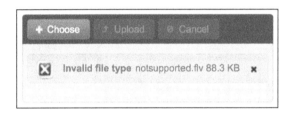

The error message **Invalid file type** can also be customized with the `invalidFileMessage` attribute.

 Specifying `allowTypes` only does a check on the client side, so for security concerns, it's advisable to implement a server-side control for an additional file type check, such as verifying the type of the file by checking it against its content. Frameworks like `simplemagic`, `http://256.com/sources/simplemagic`, can be used to achieve this.

Limiting maximum size

With the `sizeLimit` attribute, it's possible to restrict the maximum file upload size. The following definition limits the file size to a maximum of 10 KB:

```
<p:fileUpload fileUploadListener="#{fileBean.handleFileUpload}"
    sizeLimit="10240" />
```

The following image shows the error message that occurred when a file with size 2.6 MB was selected for upload:

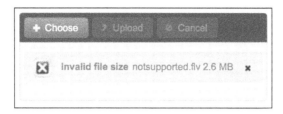

The error message **Invalid file size** can be customized with the `invalidSizeMessage` attribute.

 As of version 4.0, the default value for `sizeLimit` is set to `Long.MAX_VALUE`, which is 2^{63}-1.

Uploading multiple files

By default, selecting multiple files for uploading, via browsing after clicking on the **Choose** button, is not supported by the component. Setting the `multiple` attribute to `true` enables multiple upload for the advanced version of the component. In the multiple mode, files get uploaded in the selected order and the method bound with the `fileUploadListener` attribute gets called for each uploaded file.

```
<p:fileUpload id="multipleUpload" multiple="true" update="growl"
  fileUploadListener="#{fileBean.handleFileUpload}" />
```

 There was a known limitation of using multiple advanced file upload components in the same form. This limitation has been eliminated, starting with the PrimeFaces version 4.0.

Handling upload with client-side callbacks

The `fileUpload` component supports hooking custom JavaScript methods when the upload process starts and ends. The following code snippet shows the upload component with the `onstart` and `oncomplete` attributes showing a progress dialog box while doing the upload:

```
<p:fileUpload fileUploadListener="#{fileBean.handleFileUpload}"
  onstart="showStatus()" oncomplete="hideStatus()" />
```

The `showStatus` and `hideStatus` methods are two simple methods for showing and hiding a dialog box component, which is also a PrimeFaces component.

```
<script type="text/javascript">
  function showStatus() {
    PF('statusDialog').show();
  }
  function hideStatus() {
    PF('statusDialog').hide();
  }
</script>

<p:dialog modal="true" widgetVar="statusDialog" header="Status"
  draggable="false" closable="false">
  <p:graphicImage value="/resources/images/ajax-loader.gif" />
</p:dialog>
```

Uploading files with drag-and-drop

In supported browsers, a file can also be dragged-and-dropped for uploading with `fileUpload`, and the component itself will be the drop zone. The `dragDropSupport` attribute defines whether or not to enable drag-and-drop from the file system. By default, the value of this attribute is `true`. In order to provide drag-and-drop support, the `fileUpload` component should be in advanced mode, which is also the default mode. The definition of the `fileUpload` component for uploading files with drag-and-drop would be as follows:

```
<p:fileUpload id="upload" value="#{fileBean.file}"
  dragDropSupport="true"
  update="growl"
  fileUploadListener="#{fileBean.handleFileUpload}" />
```

PrimeFaces Cookbook Showcase application

This recipe is available in the demo web application on GitHub (`https://github.com/ova2/primefaces-cookbook/tree/second-edition`). Clone the project if you have not done it yet, explore the project structure, and build and deploy the WAR file on every Servlet 3.x compatible application server, such as *JBoss WildFly* or *Apache TomEE*.

The showcase for the recipe is available at the URLs listed in the following table:

Showcase example	URL
Basic and advanced file upload	`http://localhost:8080/primefaces-cookbook/views/chapter7/fileUpload.jsf`
Multiple file upload	`http://localhost:8080/primefaces-cookbook/views/chapter7/fileUploadMultiple.jsf`

Showcase example	URL
Filtering file types for file upload	`http://localhost:8080/primefaces-cookbook/` `views/chapter7/fileUploadFiltering.jsf`
Limiting file size for file upload	`http://localhost:8080/primefaces-cookbook/` `views/chapter7/fileUploadSizeLimit.jsf`
Client-side callback for file upload	`http://localhost:8080/primefaces-cookbook/` `views/chapter7/fileUploadCallback.` `jsf`
Uploading files with drag-and-drop	`http://localhost:8080/pf-cookbook/views/` `chapter7/fileUploadDND.jsf`

See also

For details about the `MessageUtil` class, see the *Internationalization (i18n) and Localization (L10n)* recipe in *Chapter 1, Getting Started with PrimeFaces*.

Downloading files

The `fileDownload` component can be used to stream binary contents, such as files to requesting browsers, by wrapping the components with any JSF command component, such as a button or link.

How to do it...

The value of the `fileDownload` component should be an instance of `org.primefaces.model.StreamedContent`. The concrete class `org.primefaces.model.DefaultStreamedContent` could be used in your implementation, which is also suggested by us.

The following is the backing bean implementation for the file download:

```
public class FileBean implements Serializable {
  private StreamedContent file;

  public FileBean() {
    InputStream stream = this.getClass().
      getResourceAsStream("/chapter7/PFSamplePDF.pdf");
```

```
      file = new DefaultStreamedContent(stream,
        "application/pdf", "PFSample.pdf");
    }

    public StreamedContent getFile() {
      return file;
    }

    public StreamedContent getDownloadFile() {
      return downloadFile;
    }
  }
}
```

The `fileDownload` component is wrapped by `commandButton`. The definition is given as follows:

```
<p:commandButton value="Download" ajax="false">
  <p:fileDownload value="#{fileBean.file}" />
</p:commandButton>
```

> Since the file download progress is non-AJAX, the `ajax` attribute for PrimeFaces command components that are used for wrapping the `fileDownload` component should be set to `false`.

There's more...

By default, the disposition of the downloadable content will be done with a download dialog box, which is the `attachment` mode, but setting the `contextDisposition` attribute to `inline` will make the browser try to open the file within itself without any prompt.

> Content disposition is not part of the HTTP standard, but it's widely adopted by the browsers.

Monitoring download status

File download is a non-AJAX process. So, in order to monitor the status, PrimeFaces provides the client-side `monitorDownload` method since we cannot use the `<p:ajaxStatus>` component for monitoring purposes. The method can be bound to an `onclick` event of a command component, as seen in the following code snippet:

```
<h:commandLink onclick="PrimeFaces.monitorDownload(showStatus,
  hideStatus)">
```

```
<p:graphicImage
    value="/resources/images/download/fileDownload.png" />
  <p:fileDownload value="#{fileBean.downloadFile}" />
</h:commandLink>
```

This method will trigger two methods, `showStatus` and `hideStatus`, when the download process occurs.

The `showStatus` and `hideStatus` are two simple methods for showing and hiding a dialog box component. These methods are described in the following code snippet:

```
<script type="text/javascript">
  function showStatus() {
    statusDialog').show();
  }
  function hideStatus() {
    PF('statusDialog').hide();
  }
</script>
```

The definition of the dialog box is given as follows:

```
<p:dialog modal="true" widgetVar="statusDialog" header="Status"
  draggable="false" closable="false">
  <p:graphicImage value="/resources/images/ajax-loader.gif" />
</p:dialog>
```

 File download needs a cookie named `primefaces.download` for handling monitoring purposes, so session cookies should be enabled within the browser for proper usage.

PrimeFaces Cookbook Showcase application

This recipe is available in the demo web application on GitHub (`https://github.com/ova2/primefaces-cookbook/tree/second-edition`). Clone the project if you have not done it yet, explore the project structure, and build and deploy the WAR file on every Servlet 3.x compatible application server, such as *JBoss WildFly* or *Apache TomEE*.

The showcase for the recipe is available under `http://localhost:8080/pf-cookbook/views/chapter7/fileDownload.jsf`.

Cropping images

The `imageCropper` component provides image-cropping functionality by allowing us to crop a certain region of an image, which could either be a local image or an external image. After cropping, a new image is created. It contains the cropped region and it is assigned to a `CroppedImage` instance.

How to do it...

The `org.primefaces.model.CroppedImage` class belongs to the PrimeFaces API, and the structure of the class is as follows:

```
public class CroppedImage {
   String originalFilename;
   byte[] bytes;
   int left;
   int top;
   int width;
   int height;
}
```

A simple definition of the image cropper for cropping a local image would be as shown in the following code line. The value of the component is bound with an instance of `CroppedImage`.

```
<p:imageCropper value="#{imageCropBean.croppedImageSimple}"
   image="/resources/images/crop/primefaces.jpg" />
```

When hovered over the image, the cursor of the mouse will change to crosshairs for making the crop region selection. When the region is selected, it will be highlighted with a dashed canvas and the section left outside the region will be grayed out.

 Currently, image cropping is supported on an image provided with a relative path. Cropping cannot be applied on an image presented by a `graphicImage` component.

How it works...

The `action` method for the actual crop is defined in the following code snippet. This method retrieves the cropped image and converts it to an instance of the `org.primefaces.model.StreamedContent` class to display the image with the `p:graphicImage` component.

```
StreamedContent graphicText;

public String cropSimple() throws IOException {
  graphicText = new DefaultStreamedContent(new
    ByteArrayInputStream(croppedImage.getBytes()));
  return null;
}
```

Then the cropped image could be easily displayed by using the following code snippet:

```
<p:commandButton value="Crop" action="#{imageCropBean.cropSimple}"
  update="localCroppedImage"/>
```

The `graphicText` property created within the `cropSimple` method is an instance of `StreamedContent`, and it will be visualized with the `<p:graphicImage>` component.

The backing bean containing the `graphicText` property should be defined in the session scope. The reason behind it is that the image will be fetched in a separate request from the rest of the page content and in order to retrieve the cropped image, the content should be stored in the session context.

When the `graphicImage` component is fed with an image created dynamically, as it is done in the cropping examples, its `cache` attribute should be set to `false` in order to tell the regarding browser to disable caching on the resource.

The image that will be cropped should be shown in full size in order to be processed, so there is no way to limit the size of the image with a given width/height.

One other possible implementation for cropping the image could be for saving the image to the disk and showing the saved image via a media display component, such as `graphicImage`.

```
public String cropWithSave() {
  ServletContext servletContext = (ServletContext)
    FacesContext.getCurrentInstance().getExternalContext().
    getContext();
```

```
String newFileName = servletContext.getRealPath("") +
    File.separator + "resources" + File.separator + "images" +
    File.separator + "cropped.jpg";

FileImageOutputStream imageOutput;
try {
    imageOutput = new FileImageOutputStream(
        new File(newFileName));
    imageOutput.write(croppedImageSimple.getBytes(), 0,
        croppedImageSimple.getBytes().length);
    imageOutput.close();
}
catch (Exception e) {
    throw new FacesException(
        "Error in writing cropped image.", e);
}
return null;
}
```

There's more...

The initial coordinates of the cropped region drawn on the canvas of the image can be defined with the initialCoords attribute. The notation of the attribute should follow the x, y, w, h format, where x and y stand for the *x* and *y* coordinate values, and w and h stand for width and height.

The backgroundColor attribute defines the color of the background container with the default value as black. The backgroundOpacity attribute defines the opacity of the outer image while cropping. Its default value is 0.6, and the value should be between 0 and 1.

The minSize and maxSize attributes define the minimum width and height for the cropped region in pixels with the notation [width, height].

The aspectRatio attribute defines the ratio of the cropped region as width to height. To make it a square, the value should be set to 1.

The imageCropper component provides the ability to crop external images as well. By providing the absolute URL to the image with the image attribute, it is possible to crop the image.

PrimeFaces Cookbook Showcase application

This recipe is available in the demo web application on GitHub (`https://github.com/ova2/primefaces-cookbook/tree/second-edition`). Clone the project if you have not done it yet, explore the project structure, and build and deploy the WAR file on every Servlet 3.x compatible application server, such as *JBoss WildFly* or *Apache TomEE*.

The showcase for the recipe is available under `http://localhost:8080/pf-cookbook/views/chapter7/cropImage.jsf`.

Creating dynamic image streaming programmatically

The `graphicImage` component can also render an image that is created programmatically in the server-side backing bean.

How to do it...

The following is an example that renders a PrimeFaces logo, which is read with the resource streaming mechanism:

```
<p:graphicImage value="#{dynaImageBean.graphicText}" />

public StreamedContent getGraphicText() throws IOException {
    InputStream stream =this.getClass()
      .getResourceAsStream("/chapter7/primefaces.jpg");
    return new DefaultStreamedContent(stream);
}
```

How it works...

As seen, the `getGraphicText()` method returns an instance of `StreamedContent`. PrimeFaces also provides a default implementation for the stream content, which is `org.primefaces.model.DefaultStreamedContent`. The backing bean containing the `graphicText` getter method should be defined in the session scope. The reason behind this is that the image will be fetched in a separate request from the rest of the page content, and in order to retrieve the logo image, the content should be stored in the session context.

PrimeFaces Cookbook Showcase application

This recipe is available in the demo web application on GitHub (`https://github.com/ova2/primefaces-cookbook/tree/second-edition`). Clone the project if you have not done it yet, explore the project structure, and build and deploy the WAR file on every Servlet 3.x compatible application server, such as *JBoss WildFly* or *Apache TomEE*.

The showcase for the recipe is available under `http://localhost:8080/pf-cookbook/views/chapter7/dynaImage.jsf`.

Displaying a collection of images with galleria

The `galleria` component can be used to display a collection of images with a transition effect.

How to do it...

A basic definition for the `galleria` component for viewing a static list of car images would be as follows:

```
<p:galleria>
  <p:graphicImage value="/resources/images/autocomplete/CC.png" />
  <p:graphicImage
    value="/resources/images/autocomplete/Golf.png" />
  <p:graphicImage
    value="/resources/images/autocomplete/Polo.png" />
  <p:graphicImage
    value="/resources/images/autocomplete/Touareg.png" />
</p:galleria>
```

How it works...

The definition of the `galleria` component renders a car image in a panel and four other small images in a filmstrip right below it. This component also provides built-in iteration effects for the transition to occur between the images, which are provided by the `autoPlay` attribute, set as `true` by default. The transition happens within 4000 milliseconds and can be customized with the `transitionInterval` attribute.

There's more...

The visibility of the filmstrip is enabled by default with the `showFilmstrip` attribute set as `true`. You can disable it by setting the attribute to `false`.

The width and height of the `galleria` canvas can be customized with `panelWidth` and `panelHeight` attributes. The width and height of the frames, visualized in the filmstrip, can be also be customized with the `frameWidth` and `frameHeight` attributes respectively. All values should be provided in pixels.

Transition effects

While iterating through the images, it is possible to apply transition effects. The `effect` attribute can have the values `blind`, `bounce`, `clip`, `drop`, `explode`, `fade` (the default), `fold`, `highlight`, `puff`, `pulsate`, `scale`, `shake`, `size`, `slide`, and `transfer`. The `effectSpeed` attribute can also be used to decide on the duration of the transition. Its default value is 500 milliseconds.

Displaying a collection of images

It is also possible to visualize a collection of car images that is bound through the `value` attribute of the galleria component as a collection. The `galleria` component offers data iteration on the collection with the `var` attribute.

```
<p:galleria id="withData" value-"#{galleriaBean.cars}"
  var="car" panelWidth="380" panelHeight="220">
  <p:graphicImage
    value="/resources/images/autocomplete/#{car.name}.png" />
</p:galleria>
```

Displaying captions on items

The `galleria` attribute can also display detailed information about the image as an overlay that is placed at the bottom of the image. The title of this overlay can be retrieved from the image's `title` attribute and its description can be retrieved from the `alt` attribute.

```
<p:galleria id="withDataAndCaption" value="#{galleriaBean.cars}"
   var="car" panelWidth="380" panelHeight="220"
   showCaption="true">
   <p:graphicImage
      value="/resources/images/autocomplete/#{car.name}.png"
      alt="Detail about #{car.name}" title="#{car.name}" />
</p:galleria>
```

The visual of the component will be given as follows:

PrimeFaces Cookbook Showcase application

This recipe is available in the demo web application on GitHub (`https://github.com/ova2/primefaces-cookbook/tree/second-edition`). Clone the project if you have not done it yet, explore the project structure, and build and deploy the WAR file on every Servlet 3.x compatible application, server such as *JBoss WildFly* or *Apache TomEE*.

The showcase for the recipe is available under `http://localhost:8080/pf-cookbook/views/chapter7/galleria.jsf`.

Displaying a collection of images with imageSwitch

The `imageSwitch` component can be used to display a collection of images with transition effects.

How to do it...

A basic definition for the `imageSwitch` for viewing a static list of car images would be as follows:

```
<p:imageSwitch id="simple">
  <p:graphicImage value="/resources/images/autocomplete/CC.png" />
  <p:graphicImage
    value="/resources/images/autocomplete/Golf.png" />
  <p:graphicImage
    value="/resources/images/autocomplete/Polo.png" />
  <p:graphicImage
    value="/resources/images/autocomplete/Touareg.png" />
</p:imageSwitch>
```

The snippet will be visualized as follows:

The preceding image is seen as a static image; by default, `imageSwitch` will do a slideshow on page load between the images defined. Setting the `slideshowAuto` attribute to false can disable this behavior. The speed of the transition can be defined by the `slideshowSpeed` attribute. Its default value is 3000 milliseconds.

The `imageSwitch attribute` uses effects for transition between images, and it supports over 25 different effects. The effect can be provided with the `effect` attribute and its speed can be defined by the `speed` attribute, which has 500 milliseconds as the default value. If no effect is specified, the built-in `fade` effect is used for transition. The list of the supported effects are given as follows:

- `blindX`
- `blindY`
- `blindZ`
- `cover`
- `curtainX`
- `curtainY`
- `fade`
- `fadeZoom`
- `growX`
- `growY`
- `none`
- `scrollUp`
- `scrollDown`
- `scrollLeft`
- `scrollRight`
- `scrollVert`
- `shuffle`
- `slideX`
- `slideY`
- `toss`
- `turnUp`
- `turnDown`
- `turnLeft`
- `turnRight`
- `uncover`
- `wipe`
- `zoom`

There's more...

With the client side API provided, it's also possible to do manual transition between the images of the `imageSwitch`. To trigger the slide change, two command buttons are defined, and the JavaScript defined with their `onclick` attribute executes the navigation between the images. The `previous()` and `next()` methods are provided by the `imageSwitch` component, which invokes the `cycle` method of *jQuery Cycle Plugin* with the `prev` and `next` parameters respectively.

```
<p:commandButton type="button"
  onclick="PF('manualSwitch').previous();"
  icon="ui-icon-circle-triangle-w" id="prev" />
<p:commandButton type="button"
  onclick="PF('manualSwitch').next();"
  icon="ui-icon-circle-triangle-e" id="next" />
<p:imageSwitch id="manual" widgetVar="manualSwitch"
  slideshowAuto="false">
  <p:graphicImage
    value="/resources/images/autocomplete/CC.png" />
  <p:graphicImage
    value="/resources/images/autocomplete/Golf.png" />
  <p:graphicImage
    value="/resources/images/autocomplete/Polo.png" />
  <p:graphicImage
    value="/resources/images/autocomplete/Touareg.png" />
</p:imageSwitch>
```

The visual of the component will be as follows:

In buttons, we are accessing the `imageSwitch` component via JavaScript through the value of the `widgetVar` attribute.

 slideshowAuto should be set to `false` for enabling manual transition.

Displaying a collection of images

`imageSwitch` supports the use of `<ui:repeat>` in order to provide a collection of car images dynamically.

```
<p:imageSwitch id="withData">
  <ui:repeat value="#{imageSwitchBean.cars}" var="car">
    <p:graphicImage
      value="/resources/images/autocomplete/#{car.name}.png" />
  </ui:repeat>
</p:imageSwitch>
```

PrimeFaces Cookbook Showcase application

This recipe is available in the demo web application on GitHub (`https://github.com/ova2/primefaces-cookbook/tree/second-edition`). Clone the project if you have not done it yet, explore the project structure, and build and deploy the WAR file on every Servlet 3.x compatible application server, such as *JBoss WildFly* or *Apache TomEE*.

The showcase for the recipe is available under `http://localhost:8080/pf-cookbook/views/chapter7/imageSwitch.jsf`.

Displaying a collection of images with contentFlow

The `contentFlow` component can be used to display a collection of images horizontally as a cover flow animation.

How to do it...

A basic definition for `contentFlow` for viewing a static list of car images would be as follows:

```
<p:contentFlow id="simple">
  <p:graphicImage value="/resources/images/autocomplete/CC.png"
    styleClass="content" />
```

```
  <p:graphicImage value="/resources/images/autocomplete/Golf.png"
    styleClass="content" />
  <p:graphicImage value="/resources/images/autocomplete/Polo.png"
    styleClass="content" />
  <p:graphicImage
    value="/resources/images/autocomplete/Touareg.png"
    styleClass="content" />
</p:contentFlow>
```

The visual of the component will be as follows:

The style class `content` should be applied to all of the nested images within the component. It's a built-in style implementation shipping with PrimeFaces.

There's more...

It is also possible to visualize a collection of car images that is bound through the `value` attribute of the component as a collection. The `contentFlow` component offers data iteration on the collection with the `var` attribute.

```
<p:contentFlow id="withData" value="#{contentFlowBean.cars}"
  var="car">
  <p:graphicImage
    value="/resources/images/autocomplete/#{car.name}.png"
    styleClass="content" />
</p:contentFlow>
```

Displaying captions with images

By defining a `div` as a sibling to the image given, `contentFlow` offers adding captions as information.

```
<p:contentFlow id="withCaption" value="#{contentFlowBean.cars}"
  var="car">
  <p:graphicImage
    value="/resources/images/autocomplete/#{car.name}.png"
    styleClass="content" />
  <div class="caption">#{car.name}</div>
</p:contentFlow>
```

The style class `caption` should be applied to `div`. It's a built-in style implementation shipping with PrimeFaces.

It's viable to apply the actions while handling user clicks on the caption. A sample that invokes a server-side method on the caption would be as follows:

```
<p:contentFlow id="withCaptionLink"
  value="#{contentFlowBean.cars}" var="car">
  <p:graphicImage
    value="/resources/images/autocomplete/#{car.name}.png"
    styleClass="content" />
  <div class="caption">
    <p:commandLink action="#{contentFlowBean.showMessage}"
      update="growl">
      #{car.name}
    </p:commandLink>
  </div>
</p:contentFlow>
```

PrimeFaces Cookbook Showcase application

This recipe is available in the demo web application on GitHub (`https://github.com/ova2/primefaces-cookbook/tree/second-edition`). Clone the project if you have not done it yet, explore the project structure, and build and deploy the WAR file on every Servlet 3.x compatible application server, such as *JBoss WildFly* or *Apache TomEE*.

The showcase for the recipe is available under `http://localhost:8080/pf-cookbook/views/chapter7/contentFlow.jsf`.

Embedding the multimedia content in JSF pages

The `media` component offers ways for embedding various multimedia content into a JSF page.

How to do it...

A simple definition of media component for displaying a QuickTime movie will be as follows:

```
<p:media value="/resources/media/sample_iTunes.mov"
  width="700" height="500" />
```

The visual output of the player will be as follows:

 Use the `width` and `height` attributes of the media component in order to declare the viewport of the player.

How it works...

By default, the `media` component renders the regarding HTML markup into the page according to the extension of the given file. The players and the matching extensions are listed as follows:

Player	Supported types
Flash	FLV, MP3, and SWF
PDF	PDF
QuickTime	AIF, AIFF, AAC, AU, BMP, GSM, MOV, MID, MIDI, MPG, MPEG, MP4, M4A, PSD, QT, QTIF, QIF, QTI, SND, TIF, TIFF, WAV, 3G2, and 3PG
Real	RA, RAM, RM, RPM, RV, SMI, and SMIL
Windows	ASX, ASF, AVI, WMA, and WMV

If the player cannot be resolved from the file type, for cases like when a YouTube video URL is provided to the component, the `player` attribute can be used to set the type of the player explicitly.

```
<p:media value="http://www.youtube.com/v/5aTFiNxzXF4"
    player="flash"/>
```

The visual output of the player will be as follows:

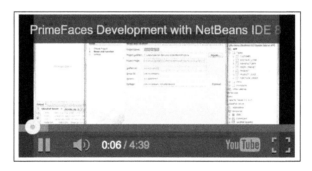

 Make sure that the URL is directly pointing to the YouTube video rather than its landing page. The URL syntax should be something like `http://www.youtube.com/v/{id_of_video}`.

There's more...

Parameters can be passed to the players according to their specification. The following is an example provided for the configuration of QuickTime player with parameters:

```
<p:media value="/resources/media/sample_iTunes.mov"
  player="quicktime" width="700" height="500">
  <f:param name="autoPlay" value="false" />
  <f:param name="controller" value="true" />
  <f:param name="volume" value="20" />
</p:media>
```

 Different proprietary players might have different configuration parameters. Please refer to the documentation of the players for further information.

Dynamic content streaming

`media` can also stream binary content provided as an instance of `StreamedContent`. Component declaration, along with method definition, is given as follows:

```
<p:media value="#{mediaBean.media}" player="quicktime" />

public StreamedContent getMedia() throws IOException {
  InputStream stream = this.getClass()
    .getResourceAsStream("/chapter7/sample_iTunes.mov");
  return new DefaultStreamedContent(stream, "video/quicktime");
}
```

PrimeFaces Cookbook Showcase application

This recipe is available in the demo web application on GitHub (`https://github.com/ova2/primefaces-cookbook/tree/second-edition`). Clone the project if you have not done it yet, explore the project structure, and build and deploy the WAR file on every Servlet 3.x compatible application server, such as *JBoss WildFly* or *Apache TomEE*.

The showcase for the recipe is available under `http://localhost:8080/pf-cookbook/views/chapter7/media.jsf`.

Capturing images with photoCam

Taking images with the attached camera and sending them to the JSF backend data model is supported by photoCam.

How to do it...

A simple definition for capturing an image with the photoCam would be as follows:

```
<p:photoCam widgetVar="pc" listener="#{photoCamBean.onCapture}"
  update="capturedImage"/>

<p:graphicImage id="capturedImage"
  value="#{photoCamBean.capturedImage}" cache="false"/>

<p:commandButton type="button" value="Capture"
  onclick="PF('pc').capture()"/>
```

How it works...

The captured image is triggered via the client-side JavaScript method, capture. The button declared in the preceding sample invokes the capture method via the widget variable defined for the photoCam component. A method expression, which will be invoked when an image is captured, is bound to the attribute. This method will handle the image captured on the server side. A sample definition for the method is as follows:

```
StreamedContent capturedImage;

public void onCapture(CaptureEvent captureEvent) {
   byte[] data = captureEvent.getData();
   capturedImage = new DefaultStreamedContent(new
     ByteArrayInputStream(data));
}
```

Since capturedImage is an instance of StreamedContent and it will be visualized with the p:graphicImage component, the backing bean containing the capturedImage object should be defined in the session scope. The reason behind that is that the image will be fetched in a separate request from the rest of the page content and in order to retrieve the captured image, the content should be stored in the session context.

When the `graphicImage` component is fed with an image created dynamically, its `cache` attribute should be set to `false` in order to tell the regarding browser to disable caching on the resource.

With PrimeFaces version 5.2, the `photoCam` component is re-implemented with an HTML5 powered version where it gracefully degrades to a Flash Player. With this version, HTML5 browser support will not be available.

There's more...

One other possible implementation for capturing the image could be saving the image to the disk and showing the saved image via a media display component such as `graphicImage`.

```
public void onCaptureWithSave(CaptureEvent captureEvent) {
  byte[] data = captureEvent.getData();
  ServletContext servletContext = (ServletContext)
    FacesContext.getCurrentInstance().getExternalContext()
    .getContext();
  String newFileName = servletContext.getRealPath("") +
  File.separator + "resources" + File.separator + "images" +
  File.separator + "captured.png";
  FileImageOutputStream imageOutput;
  try {
    imageOutput = new FileImageOutputStream(new
      File(newFileName));
    imageOutput.write(data, 0, data.length);
    imageOutput.close();
  }
  catch(Exception e) {
    throw new FacesException
    ("Error in writing captured image.", e);
  }
}
```

On arbitrary calls to the `onCaptureWithSave` method, the file created on the server will be overwritten by each method call. In order to prevent this, the name of the file can be suffixed with the current time in milliseconds or with a random number generated by `java.util.UUID`.

Authorizing access to the camera

In order to capture the image, the user might need to authorize the settings of the HTML5 Player or Flash Player, by allowing access to the camera and the microphone. The user will be notified with a dialog box of the browser or of the Flash Player before viewing the current image. The images for notifications are given as follows:

Notification of HTML5 Player

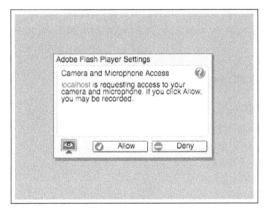

Notification of Adobe Player

PrimeFaces Cookbook Showcase application

This recipe is available in the demo web application on GitHub (`https://github.com/ova2/primefaces-cookbook/tree/second-edition`). Clone the project if you have not done it yet, explore the project structure, and build and deploy the WAR file on every Servlet 3.x compatible application server, such as *JBoss WildFly* or *Apache TomEE*.

The showcase for the recipe is available under `http://localhost:8080/pf-cookbook/views/chapter7/captureImage.jsf`.

8

Drag Me, Drop Me

In this chapter, we will cover the following topics:

- ▶ Making a component draggable
- ▶ Restricting dragging by axis, grid, and containment
- ▶ Snapping to the edges of nearest elements
- ▶ Defining droppable targets
- ▶ Restricting dropping by tolerance and acceptance
- ▶ AJAX-enhanced drag and drop
- ▶ Integrating drag and drop with data iteration components

Introduction

Drag and drop is an action, which means *grabbing* an object and *dragging* it to a different location. The components capable of being dragged and dropped enrich the Web and make a solid base for modern UI patterns. The drag and drop utilities in PrimeFaces allow us to create draggable and droppable user interfaces efficiently. They make it abstract for the developers to deal with the implementation details at the browser level.

In this chapter, we will learn about PrimeFaces' drag and drop utilities—`draggable` and `droppable`. AJAX-enhanced drag and drop, and a special integration with data iteration components, will be explained as well.

Making a component draggable

Any component can be enhanced with the draggable behavior. To enable the draggable functionality on any PrimeFaces component, we always need a component called `draggable`.

In this recipe, we will see how to make a component draggable and learn some basic features of `draggable`. To demonstrate these features, we will make several `p:panel` components draggable.

How to do it...

A component can be made draggable by using `p:draggable`. The value of the `for` attribute specifies a **search expression** for the draggable target. In our case, it matches the ID of `p:panel`.

 Chapter 1, Getting Started with PrimeFaces, provides more details on search expressions.

If the `for` attribute is omitted, the `parent` component will be selected as a draggable target. Let us make some `panel` components draggable and apply some basic features:

```
<p:panel id="pnl" header="Draggable panel with default settings">
  Drag me around
</p:panel>
<p:draggable for="pnl"/>

<p:panel id="hpnl" header="Draggable panel by handle">
  I can be only dragged by my header
</p:panel>
<p:draggable for="hpnl" handle=".ui-panel-titlebar"/>

<p:panel id="cpnl" header="Draggable panel with clone">
  I display a clone as helper while being dragged
</p:panel>
<p:draggable for="cpnl" helper="clone"/>

<p:panel id="rpnl" header="Draggable panel with revert">
  I will be returned to my start position when dragging stops
</p:panel>
<p:draggable for="rpnl" revert="true"/>

<p:panel id="opnl" header="Draggable panel with opacity">
```

```
      I use opacity for helper while being dragged
</p:panel>
<p:draggable for="opnl" opacity="0.5"/>
```

The following screenshot shows the five panels. The last panel is being dragged. Its opacity has been changed to 0.5 after the dragging starts.

How it works...

By default, any point in a dragged component can be used as a handle. To restrict the drag-start click to a specified element(s), we can use the handle option, which is a jQuery selector. The second panel is dragged by using its header only.

By default, the actual component is used as a drag indicator. The helper option allows keeping the component at its original location during dragging. This can be achieved with helper set to clone for the third panel.

If the revert option is set to true, the component will return to its starting position when the dragging stops, and the draggable component is not dropped onto a matching droppable component. The fourth panel features this behavior.

Opacity for helper, while it is being dragged, is another useful option to give the user a visual feedback. The opacity of the fifth panel is reduced when dragging.

There's more...

Other basic features are related to the attributes `cursor` and `stack`. `cursor` is a CSS cursor that is to be displayed when dragging. It is handy to set its value to `move`. `stack` is a jQuery selector. It controls the `z-index` of the set of draggable elements that match the selector and always brings them to the front. That means the draggable component always overlays the other draggables.

See also

Refer to the *Restricting dragging by axis, grid, and containment* and *Snapping to the edges of nearest elements* recipes discussed later in this chapter to learn the advanced features of `Draggable`.

PrimeFaces Cookbook Showcase application

This recipe is available in the demo web application on GitHub (`https://github.com/ova2/primefaces-cookbook/tree/second-edition`). Clone the project if you have not done it yet, explore the project structure, and build and deploy the WAR file on every Servlet 3.x compatible application server, such as *JBoss WildFly* or *Apache TomEE*.

The showcase for the recipe is available at `http://localhost:8080/pf-cookbook/views/chapter8/draggable.jsf`.

Restricting dragging by axis, grid, and containment

The dragging behavior can be limited with some configurable constraints.

In this recipe, we will see how to drag an element, either horizontally or vertically, on a grid or inside a certain section of the page.

How to do it...

The next example demonstrates three draggable panels and one draggable image. The first panel can be dragged only horizontally, the second one only vertically, and the third panel is dragged on a grid. Dragging on a grid means the dragging helper snaps to a grid—every specific x and y pixel. The image is placed within an `h:panelGroup` tag, which acts as a container for dragging. The image cannot go outside this container.

```
<p:panel id="hpnl" header="Only horizontal draggable panel">
  I can be only dragged horizontally.
</p:panel>
```

```
<p:draggable for="hpnl" axis="x"/>

<p:panel id="vpnl" header="Only vertical draggable panel">
  I can be only dragged vertically
</p:panel>
<p:draggable for="vpnl" axis="y"/>

<p:panel id="gpnl" header="Draggable panel in grid [40,50]">
  I can be only dragged in a grid
</p:panel>
<p:draggable for="gpnl" grid="40,50"/>

The image below can be only dragged within its parent's boundaries
<h:panelGroup layout="block"
  styleClass="dragContainer ui-widget-content">
  <h:graphicImage id="pic" library="images" name="logo.png"/>
</h:panelGroup>
<p:draggable for="pic" containment="parent"/>
```

The following screenshot shows the result achieved with the preceding code snippet. Especially, we can see that the image has stayed in its boundaries although the cursor has gone outside.

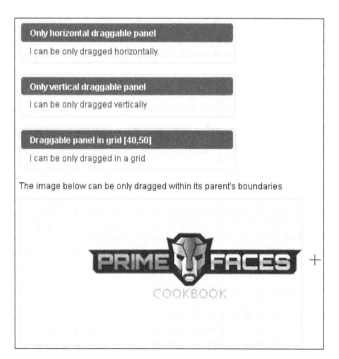

How it works...

Horizontal or vertical dragging is possible by setting the `axis` attribute as `axis="x"` or `axis="y"`, which means that the draggable element can be dragged only horizontally or only vertically, respectively.

Dragging on a grid is defined by the `grid` attribute. The value for dragging on a grid takes comma-separated dimensions. For instance, `grid="40,50"` means that the draggable element can be dragged in only 40 pixel steps horizontally and 50 vertically.

The `containment` attribute constraints dragging within the boundaries of the containment element. Possible string values are `parent`, `document`, `window`, and `[x1, y1, x2, y2]`. The setting `containment="parent"` in the preceding example means that the draggable element cannot go outside its parent.

See also

Refer to the *Snapping to the edges of nearest elements* recipe to learn about the more advanced features of `Draggable`.

PrimeFaces Cookbook Showcase application

This recipe is available in the demo web application on GitHub (`https://github.com/ova2/primefaces-cookbook/tree/second-edition`). Clone the project if you have not done it yet, explore the project structure, and build and deploy the WAR file on every Servlet 3.x compatible application server, such as *JBoss WildFly* or *Apache TomEE*.

The showcase for the recipe is available at `http://localhost:8080/pf-cookbook/views/chapter8/advancedDraggable.jsf`.

Snapping to the edges of nearest elements

With PrimeFaces, we can snap the dragged component to the inner or outer boundaries of another component (a component's DOM element).

In this recipe, we will discuss snapping and its options in detail. As an example, we will develop a big `h:panelGroup` component as a snap target and three other small `h:panelGroup` components as draggable components, with various snapping options.

How to do it...

Generally, the snapping behavior is activated by setting the attribute snap to true. The snapping behavior is configurable with two options—snapMode and snapTolerance. The first option, snapMode, determines which edges of snap elements the draggable component will snap to. The second option, snapTolerance, determines a distance in pixels the draggable component must be from the element when snapping is invoked.

```
<h:panelGroup id="snaptarget" layout="block"
  styleClass="ui-widget-content"
  style="height:150px;width:450px;">
  <p class="ui-widget-header" style="margin:0;padding:5px;">
    I'm a snap target to play with me
  </p>
  <p:draggable/>
</h:panelGroup>

<h:panelGroup id="defsnap" layout="block"
  styleClass="dragSnap ui-widget-content">
  <p>I'm with default snap and snap to all edges
    of other draggable elements</p>
</h:panelGroup>
<p:draggable for="defsnap" snap="true"/>

<h:panelGroup id="outersnap" layout="block"
  styleClass="dragSnap ui-widget-content">
  <p>I only snap to the outer edges - try with the big box</p>
</h:panelGroup>
<p:draggable for="outersnap" snap="true" snapMode="outer"/>

<h:panelGroup id="innersnap" layout="block"
  styleClass="dragSnap ui-widget-content">
  <p>I only snap to the inner edges - try with the big box</p>
</h:panelGroup>
<p:draggable for="innersnap" snap="true"
  snapMode="inner" snapTolerance="15"/>
```

The following screenshot shows the snapping for the last `h:panelGroup` tag. The component can be snapped only to the inner edges of the snap target when it is being dragged.

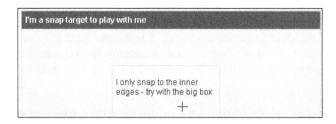

How it works...

The snapping is enabled by setting `snap` to `true`. If the `snap` attribute is set to `false` (default), no snapping occurs. The first small `h:panelGroup` has no snapping options. It snaps to the inner as well as outer boundaries of other draggable components. The second `h:panelGroup` sets `snapMode` and can only snap to the outer boundaries. Possible values of `snapMode` are `inner`, `outer`, and `both`. The third `h:panelGroup` also has a custom `snapTolerance` parameter in addition to `snapMode`, set to `inner`. This is the distance in pixels from the snap element's edges at which the snapping should occur. The default value is 20 pixels, but we have set it to `15`.

 In the current PrimeFaces implementation, a draggable component with snap set to `true` snaps to all other draggable components. This is a little bit different from jQuery's `Draggable` (`http://jqueryui.com/draggable`), where we can also specify the elements that the draggable component will snap to when it is close to the edge of such an element.

PrimeFaces Cookbook Showcase application

This recipe is available in the demo web application on GitHub (`https://github.com/ova2/primefaces-cookbook/tree/second-edition`). Clone the project if you have not done it yet, explore the project structure, and build and deploy the WAR file on every Servlet 3.x compatible application server, such as *JBoss WildFly* or *Apache TomEE*.

The showcase for the recipe is available at `http://localhost:8080/pf-cookbook/views/chapter8/snapping.jsf`.

Defining droppable targets

Any component can be enhanced with the droppable behavior. Droppable components are targets for draggable ones. To enable the droppable functionality on any PrimeFaces component, we always need a component called `droppable`.

In this recipe, we will see how to define droppable targets and will learn a client-side callback `onDrop`.

How to do it...

A component can be made droppable by using `p:droppable`. The component ID must match the `for` attribute of `p:droppable`. If the `for` attribute is omitted, the parent component will be selected as a droppable target. We will take two `h:panelGroup` components and make them droppable and draggable, respectively. In addition, we will define a client-side callback that gets invoked when a draggable component is dropped. This can be accomplished by the `onDrop` attribute, which points to a JavaScript function.

```
<h:panelGroup id="drop" layout="block" styleClass="ui-widget-
  content"
  style="height:150px; width:300px;">
  <p class="ui-widget-header" style="margin:0; padding:5px;">
    Drop here
  </p>
  <p:droppable onDrop="handleDrop"/>
</h:panelGroup>

<br/>

<h:panelGroup id="drag" layout="block"
  styleClass="dragDiv ui-widget-content">
  <p>Drag me to my target</p>
</h:panelGroup>
<p:draggable for="drag"/>
```

The client-side callback highlights the droppable `h:panelGroup` component and adds the text **Dropped!** to the paragraph tag `p`, when invoked.

```
function handleDrop(event, ui) {
  $(event.target).addClass("ui-state-highlight").
    find("p").html("Dropped!");
}
```

The following screenshot shows the result after dropping the draggable `h:panelGroup` component onto the droppable one:

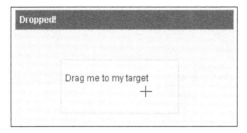

How it works...

The `onDrop` callback gets two parameters: `event` and `ui`, which are objects holding information about the drag and drop event. The droppable target is accessible by `event.target`. We use this fact to add the style class `ui-state-highlight` to the target. This class is defined by jQuery ThemeRoller.

The `event` parameter is the original browser event, and `ui` is a prepared object with the following properties:

- `ui.draggable`: This is the current draggable element, a jQuery object
- `ui.helper`: This is the current draggable helper, a jQuery object
- `ui.position`: This is the current position of the draggable helper as the `{top, left}` object
- `ui.offset`: This is the current absolute position of the draggable helper as the `{top, left}` object

See also

- The most important style classes defined by jQuery ThemeRoller are described in the *Understanding structural and skinning CSS* recipe in *Chapter 2, Theming Concepts*
- Advanced configuration and use cases of `droppable` will be discussed in the remaining three recipes of this chapter, that is, *Restricting dropping by tolerance and acceptance, AJAX-enhanced drag and drop*, and *Integrating drag and drop with data iteration components*

PrimeFaces Cookbook Showcase application

This recipe is available in the demo web application on GitHub (`https://github.com/ova2/primefaces-cookbook/tree/second-edition`). Clone the project if you have not done it yet, explore the project structure, and build and deploy the WAR file on every Servlet 3.x compatible application server, such as *JBoss WildFly* or *Apache TomEE*.

The showcase for the recipe is available at `http://localhost:8080/pf-cookbook/views/chapter8/droppable.jsf`.

Restricting dropping by tolerance and acceptance

Droppable behavior is highly configurable. There are a lot of options to restrict dropping. They are useful in matching the draggable and droppable components more precisely.

In this chapter, we will meet options for tolerance and acceptance. We will take several `h:panelGroup` components and make them droppable with different tolerance and acceptance values.

How to do it...

Tolerance specifies which mode to use for testing if a draggable component is over a droppable target. There are four different tolerance modes. They can be chosen by the `tolerance` attribute of `p:droppable`. The following code snippet shows four `h:panelGroup` components with settings for tolerance:

```
<h:panelGrid columns="4">
  <h:panelGroup id="dropFit" layout="block"
    styleClass="dropTarget ui-widget-content">
  <p class="ui-widget-header">Drop here (tolerance = fit)</p>
  <p:droppable onDrop="handleDrop" tolerance="fit"/>
  </h:panelGroup>

  <h:panelGroup id="dropIntersect" layout="block"
    styleClass="dropTarget ui-widget-content">
    <p class="ui-widget-header">Drop here (tolerance =
      intersect)</p>
    <p:droppable onDrop="handleDrop" tolerance="intersect"/>
  </h:panelGroup>

  <h:panelGroup id="dropPointer" layout="block"
    styleClass="dropTarget ui-widget-content">
```

```
    <p class="ui-widget-header">Drop here (tolerance =
      pointer)</p>
    <p:droppable onDrop="handleDrop" tolerance="pointer"/>
  </h:panelGroup>

  <h:panelGroup id="dropTouch" layout="block"
    styleClass="dropTarget ui-widget-content">
    <p class="ui-widget-header">Drop here (tolerance = touch)</p>
    <p:droppable onDrop="handleDrop" tolerance="touch"/>
  </h:panelGroup>
</h:panelGrid>

<br/>

<h:panelGroup id="drag" layout="block"
  styleClass="dragDiv ui-widget-content">
  <p>Drag me to my target</p>
  <p:draggable/>
</h:panelGroup>
```

The scope attribute is used for acceptance. Its aim is to group sets of the draggable and droppable components. Only a draggable component with the same scope value as a droppable one will be accepted during drag and drop. The following code snippet shows two draggable h:panelGroup components with different scope values. Only one can be dropped onto the droppable h:panelGroup component with the ID dropTarget2.

```
<h:panelGroup id="dropTarget2" layout="block"
  styleClass="ui-widget-content"
  style="height:120px; width:300px;">
  <p class="ui-widget-header" style="margin:0;padding:5px;">
    Drop here
  </p>
  <p:droppable onDrop="handleDrop" scope="dnd"/>
</h:panelGroup>

<br/>

<h:panelGrid columns="2">
  <h:panelGroup id="drag1" layout="block"
    styleClass="dragDiv ui-widget-content">
  <p>Drag me to my target</p>
  <p:draggable scope="dnd"/>
```

```
    </h:panelGroup>

    <h:panelGroup id="drag2" layout="block"
      styleClass="dragDiv ui-widget-content">
    <p>I'm draggable, but can't be dropped</p>
    <p:draggable scope="dummy"/>
    </h:panelGroup>
  </h:panelGrid>
```

The following screenshot demonstrates that the `handleDrop` callback is not invoked when the `h:panelGroup` with `scope` set to `dummy` gets dropped onto the `h:panelGroup` with `scope` set to `dnd`:

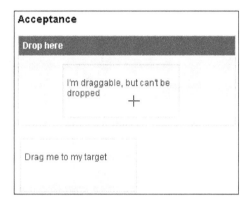

How it works...

The following table lists four tolerance modes that define the way to accept a `draggable`:

Mode	Description
fit	Draggable component should overlap the droppable component entirely
intersect	Draggable component should overlap the droppable component by at least 50 percent
pointer	Mouse pointer should overlap the droppable
touch	Draggable should overlap the droppable by any amount

There's more...

In addition to `scope`, there is also the `accept` attribute. This is the jQuery selector that defines the accepted components. Only the draggable components matching the selector will be accepted by the droppable component.

PrimeFaces Cookbook Showcase application

This recipe is available in the demo web application on GitHub (`https://github.com/ova2/primefaces-cookbook/tree/second-edition`). Clone the project if you have not done it yet, explore the project structure, and build and deploy the WAR file on every Servlet 3.x compatible application server, such as *JBoss WildFly* or *Apache TomEE*.

The showcase for the recipe is available at `http://localhost:8080/pf-cookbook/views/chapter8/advancedDroppable.jsf`.

AJAX-enhanced drag and drop

The user's client-side drag and drop interactions can be posted to the server. Drag and drop has only one (default) AJAX behavior event provided by the droppable component, which is processed when a valid draggable component is dropped. That is the `drop` event. If we define a listener, it will be invoked by passing an event instance of the type `org.primefaces.event.DragDrop` as parameter. This parameter holds information about the dragged and dropped components. Through this information, the server-side state of the draggable/droppable items can be updated.

In this recipe, we will develop a workflow simulating the process of pizza ordering. The pizza ordering should occur by drag and drop. Users should be able to select any available Turkish pizza and drag and drop it onto the order list. The remove functionality, capable of drag and drop, should be included as well. For this purpose, we will implement a trash for the items removed from the pizza items in the order list.

How to do it...

The following screenshots demonstrate the entire workflow:

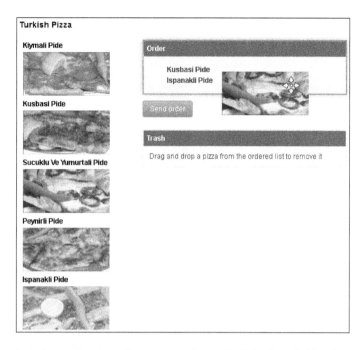

The first screenshot shows the dragging process from the list of available pizzas to the order list.

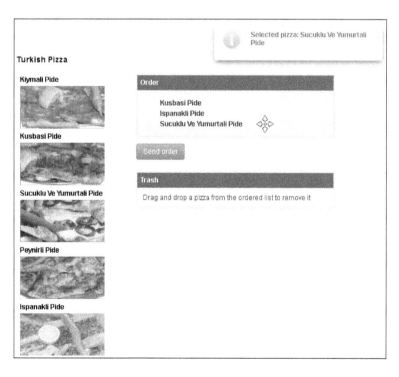

The second screenshot shows what happens when the dragged pizza image is dropped into the order list. A growl component is displayed with the currently selected pizza name.

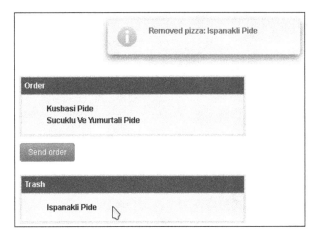

The last screenshot demonstrates the removal process. One pizza has been dragged from the order list and dropped into the trash list.

We will make the five pizza image tags `h:graphicImage` draggable.

```
<p:growl id="growl" escape="false"/>

<h:panelGrid id="selectPizza" columns="1">
  <h:outputText value="Kiymali Pide" styleClass="text"/>
  <h:graphicImage id="pizza1" styleClass="pizzaimage"
    library="images" name="dragdrop/pizza1.png"
    title="Kiymali Pide"/>

  <h:outputText value="Kusbasi Pide" styleClass="text"/>
  <h:graphicImage id="pizza2" styleClass="pizzaimage"
    library="images" name="dragdrop/pizza2.png"
    title="Kusbasi Pide"/>

  <h:outputText value="Sucuklu Ve Yumurtali Pide"
    styleClass="text"/>
  <h:graphicImage id="pizza3" styleClass="pizzaimage"
    library="images" name="dragdrop/pizza3.png"
    title="Sucuklu Ve Yumurtali Pide"/>

  <h:outputText value="Peynirli Pide" styleClass="text"/>
```

```
<h:graphicImage id="pizza4" styleClass="pizzaimage"
  library="images" name="dragdrop/pizza4.png"
  title="Peynirli Pide"/>

<h:outputText value="Ispanakli Pide" styleClass="text"/>
<h:graphicImage id="pizza5" styleClass="pizzaimage"
  library="images" name="dragdrop/pizza5.png"
  title="Ispanakli Pide"/>
</h:panelGrid>

<p:draggable for="pizza1" helper="clone" revert="true"
  cursor="move"/>
<p:draggable for="pizza2" helper="clone" revert="true"
  cursor="move"/>
<p:draggable for="pizza3" helper="clone" revert="true"
  cursor="move"/>
<p:draggable for="pizza4" helper="clone" revert="true"
  cursor="move"/>
<p:draggable for="pizza5" helper="clone" revert="true"
  cursor="move"/>
```

Two h:panelGroup tags will be made droppable. One h:panelGroup tag is intended
to be used for the order list and one is for items removed from the order list. Droppable
p:droppable tags will get AJAX behaviors p:ajax attached with corresponding listeners in
each case. One listener should be invoked on pizza ordering and another on pizza removal.

```
<h:panelGroup id="order" layout="block" styleClass="ui-widget-
  content"
  style="width:350px; padding:1px;">
  <p class="ui-widget-header" style="margin:0;padding:5px;">
    Order
  </p>

  <h:panelGroup layout="block" style="padding:10px;"
    rendered="#{empty ajaxDragDrop.orderedPizza}">
    Please drag and drop any available pizza to order it
  </h:panelGroup>

  <p:dataList id="orderedPizza"
    value="#{ajaxDragDrop.orderedPizza}" var="op"
    rendered="#{not empty ajaxDragDrop.orderedPizza}">
    <h:panelGroup id="op" styleClass="text" layout="block">
      <f:attribute name="pizza" value="#{op}"/>
```

```
            <h:outputText value="#{op}"/>
        </h:panelGroup>

        <p:draggable for="op" revert="true" cursor="move"
          scope="trash"/>
    </p:dataList>

    <p:droppable id="drop1" for="order" accept=".pizzaimage"
      tolerance="touch" activeStyleClass="ui-state-default"
      hoverStyleClass="ui-state-hover">
        <p:ajax listener="#{ajaxDragDrop.onPizzaOrder}"
          update="order growl"/>
    </p:droppable>
</h:panelGroup>

<p:commandButton value="Send order" action="#
  {ajaxDragDrop.sendOrder}"
  update="growl" style="margin:10px 0 20px 0;"/>

<h:panelGroup id="trash" layout="block" styleClass="ui-widget-
  content"
  style="width:350px; padding:1px;">
    <p class="ui-widget-header" style="margin:0;
      padding:5px;">Trash</p>

    <h:panelGroup layout="block" style="padding:10px;"
      rendered="#{empty ajaxDragDrop.removedPizza}">
        Drag and drop a pizza from the ordered list to remove it
    </h:panelGroup>

    <p:dataList value="#{ajaxDragDrop.removedPizza}" var="rp"
      rendered="#{not empty ajaxDragDrop.removedPizza}">
        <h:panelGroup styleClass="text" layout="block">
          <h:outputText value="#{rp}"/>
        </h:panelGroup>
    </p:dataList>

    <p:droppable id="drop2" for="trash" scope="trash"
      tolerance="touch"
      activeStyleClass="ui-state-default"
      hoverStyleClass="ui-state-hover">
        <p:ajax listener="#{ajaxDragDrop.onPizzaRemove}"
          update="order trash growl"/>
    </p:droppable>
</h:panelGroup>
```

The corresponding CDI bean `AjaxDragDrop` adds an ordered pizza to the `orderedPizza` list, and moves the pizza to the `removedPizza` list when it gets removed. This happens in the listeners `onPizzaOrder` and `onPizzaRemove`, respectively.

```
@Named
@ViewScoped
public class AjaxDragDrop implements Serializable {

  private List<String> orderedPizza = new ArrayList<String>();
  private List<String> removedPizza = new ArrayList<String>();

  public List<String> getOrderedPizza() {
    return orderedPizza;
  }

  public List<String> getRemovedPizza() {
    return removedPizza;
  }

  public void onPizzaOrder(DragDropEvent event) {
    HtmlGraphicImage image = (HtmlGraphicImage) event.
      getComponent().findComponent(event.getDragId());
    String pizza = image != null ? image.getTitle() : "";

    orderedPizza.add(pizza);

    FacesMessage msg = new FacesMessage
      (FacesMessage.SEVERITY_INFO,
      "Selected pizza: " + pizza, null);
    FacesContext.getCurrentInstance().addMessage(null, msg);
  }

  public void onPizzaRemove(DragDropEvent event) {
    DataList dataList = (DataList) event.
      getComponent().findComponent("orderedPizza");

    FacesContext fc = FacesContext.getCurrentInstance();
    dataList.invokeOnComponent(fc, event.getDragId(),
      new ContextCallback() {
      public void invokeContextCallback(FacesContext fc,
        UIComponent comp) {
          HtmlPanelGroup pGroup = (HtmlPanelGroup)comp;
```

```
            String pizza = pGroup != null ?
              (String) pGroup.getAttributes().get("pizza") :
              "";

            orderedPizza.remove(pizza);
            removedPizza.add(pizza);

            FacesMessage msg = new FacesMessage(
              FacesMessage.SEVERITY_INFO,
              "Removed pizza: " + pizza, null);
            fc.addMessage(null, msg);
        }
    });
}

public String sendOrder() {
    StringBuilder sb = new StringBuilder("You have ordered:");
    for (String pizza : orderedPizza) {
        sb.append("<br/>");
        sb.append(pizza);
    }

    FacesMessage msg = new FacesMessage(
      FacesMessage.SEVERITY_INFO, sb.toString(), null);
    FacesContext.getCurrentInstance().addMessage(null, msg);

    return null;
}
}
```

How it works...

To make h:graphicImage draggable, we use p:draggable with proper options:
helper="clone", revert="true", and cursor="move". The draggable images have
the title attributes set to the pizza names. This is important for getting the dropped
pizza's name in the onPizzaOrder listener by means of the findComponent() call.
The draggable h:panelGroup tag in the order list has, in contrast to h:graphicImage,
f:attribute with the pizza name as the value. This allows us to get the dropped pizza's
name from the component's attribute map in the onPizzaRemove listener by means of
the invokeOnComponent() call. Client IDs of draggable/droppable components can be
accessed by getDragId() or getDropId() on a DragDropEvent instance.

Refer to the JSF 2 API documentation (`http://javaserverfaces.java.net/nonav/docs/2.2/javadocs/javax/faces/component/UIComponent.html`) to read more about `findComponent()` and `invokeOnComponent()`.

Last but not least, we use different ways to accept `draggable`. In the case of images, we set `accept` to `.pizzaimage`. The `accept` attribute defines a jQuery selector for the accepted draggable components. In the case of items in the order list, we set `scope` to `trash`. The `scope` attribute is an alternative way to match the droppable and accepted draggable components. What is easier to use in each particular case depends on the code.

There's more...

We used two style classes with `p:droppable`:

- `activeStyleClass` set to `ui-state-default`
- `hoverStyleClass` set to `ui-state-hover`

They are used for better visual effects when dragging/dropping. If `activeStyleClass` is specified, the class will be added to the droppable component while an acceptable draggable component is being dragged. If `hoverStyleClass` is specified, the class will be added to the droppable component while an acceptable draggable component is being dragged over it.

PrimeFaces Cookbook Showcase application

This recipe is available in the demo web application on GitHub (`https://github.com/ova2/primefaces-cookbook/tree/second-edition`). Clone the project if you have not done it yet, explore the project structure, and build and deploy the WAR file on every Servlet 3.x compatible application server, such as *JBoss WildFly* or *Apache TomEE*.

The showcase for the recipe is available at `http://localhost:8080/pf-cookbook/views/chapter8/ajaxDragDrop.jsf`.

Integrating drag and drop with data iteration components

The `droppable` component has a special integration with the data iteration components extending `javax.faces.component.UIData`. Such PrimeFaces components are `dataTable`, `dataGrid`, `dataList`, `dataScroller`, `carousel`, and `ring`. The component tag `p:droppable` defines a data source option as an ID of the data iteration component that needs to be connected with `droppable`.

In this recipe, we will introduce a `dataGrid` component containing some imaginary documents and make these documents draggable in order to drop them onto a recycle bin. The `dataGrid` component will act as a data source for the droppable Recycle Bin.

How to do it...

For the purpose of better understanding the developed code, pictures come first. The first screenshot shows what happens when we start to drag a document. The **Recycle Bin** area gets highlighted as follows:

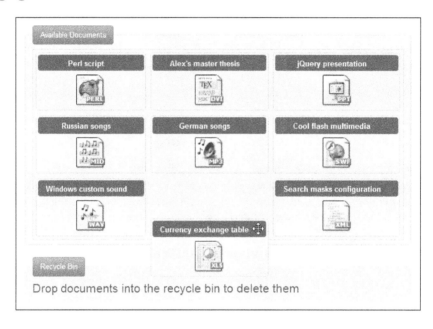

What it looks like after dropping three documents onto the Recycle Bin is reproduced in the following screenshot:

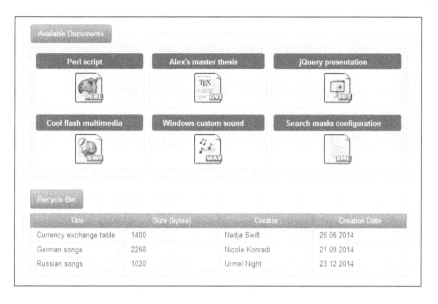

Available documents are represented as images within `p:dataGrid`. They are placed in the `panel` components, which are made draggable. The dragging occurs via the panel's titlebar. The titlebar contains the document's title (name). The recycle bin is represented by a `p:fieldset` tag with the ID `deletedDocs`. `Fieldset` is made droppable. It also contains a `p:dataTable` with the currently deleted document items. Whenever a document is being dragged and dropped into the Recycle Bin, an AJAX listener is invoked. In the listener, the dropped document is removed from the list of all available documents and added to the list of deleted documents. Data iteration components will be updated after that in order to display the correct data. The code snippet, in XHTML, looks as follows:

```
<p:fieldset legend="Available Documents">
  <p:dataGrid id="availableDocs" columns="3" var="doc"
    value="#{integrationDragDrop.availableDocs}">
    <p:column>
      <p:panel id="pnl" header="#{doc.title}"
        style="text-align:center">
        <h:graphicImage library="images"
          name="dragdrop/#{doc.extension}.png"/>
      </p:panel>
      <p:draggable for="pnl" revert="true"
        handle=".ui-panel-titlebar"
```

```
            stack=".ui-panel" cursor="move"/>
      </p:column>
    </p:dataGrid>
  </p:fieldset>

  <p:fieldset id="deletedDocs" legend="Recycle Bin" style="margin-
    top:20px">
    <p:outputPanel id="dropArea">
      <h:outputText value="Drop documents into the recycle bin to
        delete them"
        rendered="#{empty integrationDragDrop.deletedDocs}"
        style="font-size:20px;"/>

      <p:dataTable var="doc"
        value="#{integrationDragDrop.deletedDocs}"
        rendered="#{not empty integrationDragDrop.deletedDocs}">

        <p:column headerText="Title">
          <h:outputText value="#{doc.title}"/>
        </p:column>
        <p:column headerText="Size (bytes)">
          <h:outputText value="#{doc.size}"/>
        </p:column>
        <p:column headerText="Creator">
          <h:outputText value="#{doc.creator}"/>
        </p:column>
        <p:column headerText="Creation Date">
          <h:outputText value="#{doc.creationDate}">
            <f:convertDateTime pattern="dd.MM.yyyy"/>
          </h:outputText>
        </p:column>
      </p:dataTable>
    </p:outputPanel>
  </p:fieldset>

  <p:droppable id="droppable" for="deletedDocs" tolerance="touch"
    activeStyleClass="ui-state-highlight"
    datasource="availableDocs">
    <p:ajax listener="#{integrationDragDrop.onDocumentDrop}"
      update="dropArea availableDocs"/>
  </p:droppable>
```

The model class `Document` contains the document properties.

```java
public class Document implements Serializable {

  private String title;
  private int size;
  private String creator;
  private Date creationDate;
  private String extension;

  public Document(String title, int size, String creator,
    Date creationDate, String extension) {
    this.title = title;
    this.size = size;
    this.creator = creator;
    this.creationDate = creationDate;
    this.extension = extension;
  }

  // getters / setters
  ...
}
```

The bean `IntegrationDragDrop` creates available documents (they can be loaded from a document management system, database, or filesystem), holds two lists for the data iteration components, and provides the AJAX listener `onDocumentDrop`.

```java
@Named
@ViewScoped
public class IntegrationDragDrop implements Serializable {

  private List<Document> availableDocs =
    new ArrayList<Document>();
  private List<Document> deletedDocs =
    new ArrayList<Document>();

  @PostConstruct
  public void initialize() {
    availableDocs.add(new Document("Perl script", 120,
      "Sara Schmidt", getCreationDate(), "perl"));
    ...
  }

  public List<Document> getAvailableDocs() {
    return availableDocs;
```

```
    }

    public List<Document> getDeletedDocs() {
      return deletedDocs;
    }

    public void onDocumentDrop(DragDropEvent ddEvent) {
      Document doc = (Document) ddEvent.getData();
      deletedDocs.add(doc);
      availableDocs.remove(doc);
    }

    private Date getCreationDate() {
      Random random = new Random();
      int day = random.nextInt(30);
      int month = random.nextInt(Calendar.DECEMBER + 1);
      int year = 2014;
      GregorianCalendar calendar =
        new GregorianCalendar(year, month, day);

      return calendar.getTime();
    }
  }
```

How it works...

We make the second `p:fieldset` tag droppable, and connect it to the `p:dataList` tag with the ID `availableDocs`. This is done by setting `datasource` to `availableDocs` on `p:droppable`. The AJAX listener `onDocumentDrop`, attached by the `p:ajax` tag, is invoked on the `drop` event. Thanks to `datasource`, we can now access the dropped document instance in the listener: `Document doc = (Document)ddEvent.getData()`.

PrimeFaces Cookbook Showcase application

This recipe is available in the demo web application on GitHub (`https://github.com/ova2/primefaces-cookbook/tree/second-edition`). Clone the project if you have not done it yet, explore the project structure, and build and deploy the WAR file on every Servlet 3.x compatible application server, such as *JBoss WildFly* or *Apache TomEE*.

The showcase for the recipe is available at `http://localhost:8080/pf-cookbook/views/chapter8/dragDropIntegration.jsf`.

9
Creating Charts and Maps

In this chapter, we will cover the following topics:

- Creating line, area, bar, and pie charts
- Creating combined charts
- Updating live data in charts with polling
- Interacting with charts via AJAX
- Basic mapping with GMaps
- Adding, selecting, and dragging markers in maps
- Creating rectangles, circles, polylines, and polygons in maps
- Enabling InfoWindow and streetView on maps

Introduction

In this chapter, we will cover chart creation with PrimeFaces' extensive charting features and create maps based on Google Maps. PrimeFaces offers basic and advanced charting with its easy-to-use and user-friendly charting infrastructure. Along with basic charting, live updating of chart data and interaction with charts via the AJAX mechanism will also be covered. In version 5.0, chart components were re-implemented in order to overcome limitations. Now, they are more model-driven instead of implementing with component attributes.

Throughout the chapter, we will cover mapping abilities, such as drawing polylines and polygons, and then move on to advanced topics such as handling markers and events and adding information panels and controls on map as overlays.

Creating line, area, bar, and pie charts

PrimeFaces offers one base component named `chart`, which provides different charting according to the provided `type` attribute. In this recipe, we will create line, area, bar, and pie charts using this component.

How to do it...

A basic definition of a line chart with two series of data is given here:

```
<p:chart type="line" model="#{chartBean.model}"
  style="height:250px" />
```

The model defined for the line chart is given here:

```
private LineChartModel createLineModel() {
  LineChartModel model = new LineChartModel();
  LineChartSeries sales = new LineChartSeries();
  sales.setLabel("Sales");
  sales.set(2004, 1000);
  sales.set(2005, 1170);
  sales.set(2006, 660);
  sales.set(2007, 1030);

  LineChartSeries expenses = new LineChartSeries();
  expenses.setLabel("Expenses");
  expenses.set(2004, 400);
  expenses.set(2005, 460);
  expenses.set(2006, 1120);
  expenses.set(2007, 540);

  model.addSeries(sales);
  model.addSeries(expenses);
  model.setTitle("Company Performance");

  return model;
}
```

The visual output of the chart is given here:

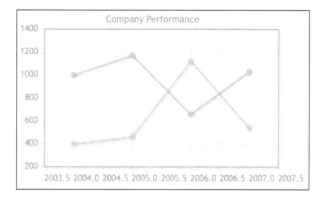

> It's advised that you specify the height for your charts via the `style` attribute to render them properly on the page.

There's more...

By default, the `chart` component renders axis labels with decimal points, and sometimes, it might not make sense for values such as years. To disable this, a JavaScript definition should be added and attached to the chart with the extender definition of the model, as given here:

```
model.setExtender("chart");
```

The value defined in the extender will be the name for the JavaScript method. Then, we can access the axis that we'd like to correct and set its format as follows:

```
<script type="text/javascript">
  function chart() {
    this.cfg.axes.xaxis.tickOptions = {
      formatString : '%d'
    };
  }
</script>
```

Creating area charts

To create area charts, we will use `LineChartModel` and its series given when creating the line chart, but we will set `fill` to `true` here:

```
sales.setFill(true);
expenses.setFill(true);
```

The visual output is as follows:

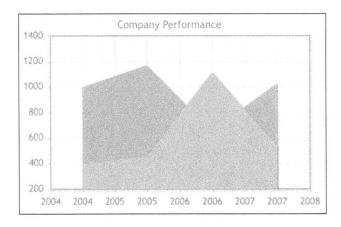

Creating bar charts

It's also possible to create a bar chart using the same chart series. The model that will be used for binding should be an instance of `BarChartModel` and `type` should be set to `bar`. Here's how you can create the bar chart:

```
<p:chart type="bar" model="#{chartBean.barModel}" />
```

The visual output of the bar chart is given here:

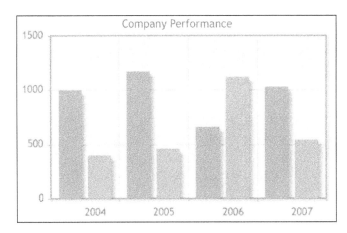

Creating pie charts

To create a pie chart, we need to define an instance of `PieChartModel` and set values into it by configuring its legends and labels as follows:

```
PieChartModel model = new PieChartModel();
model.setLegendPosition("w");
model.setShowDataLabels(true);
model.set("Work", 11);
model.set("Eat", 2);
model.set("Commute", 2);
model.set("Watch TV", 2);
model.set("Sleep", 7);
```

The definition of the chart component for the model is as follows:

```
<p:chart type="pie" model="#{chartBean.pieModel}" />
```

The visual output of the pie chart with legends is given here:

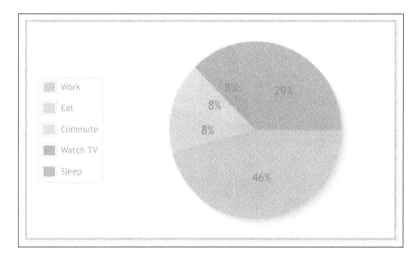

PrimeFaces Cookbook Showcase application

This recipe is available in the demo web application on GitHub (`https://github.com/ova2/primefaces-cookbook/tree/second-edition`). Clone the project if you have not done it yet, explore the project structure, and build and deploy the WAR file on application servers compatible with Servlet 3.x, such as *JBoss WildFly* and *Apache TomEE*.

The showcase for the recipe is available at `http://localhost:8080/pf-cookbook/views/chapter9/chart.jsf`.

Creating combined charts

The `chart` component supports combining multiple data series into one cartesian model.

How to do it...

A basic definition for a chart with one line and bar model is given here:

```
<p:chart type="bar" model="#{chartBean.combinedModel}"
   style="height:250px" />
```

The combined model definition is given here:

```
CartesianChartModel combinedModel = new BarChartModel();

public CartesianChartModel getCombinedModel() {
   LineChartSeries sales = new LineChartSeries();
   sales.setLabel("Sales");
   sales.set(2004, 1000);
   sales.set(2005, 1170);
   sales.set(2006, 660);
   sales.set(2007, 1030);

   BarChartSeries expenses = new BarChartSeries();
   expenses.setLabel("Expenses");
   expenses.set("2004", 400);
   expenses.set("2005", 460);
   expenses.set("2006", 1120);
   expenses.set("2007", 540);

   combinedModel.addSeries(sales);
   combinedModel.addSeries(expenses);

   return combinedModel;
}
```

The visual output of the chart is given here:

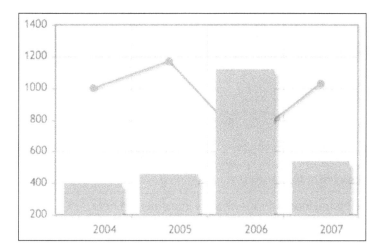

 The implementation could either be based on BarChartModel, as given in the preceding graph, or it can be done the other way around by first taking LineChartModel and then adding the series into it.

PrimeFaces Cookbook Showcase application

This recipe is available in the demo web application on GitHub (https://github.com/ova2/primefaces-cookbook/tree/second-edition). Clone the project if you have not done it yet, explore the project structure, and build and deploy the WAR file on application servers compatible with Servlet 3.x, such as *JBoss WildFly* and *Apache TomEE*.

The showcase for the recipe is available at http://localhost:8080/pf-cookbook/views/chapter9/combinedChart.jsf.

Updating live data in charts with polling

The chart component nicely integrates with the `<p:poll>` component to update itself with an ever-changing data model.

How to do it...

A basic definition for a chart with live data is given here:

```
<p:poll interval="2" update="live" />
<p:chart id="live" type="pie" model="#{chartBean.livePieModel}"
  style="height:250px" />
```

The randomly generated model for the chart is implemented here:

```
public PieChartModel getLivePieModel() {
   int random1 = (int)(Math.random() * 1000);
   int random2 = (int)(Math.random() * 1000);

   liveChartModel.getData().put("Candidate 1", random1);
   liveChartModel.getData().put("Candidate 2", random2);
   liveChartModel.setLegendPosition("w");
   liveChartModel.setShowDataLabels(true);

   return liveChartModel;
}
```

The visual output will be updated every 2 seconds, and the new model will be rendered with its randomly generated values.

PrimeFaces Cookbook Showcase application

This recipe is available in the demo web application on GitHub (`https://github.com/ova2/primefaces-cookbook/tree/second-edition`). Clone the project if you have not done it yet, explore the project structure, and build and deploy the WAR file on application servers compatible with Servlet 3.x, such as *JBoss WildFly* and *Apache TomEE*.

The showcase for the recipe is available at `http://localhost:8080/pf-cookbook/views/chapter9/pollingChart.jsf`.

Interacting with charts via AJAX

The `chart` component offers AJAX behavior events to interact with the chart by item selection.

How to do it...

A basic definition for a chart with `<p:ajax>` bundled inside is given here:

```
<p:chart type="bar" id="withAjax" model="#{chartBean.barModel}"
  style="height:250px">
  <p:ajax event="itemSelect" listener="#{chartBean.itemSelect}"
    update="growl" />
</p:chart>
```

The `itemSelect` method retrieves an instance of `org.primefaces.event.ItemSelectEvent`, which enables us to access the item index and series index of the selected chart item. The usage of the `itemSelect` method is given here:

```
public void itemSelect(ItemSelectEvent event) {
  MessageUtil.addInfoMessageWithoutKey("Item selected",
    "Item Index:" + event.getItemIndex() +
    ", Series Index: " + event.getSeriesIndex());
}
```

PrimeFaces Cookbook Showcase application

This recipe is available in the demo web application on GitHub (`https://github.com/ova2/primefaces-cookbook/tree/second-edition`). Clone the project if you have not done it yet, explore the project structure, and build and deploy the WAR file on application servers compatible with Servlet 3.x, such as *JBoss WildFly* and *Apache TomEE*.

The showcase for the recipe is available at `http://localhost:8080/pf-cookbook/views/chapter9/chartInteraction.jsf`.

Basic mapping with GMaps

The `gmap` component provides ways to integrate Google Maps into JSF applications. It is built upon Google Maps API V3.

How to do it...

In order to use the component, the Google Maps API script should be referenced from the page, ideally in the header section:

```
<script src="http://maps.google.com/maps/api/js?sensor=true"
  type="text/javascript"></script>
```

The `sensor` parameter in the URL is mandatory, and it specifies whether the application requires a sensor, such as a GPS locator.

A simple definition of placing a map canvas on page is given here:

```
<p:gmap center="41.106261, 29.057465" zoom="10" type="hybrid"
  style="width:600px;height:400px" />
```

This output will be rendered as follows:

How it works...

The `gmap` component depicts four attributes that should be set, as shown in the previous example, in order to use the map canvas properly. The `center` attribute defines the center of the map in the `[latitude, longitude]` format. The `zoom` attribute defines the zoom level of the map. Zoom levels between `0` (the lowest zoom level, in which the entire world can be seen on one map) and `21+` (down to individual buildings) are possible. The `type` attribute declares the type of the map with one of the following values: `roadmap` (the default value), `satellite`, `hybrid`, or `terrain`. The `style` attribute could be used to define dimensions of the map canvas.

There's more...

It is also possible to bind the component to a model with an instance of `org.primefaces.model.map.MapModel`. PrimeFaces provides `org.primefaces.model.map.DefaultMapModel` as the default model implementation. `DefaultMapModel` is a wrapper class for markers, polylines, polygons, circles, and rectangles. Here's how you can bind the `gmap` component to a model:

```
<p:gmap center="41.106261, 29.057465" zoom="10" type="roadmap"
  style="width:600px;height:400px"
  model="#{mapBean.markerModel}" />
```

Configuring controls

The `gmap` component provides the `disableDefaultUI` attribute. By setting it to `true`, controls will be removed regardless of the status of other attributes. The `disabledDoubleClickZoom` attribute disables zooming on double-click. The `draggable` attribute defines the "draggability" of the map; it could be used to define static maps, which means no panning.

> The `gmap` component provides two attributes—`navigationControl` and `mapTypeControl`—to set the visibility of map controls. The `mapTypeControl` attribute enables/disables the map type control that lets the user toggle between map types (such as **Map** and **Satellite**). By default, this control is visible and appears in the top-right corner of the map. The visibility of the navigation controls can be set with the `navigationControl` attribute.
>
> In version 5.2, the `navigationControl` and `mapTypeControl` attributes do not work as expected. Please use the `disableDefaultUI` attribute to enable/disable all controls.

PrimeFaces Cookbook Showcase application

This recipe is available in the demo web application on GitHub (`https://github.com/ova2/primefaces-cookbook/tree/second-edition`). Clone the project if you have not done it yet, explore the project structure, and build and deploy the WAR file on application servers compatible with Servlet 3.x, such as *JBoss WildFly* and *Apache TomEE*.

The showcase for the recipe is available at `http://localhost:8080/pf-cookbook/views/chapter9/map.jsf`.

Adding, selecting, and dragging markers in maps

It is possible to add markers onto the map via a data model and then select or drag it by interacting with the map.

How to do it...

The marker should be an instance of `org.primefaces.model.map.Marker`. Markers can be easily constructed by providing an instance of `org.primefaces.model.map.LatLng` to define their position. The `latitude` and `longitude` values could be provided to the `LatLng` class as constructor parameters. Markers will be added to the data model via the `addOverlay` method. This is shown in the following code:

```
MapModel markerModel = new DefaultMapModel();
markerModel.addOverlay(new Marker(new LatLng(41.073399,
    29.051971), "Bosphorus"));
markerModel.addOverlay(new Marker(new LatLng(41.118418,
    29.134026), "Bosphorus"));
```

The attributes of `org.primefaces.model.map.Marker` are listed in the following table:

Property	Default	Type	Description
title	null	String	This is the text to display on rollover
latlng	null	LatLng	This is the location of the marker
icon	null	String	This is the foreground image of the marker
shadow	null	String	This is the shadow image of the marker
cursor	pointer	String	This is the cursor to display on rollover
draggable	False	Boolean	This defines whether the marker can be dragged
clickable	True	Boolean	This defines whether the marker can be clicked

Property	Default	Type	Description
flat	False	Boolean	This is the shadow image not displayed when set to `true`
visible	True	Boolean	This defines the visibility of the marker

There's more...

The `gmap` component offers the `overlaySelect` and `markerDrag` AJAX behavior events to handle the selection and dragging of the markers placed on the map.

Selecting markers

The definition of `<p:ajax>`, along with the listener method, is given here:

```
<p:gmap ...>
  <p:ajax event="overlaySelect"
    listener="#{mapBean.onMarkerSelect}" update="growl" />
</p:gmap>

public void onMarkerSelect(OverlaySelectEvent event) {
  Marker selectedMarker = (Marker) event.getOverlay();
  MessageUtil.addInfoMessageWithoutKey(selectedMarker.getTitle(),
    selectedMarker.getLatlng().toString());
}
```

Dragging markers

To have draggable markers, each marker's `draggable` attribute should be set to `true` first. Then, the definition of `<p:ajax>`, along with the listener method, can be performed, as shown here:

```
<p:gmap ...>
  <p:ajax event="markerDrag"
    listener="#{mapBean.onMarkerDrag}" update="growl" />
</p:gmap>

public void onMarkerDrag(MarkerDragEvent event) {
  MessageUtil.addInfoMessage("marker.dragged",
    event.getMarker().getLatlng().toString());
}
```

PrimeFaces Cookbook Showcase application

This recipe is available in the demo web application on GitHub (`https://github.com/ova2/primefaces-cookbook/tree/second-edition`). Clone the project if you have not done it yet, explore the project structure, and build and deploy the WAR file on application servers compatible with Servlet 3.x, such as *JBoss WildFly* and *Apache TomEE*.

The showcase for the recipe is available at `http://localhost:8080/pf-cookbook/views/chapter9/mapMarkers.jsf`.

Creating rectangles, circles, polylines, and polygons in maps

The `gmap` component supports the drawing of rectangles, circles, polylines, and polygons on the map canvas.

How to do it...

All drawings can be implemented as an instance of `DefaultMapModel`, as stated here:

```
private MapModel rectangleModel = new DefaultMapModel();
private MapModel circleModel = new DefaultMapModel();
private MapModel polylineModel = new DefaultMapModel();
private MapModel polygonModel = new DefaultMapModel();
```

All models contain instances of `LatLng`, where they define the points for the drawings. The rectangle model can be defined with two points, upper-left and lower-right, which are wrapped in an instance of `LatLngBounds`. This is shown in the following code:

```
rectangleModel.addOverlay(new Rectangle(new LatLngBounds(
    new LatLng(41.073399, 29.051971),
    new LatLng(41.118418, 29.134026))));
```

The circle model accepts a point and the radius value to be defined:

```
Circle circle =new Circle(new LatLng(41.073399, 29.051971), 5000);
circleModel.addOverlay(circle);
```

The polyline drawings can be defined with a list of points, as shown here:

```
Polyline polyline = new Polyline();
polyline.getPaths().add(new LatLng(41.073399, 29.051971));
polyline.getPaths().add(new LatLng(41.118418, 29.134026));
polyline.getPaths().add(new LatLng(41.027807, 29.049973));
polylineModel.addOverlay(polyline);
```

The polygon's definition is similar to the polyline's, but the output will be a closed drawing filled inside. The opacity of the filling can be configured with the `setFillOpacity()` method of the polygon model. This is shown in the following code:

```
Polygon polygon = new Polygon();
polygon.getPaths().add(new LatLng(41.073399, 29.051971));
polygon.getPaths().add(new LatLng(41.118418, 29.134026));
polygon.getPaths().add(new LatLng(41.027807, 29.049973));
polygonModel.addOverlay(polygon);
```

Binding these models to the `<p:gmap>` component separately will do the trick, as shown in the following screenshot:

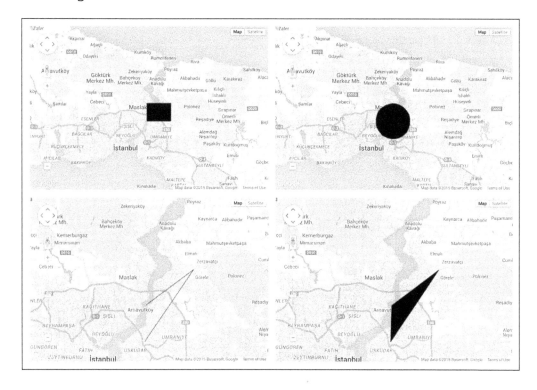

PrimeFaces Cookbook Showcase application

This recipe is available in the demo web application on GitHub (`https://github.com/ova2/primefaces-cookbook/tree/second-edition`). Clone the project if you have not done it yet, explore the project structure, and build and deploy the WAR file on application servers compatible with Servlet 3.x, such as *JBoss WildFly* and *Apache TomEE*.

The showcase for the recipe is available at `http://localhost:8080/pf-cookbook/views/chapter9/mapDrawings.jsf`.

Enabling InfoWindow and streetView on maps

The gmap component uses the gmapInfoWindow helper component to display a component that renders two markers with an information window attached.

How to do it...

A basic definition of gmap with the information window is given here:

```
<p:gmap id="withInformation" center="41.106261, 29.057465"
  zoom="10" type="roadmap" style="width:600px;height:400px"
  model="#{mapBean.markerModel}">
  <p:ajax event="overlaySelect"
    listener="#{mapBean.selectMarker}" />
  <p:gmapInfoWindow id="infoWindow">
    <p:graphicImage
      value="/resources/images/map/#{mapBean.selected
        Marker.data}" />
  </p:gmapInfoWindow>
</p:gmap>
```

The visual output is shown here:

There's more...

It is possible to enable the street view by setting the `streetView` attribute to `true`. Then, the user will be able to drag the human icon onto the blue lines on the map, which depict the viewable streets/roads. This is shown in the following screenshot:

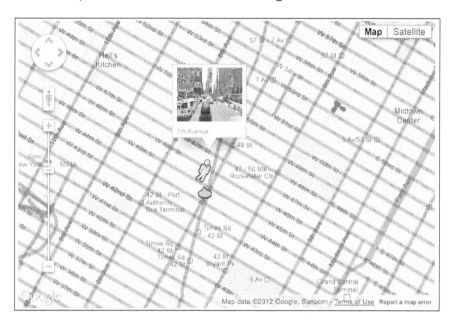

PrimeFaces Cookbook Showcase application

This recipe is available in the demo web application on GitHub (`https://github.com/ova2/primefaces-cookbook/tree/second-edition`). Clone the project if you have not done it yet, explore the project structure, and build and deploy the WAR file on application servers compatible with Servlet 3.x, such as *JBoss WildFly* and *Apache TomEE*.

The showcase for the recipe is available at `http://localhost:8080/pf-cookbook/views/chapter9/mapInfoView.jsf`.

10

Client-side Validation

In this chapter, we will cover the following topics:

- ▸ Configuring and getting started with CSV
- ▸ Instant validation with p:clientValidator
- ▸ Bean Validation and transformation
- ▸ Extending CSV with JSF
- ▸ Extending CSV with Bean Validation

Introduction

Validation exists to ensure that the application is robust against all forms of input data. Invalid data can cause unexpected execution errors, break assumptions elsewhere in your application, introduce errors, and even let someone hijack your data to attack your software. Every software should have server-side validation.

In addition, validation on the client side enables quick feedback for the users without a round trip to the server. That means client-side validation is faster and enables the user to fix problems without sending input data to the server. We can say that server-side validation is a *must-have* and client-side validation is *nice to have* for every software.

In this chapter, we will learn how to implement **Client-side Validation** (**CSV**) with PrimeFaces. PrimeFaces Client Side Validation Framework is the most complete and advanced CSV solution for **JavaServer Faces** (**JSF**). It implements an API for JSF validation within the browser. This implementation is compatible with the server-side implementation so that users do not experience different behaviors on the client and server sides. They can use the same standard JSF validators and converters without worrying about implementation details. A few of the other features of PrimeFaces CSV are:

▸ Supporting `process` and `update` attributes for AJAX

▸ Utilizing PrimeFaces message components for CSV

▸ Supporting i18n validation messages configured on the client side

▸ Instant validation for various events

▸ Integrating CSV with Bean Validation

▸ Ease of writing custom validators and converters

 CSV only works for PrimeFaces components; standard `h:*` components are not supported.

Configuring and getting started with CSV

PrimeFaces CSV is easy to configure. It works with AJAX and non-AJAX requests. It supports partial processing and updating on the client side. There is almost no effort for the users if they plan to add a CSV support to their web applications.

In this recipe, we will see how to configure and use PrimeFaces Client Side Validation Framework. We will develop input components with attached standard validators and converters and see how client-side validation works in action. We will also learn how the text for validation messages can be customized in JavaScript to be used with PrimeFaces CSV.

Getting ready

CSV is disabled by default. To enable the CSV Framework, a configuration parameter in `web.xml` is required:

```
<context-param>
  <param-name>
    primefaces.CLIENT_SIDE_VALIDATION
  </param-name>
  <param-value>true</param-value>
</context-param>
```

Now, you are able to use CSV by setting the `validateClient` attribute to `true` for command components such as `p:commandButton` or `p:commandLink`. After that, a click on a button or link validates the form fields on the client side and displays validation errors in message components.

How to do it...

For demonstration purposes, we will create a bean with seven properties, which have various data types:

```
@Named
@ViewScoped
public class BasicCsvBean implements Serializable {

  private String string1;
  private String string2;
  private String string3;
  private Integer int1;
  private Double double1;
  private Double double2;
  private Date date1;

  // getters / setters
  ...
}
```

The bean's properties are bound to the values of input components. Furthermore, a few standard JSF validators and converters are attached to the input components. The following code shows this:

```
<p:messages id="messages"/>

<h:panelGrid id="grid" columns="2" cellpadding="3"
  style="margin-bottom:10px;">
  <p:outputLabel for="text1" value="Text1"/>
  <p:inputText id="text1" value="#{basicCsvBean.string1}"
    required="true" label="Text1"/>

  <p:outputLabel for="text2" value="Text2"/>
  <p:inputText id="text2" value="#{basicCsvBean.string2}"
    label="Text2">
    <f:validateLength minimum="5" maximum="8"/>
  </p:inputText>
```

```
    <p:outputLabel for="text3" value="Text3"/>
    <p:inputText id="text3" value="#{basicCsvBean.string3}"
      label="Text3">
      <f:validateRegex pattern="^[\d]+$"/>
    </p:inputText>

    <p:outputLabel for="int1" value="Integer1"/>
    <p:inputText id="int1" value="#{basicCsvBean.int1}"
      label="Integer1">
      <f:convertNumber integerOnly="true"/>
    </p:inputText>

    <p:outputLabel for="double1" value="Double1"/>
    <p:inputText id="double1" value="#{basicCsvBean.double1}"
      label="Double1">
      <f:validateDoubleRange minimum="5.5" maximum="8.5"/>
    </p:inputText>

    <p:outputLabel for="double2" value="Double2"/>
    <p:inputText id="double2" value="#{basicCsvBean.double2}"
      label="Double2">
      <f:convertNumber type="currency" currencySymbol="$"/>
    </p:inputText>

    <p:outputLabel for="date1" value="Date1"/>
    <p:inputText id="date1" value="#{basicCsvBean.date1}"
      label="Date1">
      <f:convertDateTime pattern="dd.MM.yyyy"/>
    </p:inputText>
  </h:panelGrid>

  <p:commandButton validateClient="true"
    value="Submit (Non-Ajax)" ajax="false"
    style="margin-right:5px"
    onclick="PF('inputValuesWdgt').hide()"/>
  <p:commandButton validateClient="true"
    value="Submit (Ajax)"
    process="grid" update="grid messages inputValues"
    onclick="PF('inputValuesWdgt').hide()"
    oncomplete="PF('inputValuesWdgt').show()"/>

  <p:dialog header="Input values" closeOnEscape="true"
    visible="#{facesContext.postback and
```

```
    !facesContext.validationFailed}"
    widgetVar="inputValuesWdgt">
    <h:panelGrid id="inputValues" columns="1" cellpadding="3">
      <h:outputText value="#{basicCsvBean.string1}"/>
      <h:outputText value="#{basicCsvBean.string2}"/>
      <h:outputText value="#{basicCsvBean.string3}"/>
      <h:outputText value="#{basicCsvBean.int1}"/>
      <h:outputText value="#{basicCsvBean.double1}"/>
      <h:outputText value="#{basicCsvBean.double2}">
        <f:convertNumber type="currency" currencySymbol="$"/>
      </h:outputText>
      <h:outputText value="#{basicCsvBean.date1}">
        <f:convertDateTime pattern="dd.MM.yyyy"/>
      </h:outputText>
    </h:panelGrid>
  </p:dialog>
```

Two command buttons process the input components in non-AJAX and AJAX cases, respectively. In the AJAX case, the inputs, the `messages` component, and the content of a dialog are updated. The `p:messages` tag displays errors if validation fails and `p:dialog` displays the submitted values if everything is OK. A failed validation is shown here:

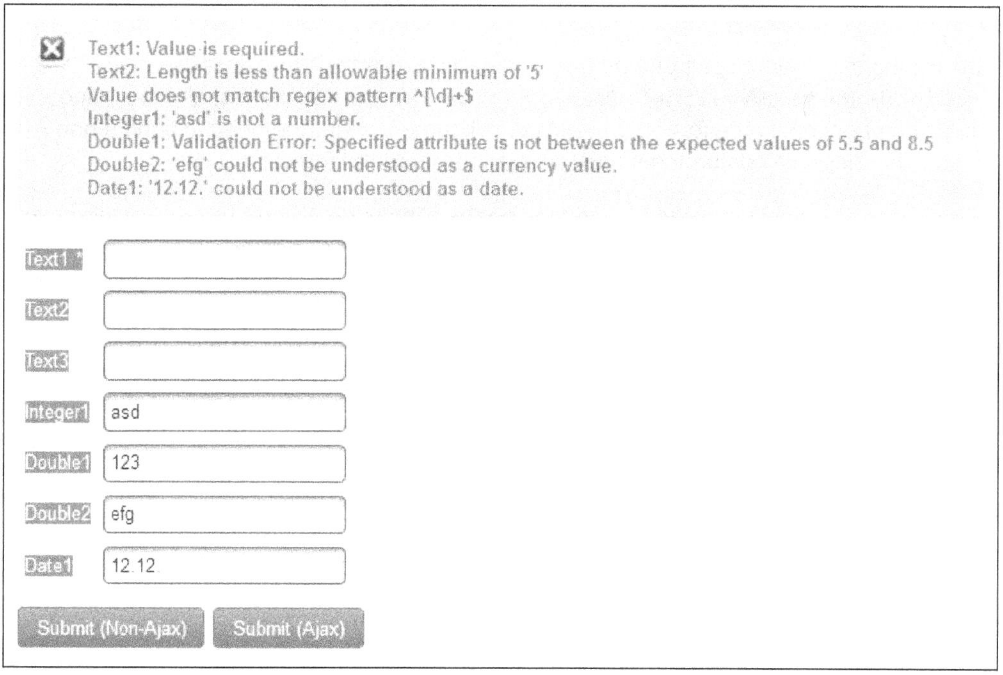

The `dialog` looks like this:

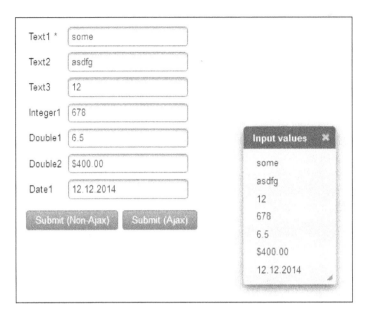

How it works...

In the example, the input components are validated on the client side because `p:commandButton` has `validateClient="true"`. In non-AJAX cases, all visible and editable components in the form (`h:form`) get validated without the need to send a non-AJAX request. The message components must be placed inside the form too.

In AJAX cases, the whole processing happens on the client side. If the `process` attribute is enabled, the components that would be processed on the server side get validated on the client side. If the `update` attribute is defined, the components that would be updated on the server side get updated on the client side.

 Note the advantage of `p:outputLabel`, which is highlighted in red on an attempt to update it when the corresponding input field is invalid.

PrimeFaces message components have client-side renderers for CSV support; these are `p:message`, `p:messages`, and `p:growl`. Lots of options for these components, such as `showSummary`, `showDetail`, `globalOnly`, and `redisplay`, are supported on the client side as well.

There's more...

The text for validation messages is retrieved from client-side bundles. PrimeFaces only provides bundles in the English language. The default text is located in the *validation.js* and *beanvalidation.js* files that are included by PrimeFaces automatically.

> For more languages, please follow the instructions for PrimeFaces Locales `http://code.google.com/p/primefaces/wiki/PrimeFacesLocales`.

Default text can be easily customized. The next JavaScript snippet overwrites the PrimeFaces' default text for missing values in the required fields and the `f:validateLength` and `f:validateRegex` validators. This text is displayed in the first picture showed earlier. Here's the JavaScript snippet that is being discussed:

```
PrimeFaces.locales['en'] = {
  messages: PrimeFaces.locales['en_US'].messages
};

$.extend(PrimeFaces.locales['en'].messages, {
  'javax.faces.component.UIInput.REQUIRED':
    '{0}: Value is required.',
  'javax.faces.validator.LengthValidator.MINIMUM':
    '{1}: Length is less than allowable minimum of \'{0}\'',
  'javax.faces.validator.LengthValidator.MAXIMUM':
    '{1}: Length is greater than allowable maximum of \'{0}\'',
  'javax.faces.validator.RegexValidator.NOT_MATCHED':
    'Value does not match regex pattern {0}'
});
```

The JavaScript snippet can be placed in the `lang_en.js` file in the `resources/js` folder and included on a page via `h:outputScript`. This is shown in the following code:

```
<h:outputScript library="js"
  name="lang_#{facesContext.viewRoot.locale.language}.js"/>
```

The same approach can be applied to all other languages in a multilanguage web application.

> We get the language from `ViewRoot`, but getting the language from a bean, such as #{userBean.language}, is possible too.

See also

Consider the use of `p:clientValidator` if you would like to validate user' inputs instantly. This use case is described in the next recipe, *Instant validation with p:clientValidator*.

PrimeFaces Cookbook Showcase application

This recipe is available in the demo web application on GitHub (`https://github.com/ova2/primefaces-cookbook/tree/second-edition`). Clone the project if you have not done it yet, explore the project structure, and build and deploy the WAR file on application servers compatible with Servlet 3.x, such as *JBoss WildFly* and *Apache TomEE*.

The showcase for the recipe is available at `http://localhost:8080/pf-cookbook/views/chapter10/basicCsv.jsf`.

Instant validation with p:clientValidator

Sometimes, users don't want to fill all form elements and hit `p:commandButton` or `p:commandLink` to get feedback about valid values. They would like to get feedback immediately, for example, during typing or while leaving a field. CSV allows us to validate input values instantly on the client side by means of `p:clientValidator`.

In this recipe, we will meet `p:clientValidator` and develop an example with instant validation on the `change`, `keyup`, and `blur` events.

How to do it...

First, we have to create a bean with three properties, as shown here:

```
@Named
@ViewScoped
public class InstantCsvBean implements Serializable {

  private String value1;
  private Integer value2;
  private Date value3;

  // getters / setters
}
```

In Facelets, the properties are bound to the values of p:inputText. Every p:inputText tag will obtain an attached p:clientValidator tag with a specified event. A missing event means the change event, which is set as default in this case. This is shown in the following code:

```
<h:panelGrid columns="3" cellpadding="3">
  <p:outputLabel for="text" value="Validation on change"/>
  <p:inputText id="text" value="#{instantCsvBean.value1}">
    <f:validateLength minimum="2" maximum="4"/>
    <p:clientValidator/>
  </p:inputText>
  <p:message for="text"/>

  <p:outputLabel for="int" value="Validation on keyup"/>
  <p:inputText id="int" value="#{instantCsvBean.value2}">
    <p:clientValidator event="keyup"/>
  </p:inputText>
  <p:message for="int"/>

  <p:outputLabel for="date" value="Validation on blur"/>
  <p:inputText id="date" value="#{instantCsvBean.value3}">
    <f:convertDateTime pattern="dd.MM.yyyy"/>
    <p:clientValidator event="blur"/>
  </p:inputText>
  <p:message for="date"/>
</h:panelGrid>
```

How it works...

The first attached p:clientValidator tag validates the String value if it has a length between two and four characters. Validation occurs at the time when the input value has been changed and the focus has left the field (onchange event). The second p:clientValidator tag validates the Integer value when the user is typing into the input field (onkeyup event). The third p:clientValidator tag validates the Date value when the input field loses the focus (onblur event). The onblur event is most often used with form validation. Connected p:message components are updated automatically on the mentioned events. They display validation errors as usual in these cases.

PrimeFaces Cookbook Showcase application

This recipe is available in the demo web application on GitHub (`https://github.com/ova2/primefaces-cookbook/tree/second-edition`). Clone the project if you have not done it yet, explore the project structure, and build and deploy the WAR file on application servers compatible with Servlet 3.x, such as *JBoss WildFly* and *Apache TomEE*.

The showcase for the recipe is available at `http://localhost:8080/pf-cookbook/views/chapter10/instantCsv.jsf`.

Bean Validation and transformation

Validating input received from the user to maintain data integrity is an important part of application logic. Validation of data can take place at different layers in an application. Bean Validation (`http://beanvalidation.org`) is a validation model available as part of the Java EE 6 platform, which allows validation by constraints in the form of annotations placed on a field, method, or class. JSF 2.2 supports validation placed on fields (properties and their getters/setters) in managed beans as well as Spring and CDI beans. Validation on the class level is not supported as long as you do not use utilities such as OmniFaces (`http://showcase.omnifaces.org/validators/validateBean`).

The PrimeFaces' CSV has a built-in integration with Bean Validation. Constraints defined with annotations can be validated on the client side by the CSV Framework.

In this recipe, we will develop an example with all available standard Bean Validation constraints. These constraints correspond to the `@AssertFalse`, `@AssertTrue`, `@DecimalMax`, `@DecimalMin`, `@Digits`, `@Future`, `@Past`, `@Max`, `@Min`, `@NotNull`, `@Null`, `@Pattern`, and `@Size` annotations. PrimeFaces provides client-side validators for all mentioned annotations.

Getting ready

To enable Bean Validation, a Maven artifact for the Validation API is required. The following dependency in `pom.xml` ensures that we can use Bean Validation Framework:

```
<dependency>
  <groupId>javax.validation</groupId>
  <artifactId>validation-api</artifactId>
  <version>1.1.0.Final</version>
  <scope>provided</scope>
</dependency>
```

How to do it...

We put all constraint annotations in the `BVBean` bean on its properties, as shown in the following code:

```
@Named(value = "bvBean")
@ViewScoped
public class BVBean implements Serializable {

    @AssertFalse
    private boolean supported;

    @AssertTrue
    private boolean active;

    @DecimalMin("5.00") @DecimalMax("30.00")
    private BigDecimal discount;

    @Digits(integer = 6, fraction = 2)
    private Double price;

    @Future
    private Date eventDate;

    @Past
    private Date birthday;

    @Min(5) @Max(10)
    private int quantity;

    @NotNull
    private String username;

    @Null
    private String unusedString;

    @Pattern(regexp = "\\(\\d{3}\\)\\d{3}-\\d{4}")
    private String phoneNumber;

    @Size(min = 2, max = 50)
    private String briefMessage;

    // getters / setters
    ...
}
```

In Facelets, the properties are bound to the values of `p:selectBooleanCheckbox` and `p:inputText`. This is shown in the following code:

```
<p:messages id="messages"/>

<h:panelGrid id="grid" columns="2" cellpadding="3"
  style="margin-bottom:10px;">
  <p:outputLabel for="input1" value="Boolean @AssertFalse"/>
  <p:selectBooleanCheckbox id="input1" value="#{bvBean.supported}"/>

  <p:outputLabel for="input2" value="Boolean @AssertTrue"/>
  <p:selectBooleanCheckbox id="input2" value="#{bvBean.active}"/>

  <p:outputLabel for="input3" value="BigDecimal @DecimalMin /
    Max"/>
  <p:inputText id="input3" value="#{bvBean.discount}"/>

  <p:outputLabel for="input4" value="Double @Digits"/>
  <p:inputText id="input4" value="#{bvBean.price}"/>

  <p:outputLabel for="input5" value="Date @Future"/>
  <p:inputText id="input5" value="#{bvBean.eventDate}">
    <f:convertDateTime pattern="MM/dd/yyyy"/>
  </p:inputText>

  <p:outputLabel for="input7" value="Date @Past"/>
  <p:inputText id="input7" value="#{bvBean.birthday}">
    <f:convertDateTime pattern="MM/dd/yyyy"/>
  </p:inputText>

  <p:outputLabel for="input8" value="int @Min / @Max"/>
  <p:inputText id="input8" value="#{bvBean.quantity}"/>

  <p:outputLabel for="input9" value="String @NotNull"/>
  <p:inputText id="input9" value="#{bvBean.username}"/>

  <p:outputLabel for="input10" value="String @Null"/>
  <p:inputText id="input10" value="#{bvBean.unusedString}"/>

  <p:outputLabel for="input11" value="String @Pattern"/>
  <p:inputText id="input11" value="#{bvBean.phoneNumber}"/>
```

```
    <p:outputLabel for="input12" value="String @Size"/>
    <p:inputText id="input12" value="#{bvBean.briefMessage}"/>
  </h:panelGrid>

  <p:commandButton validateClient="true"
    value="Submit" ajax="false"
    onclick="PF('inputValuesWdgt').hide()"/>
```

If validation fails, errors are shown in `p:messages`. Otherwise, valid input values are shown in `p:dialog` on postback. The following code shows this:

```
<p:dialog header="Input values" closeOnEscape="true"
  visible="#{facesContext.postback and
    !facesContext.validationFailed}"
  widgetVar="inputValuesWdgt">
  <h:panelGrid id="inputValues" columns="1" cellpadding="3">
    <h:outputText value="#{bvBean.supported}"/>
    <h:outputText value="#{bvBean.active}"/>
    <h:outputText value="#{bvBean.discount}"/>
    <h:outputText value="#{bvBean.price}"/>
    <h:outputText value="#{bvBean.eventDate}">
      <f:convertDateTime pattern="MM/dd/yyyy"/>
    </h:outputText>
    <h:outputText value="#{bvBean.birthday}">
      <f:convertDateTime pattern="MM/dd/yyyy"/>
    </h:outputText>
    <h:outputText value="#{bvBean.quantity}"/>
    <h:outputText value="#{bvBean.username}"/>
    <h:outputText value="#{bvBean.unusedString}"/>
    <h:outputText value="#{bvBean.phoneNumber}"/>
    <h:outputText value="#{bvBean.briefMessage}"/>
  </h:panelGrid>
</p:dialog>
```

How it works...

In the example, the input components are validated on the client side by setting `validateClient="true"` on `p:commandButton`. Thanks to PrimeFaces' built-in client-side validators and converters, we do not need to deal with writing any JavaScript code. However, there is one specialty of the `@NotNull` constraint—that input is required. By default, JSF treats no input as an empty string. In this case, an empty string will pass this validation constraint. However, if you set the `javax.faces.INTERPRET_EMPTY_STRING_SUBMITTED_VALUES_AS_NULL` context parameter in `web.xml` to `true`, the value of the bean property is passed to the Bean Validation runtime as a `null` value, causing the `@NotNull` constraint to fail.

There's more...

PrimeFaces can take certain Bean Validation constraints and transform them into component and HTML attributes. These transformations avoid manual maintenance of these attributes for component tags. For instance, the `required` and `maxlength` attributes are not required to be set when the `@NotNull` and `@Size` annotations are available. Transformation is enabled by setting the following context parameter in `web.xml`:

```
<context-param>
  <param-name>primefaces.TRANSFORM_METADATA</param-name>
  <param-value>true</param-value>
</context-param>
```

Now, you can write the following in a bean:

```
@NotNull
@Max(140)
private String sms;
```

You can omit the `required` and `maxlength` attributes for `p:inputText` because the HTML output gets `maxlength="140"` from the `@Max(140)` annotation, and the component's `required` attribute is set to `true` due to the `@NotNull` annotation:

```
<p:inputText value="#{bean.sms}"/>
```

See also

- ▸ PrimeFaces provides messages in the *beanvalidation.js* file that can be customized, as described in the *Configuring and getting started with CSV* recipe
- ▸ The *Extending CSV with Bean Validation* recipe shows you how to write custom validators for Bean Validation and how to add new messages

PrimeFaces Cookbook Showcase application

This recipe is available in the demo web application on GitHub (`https://github.com/ova2/primefaces-cookbook/tree/second-edition`). Clone the project if you have not done it yet, explore the project structure, and build and deploy the WAR file on application servers compatible with Servlet 3.x, such as *JBoss WildFly* and *Apache TomEE*.

The showcase for the recipe is available at `http://localhost:8080/pf-cookbook/views/chapter10/bvCsv.jsf`.

Extending CSV with JSF

The Client Side Validation API makes it possible to write our own validators and converters. The writing process is straightforward.

In this recipe, we will develop a custom JSF validator that validates any Unicode strings. The validator will check whether an input value consists of letters, spaces, hyphens, and apostrophes. Any other characters are not allowed. This is a common requirement for validating names of persons, addresses, and similar inputs. We will use the CSV API to implement both server-side and client-side validators. After that, we will see validation in action.

How to do it...

A custom JSF validator must implement two interfaces: `javax.faces.validator.Validator` and `org.primefaces.validate.ClientValidator`. The first interface defines a well-known `validate()` method, and the second one defines the `getMetadata()` and `getValidatorId()` methods. Implementing the `getMetadata()` method should provide optional metadata. Implementing the `getValidatorId()` method should provide a unique ID. Both pieces of information are used in the client-side validator implemented in JavaScript. As metadata, we would like to use a custom parameter for the fixed localized message. The parameter will, therefore, be exposed to the JavaScript code. We will start with the server-side implementation. The complete validator code looks like this:

```
@FacesValidator("org.primefaces.cookbook.UnicodeValidator")
public class UnicodeValidator
  implements Validator, ClientValidator, Serializable {

  private static final String MESSAGE_METADATA = "data-param";
  private static final String REGEX =
    "[\\p{L}\\-\\'\\´\\`\\s]+";

  private String msgparam;

  @Override
  public void validate(FacesContext context,
    UIComponent component,
    Object value) throws ValidatorException {
    if (value == null) {
      return;
    }
```

```
        boolean valid = value.toString().matches(REGEX);
        if (!valid) {
          String param = MessageUtil.getMessage(msgparam);
          String msg = MessageUtil.getMessage(
            "invalid.unicode", param);
          throw new ValidatorException(new FacesMessage(
            FacesMessage.SEVERITY_ERROR, null, msg));
        }
      }

      @Override
      public Map<String, Object> getMetadata() {
        Map<String, Object> metadata =
          new HashMap<String, Object>();
        String param = MessageUtil.getMessage(msgparam);
        metadata.put(MESSAGE_METADATA, param);

        return metadata;
      }

      @Override
      public String getValidatorId() {
        return UnicodeValidator.class.getSimpleName();
      }

      public String getMsgparam() {
        return msgparam;
      }

      public void setMsgparam(String msgparam) {
        this.msgparam = msgparam;
      }
    }
```

We use the `[\\p{L}\\-\\'\\´\\`\\s]`+ regular expression to validate user input.
`MessageUtil` is a utility class used to get message text from resource bundles. It is not
specified here. The `msgparam` property is mentioned in the preceding variable parameter
for the localized message. The validator should be registered in `facelet-taglib`:

```xml
<?xml version="1.0"?>
<facelet-taglib version="2.2" ...>
  <namespace>
    http://primefaces.org/ui/cookbook
  </namespace>
```

```
<tag>
  <tag-name>validateUnicode</tag-name>
  <validator>
    <validator-id>
      org.primefaces.cookbook.UnicodeValidator
    </validator-id>
  </validator>
  <attribute>
    <name>msgparam</name>
    <required>true</required>
    <type>java.lang.String</type>
  </attribute>
</tag>
</facelet-taglib>
```

The message keys and text for this example are defined in property files acting as resource bundles. The English version looks like this:

```
firstName=First Name
lastName=Last Name
invalid.unicode={0} may only contain letters, spaces, hyphens and
  apostrophes
```

Let's go to the client-side implementation. First, we have to create a JavaScript file, say `validators.js`, and register there our own validator in the `PrimeFaces.validator` namespace with the name `UnicodeValidator`. This name is the unique ID mentioned earlier. The function to be implemented is called `validate()`. It has two parameters—the element itself and the current input value to be validated. The following code shows this:

```
PrimeFaces.validator['UnicodeValidator'] = {
  regex: XRegExp("^[\\p{L}-'´`\\s]+$"),

  MESSAGE_ID: 'invalid.unicode',

  validate: function (element, value) {
    if (!this.regex.test(value)) {
      throw PrimeFaces.util.ValidationContext.getMessage(
        this.MESSAGE_ID, element.data('param'));
    }
  }
};
```

Second, we have to create a JavaScript file for localized messages, for example, `lang_en.js`. The messages should be the same as already defined in the server-side resource bundles. The following code shows this:

```
PrimeFaces.locales['en'] = {
  messages : PrimeFaces.locales['en_US'].messages
};


$.extend(PrimeFaces.locales['en'].messages, {

  ...


  'invalid.unicode':
  '{0} may only contain letters, spaces, hyphens and apostrophes'
});
```

The bean contains two properties of the `String` type. The following code shows this:

```
@Named
@ViewScoped
public class ExtendCsvBean implements Serializable {

  private String firstName;
  private String lastName;

  // getters / setters
  ...
}
```

Now, we can take the `xmlns:book="http://primefaces.org/ui/cookbook"` namespace from `facelet-taglib` and write the following XHTML snippet:

```
<h:panelGrid columns="3" cellpadding="3"
  style="margin-bottom:10px;">
  <p:outputLabel for="firstName" value="First Name"/>
  <p:inputText id="firstName"
    value="#{extendCsvBean.firstName}">
    <book:validateUnicode msgparam="firstName"/>
  </p:inputText>
  <p:message for="firstName"/>
```

```
<p:outputLabel for="lastName" value="Last Name"/>
<p:inputText id="lastName"
  value="#{extendCsvBean.lastName}">
  <book:validateUnicode msgparam="lastName"/>
</p:inputText>
<p:message for="lastName"/>
</h:panelGrid>

<p:commandButton validateClient="true"
  value="Submit" ajax="false"/>
```

The `book:validateUnicode` validator is attached to `p:inputText`:

 Using `<f:validator validatorId=" org.primefaces.cookbook.UnicodeValidator"/>` could be possible too if we were not using any attributes for the validator tag.

In the last step, all required JavaScript files have to be included on the page. Besides `lang_en.js` and `validators.js`, we need to include a JavaScript library for extensible regular expressions supporting Unicode and more (`http://xregexp.com`). The following code shows this:

```
<h:outputScript library="js" name="chapter10/lang_en.js"/>
<h:outputScript library="js" name="chapter10/xregexp-all.js"/>
<h:outputScript library="js" name="chapter10/validators.js"/>
```

Validation happens on the client-side without a round trip to the server. Setting `validateClient="false"` would trigger a server-side validation. The following screenshot shows the end result when validation fails:

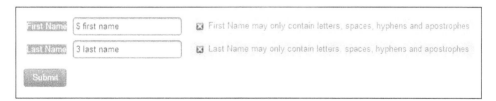

How it works...

The `getMetadata()` method provides a map with name-value pairs. The metadata is exposed in the rendered HTML. The values can be accessed on the client side via `element.data(name)`, where `element` is a jQuery object for the underlying native HTML element. The metadata in the example is rendered as follows:

```
<input data-param="First Name" .../>

<input data-param="Second Name" .../>
```

Client-side validation happens by means of the useful JavaScript library, *XRegExp*. We need this library because the native JavaScript regular expressions do not support Unicode (the `\\p{L}` expression in the regex). If validation fails, we throw an exception by invoking `throw PrimeFaces.util.ValidationContext.getMessage(text, parameter)`.

There's more...

Client-side converters can be implemented similarly. On the server side, PrimeFaces provides the `org.primefaces.convert.ClientConverter` interface with the `getMetadata()` and `getConverterId()` methods. The meaning of these methods is the same as for validators. On the client side, you need to override the `convert: function(element, submittedValue){}` function returning a converted JavaScript object. All client-side converters are defined in the `PrimeFaces.converter` namespace.

> Refer to the PrimeFaces sources and explore the standard converters in the `validation.js` file to understand the writing of custom converters.

See also

Extending CSV with Bean Validation is the topic of the next recipe, *Extending CSV with Bean Validation*.

PrimeFaces Cookbook Showcase application

This recipe is available in the demo web application on GitHub (`https://github.com/ova2/primefaces-cookbook/tree/second-edition`). Clone the project if you have not done it yet, explore the project structure, and build and deploy the WAR file on application servers compatible with Servlet 3.x, such as *JBoss WildFly* and *Apache TomEE*.

The showcase for the recipe is available at `http://localhost:8080/pf-cookbook/views/chapter10/extendJsfCsv.jsf`.

Extending CSV with Bean Validation

Although the Bean Validation API defines a whole set of standard constraint annotations, one can easily think of situations in which these standard annotations will not suffice. For these cases, you will be able to create custom constraints for specific validation requirements. The Client Side Validation API in PrimeFaces works seamlessly with custom constraints.

In this recipe, we will develop a special custom constraint and validators to validate a **Card Verification Code** (**CVC**). CVC is used as a security feature with a bank card number. It is a number with a length between three and four digits. For instance, MasterCard and Visa require three digits, and American Express requires four digits. Therefore, the CVC validation will depend on the selected bank card. The user can select a bank card using `p:selectOneMenu`, type a CVC into `p:inputText`, and submit the input after that.

How to do it...

We will start with a custom annotation used for the CVC field. The following code shows this:

```java
import org.primefaces.validate.bean.ClientConstraint;
import javax.validation.Constraint;
import javax.validation.Payload;
import java.lang.annotation.Retention;
import java.lang.annotation.RetentionPolicy;
import java.lang.annotation.Target;
import static java.lang.annotation.ElementType.FIELD;
import static java.lang.annotation.ElementType.METHOD;

@Constraint(validatedBy = CvcConstraintValidator.class)
@ClientConstraint(resolvedBy = CvcClientConstraint.class)
@Target({FIELD, METHOD})
@Retention(RetentionPolicy.RUNTIME)
public @interface ValidCVC {

  String message() default "{invalid.cvc.message}";

  Class<?>[] groups() default {};

  Class<? extends Payload>[] payload() default {};

  // identifier of the select menu with cards
  String forCardMenu() default "";
}
```

@Constraint is a regular annotation from the Bean Validation API, and @ClientConstraint is one from PrimeFaces CSV Framework, which helps to resolve metadata. The developed annotation defines the invalid.cvc.message message key and has the forCardMenu custom property. The value of this property is any search expression in terms of **PrimeFaces Selectors** (**PFS**) to reference the select menu with bank cards. This is necessary because the valid CVC value depends on the selected card.

The goal of CvcConstraintValidator is the validation of the input length. This is shown in the following code:

```
public class CvcConstraintValidator
  implements ConstraintValidator<ValidCVC, Integer> {

  @Override
  public void initialize(ValidCVC validCVC) {
  }

  @Override
  public boolean isValid(Integer cvc,
    ConstraintValidatorContext context) {
    if (cvc == null || cvc < 0) {
      return false;
    }

    int length = (int) (Math.log10(cvc) + 1);
    return (length >= 3 && length <= 4);
  }
}
```

The goal of CvcClientConstraint is the preparation of metadata. This is shown in the following code:

```
public class CvcClientConstraint
  implements ClientValidationConstraint {

  private static final String CARDMENU_METADATA =
    "data-forcardmenu";

  @Override
  public Map<String, Object> getMetadata(
    ConstraintDescriptor constraintDescriptor) {
    Map<String, Object> metadata =
      new HashMap<String, Object>();
    Map attrs = constraintDescriptor.getAttributes();
    String forCardMenu = (String) attrs.get("forCardMenu");
    if (StringUtils.isNotBlank(forCardMenu)) {
```

```
            metadata.put(CARDMENU_METADATA, forCardMenu);
        }

        return metadata;
    }

    @Override
    public String getValidatorId() {
        return ValidCVC.class.getSimpleName();
    }
}
```

Let's go to the client-side implementation. First, we have to create a JavaScript file, say `validators.js`, and register there our own validator in the `PrimeFaces.validator` namespace with the name `ValidCVC`. This name is a unique ID returned by the `getValidatorId()` method (see the `CvcClientConstraint` class). The function to be implemented is called `validate()`. It has two parameters—the element itself and the current input value to be validated. This is shown in the following code:

```
PrimeFaces.validator['ValidCVC'] = {
    MESSAGE_ID: 'invalid.cvc',

    validate: function (element, value) {
        // find out selected menu value
        var forCardMenu = element.data('forcardmenu');
        var selOption = forCardMenu ?
            PrimeFaces.expressions.SearchExpressionFacade.
            resolveComponentsAsSelector(forCardMenu).
            find("select").val() : null;

        var valid = false;
        if (selOption && selOption === 'MCD') {
            // MasterCard
            valid = value > 0 && value.toString().length == 3;
        } else if (selOption && selOption === 'AMEX') {
            // American Express
            valid = value > 0 && value.toString().length == 4;
        }

        if (!valid) {
            throw PrimeFaces.util.ValidationContext.
                getMessage(this.MESSAGE_ID);
        }
    }
};
```

Secondly, we have to create a JavaScript file for localized messages, for example, `lang_en.js`. The following code shows this:

```
PrimeFaces.locales['en'] = {
  messages : PrimeFaces.locales['en_US'].messages
};

$.extend(PrimeFaces.locales['en'].messages, {
  ...

  'invalid.cvc':
    'Card Validation Code is invalid'
});
```

The bean has two required properties annotated with `@NotNull`. In addition, the `cvc` property is annotated with our custom annotation `@ValidCVC`. The value of the `forCardMenu` attribute points to the style class of `p:selectOneMenu`, which lists the available bank cards. This is shown in the following code:

```
@Named
@ViewScoped
public class ExtendCsvBean implements Serializable {

  @NotNull
  private String card;
  @NotNull
  @ValidCVC(forCardMenu = "@(.card)")
  private Integer cvc;

  public void save() {
    RequestContext.getCurrentInstance().execute(
      "alert('Saved!')");
  }

  // getters / setters
  ...
}
```

In the XHTML fragment, we have a select menu with two bank cards and an input field for CVC. The p:commandButton component validates the fields and executes the save() method on postback. This is shown in the following code:

```
<h:panelGrid id="pgrid" columns="3" cellpadding="3"
  style="margin-bottom:10px;">
  <p:outputLabel for="card" value="Card"/>
  <p:selectOneMenu id="card" styleClass="card"
    value="#{extendCsvBean.card}">
    <f:selectItem itemLabel="Please select a card"
      itemValue="#{null}"/>
    <f:selectItem itemLabel="MasterCard"
      itemValue="MCD"/>
    <f:selectItem itemLabel="American Express"
      itemValue="AMEX"/>
  </p:selectOneMenu>
  <p:message for="card"/>

  <p:outputLabel for="cvc" value="CVC"/>
  <p:inputText id="cvc" value="#{extendCsvBean.cvc}"/>
  <p:message for="cvc"/>
</h:panelGrid>

<p:commandButton validateClient="true" value="Save"
  process="@this pgrid" update="pgrid"
  action="#{extendCsvBean.save}"/>
```

As illustrated, neither p:selectOneMenu nor p:inputText specifies the required attribute. We can achieve the transformation of the @ NotNull annotation to the required attribute with the value true if we set the primefaces.TRANSFORM_METADATA context parameter to true. More details on this feature are available in the *Bean Validation and transformation* recipe.

In the last step, all required JavaScript files have to be included on the page. The following code shows this:

```
<h:outputScript library="js" name="chapter10/lang_en.js"/>
<h:outputScript library="js" name="chapter10/validators.js"/>
```

The next two pictures show what happens when validations fails:

If everything is ok, an alert box with the text **Saved!** is displayed to the user:

The `invalid.cvc.message` message key and the text should be put in resource bundles named `ValidationMessages`, for example, `ValidationMessages_en.properties`. `ValidationMessages` is the standard name specified in the Bean Validation specification. The property files should be located in the application classpath and contain the following entry: `invalid.cvc.message=Card Validation Code is invalid`. This configuration is important for server-side validation.

The `getMetadata()` method in the `CvcClientConstraint` class provides a map with name-value pairs. The metadata is exposed in the rendered HTML. The values can be accessed on the client side via `element.data(name)`, where `element` is a jQuery object for the underlying native HTML element. The CVC field with the metadata is rendered as shown here:

```
<input type="text" data-forcardmenu="@(.card)"
    data-p-con="javax.faces.Integer" data-p-required="true"...>
```

The most interesting part is the implementation of the client-side validator. The value to be validated is already numeric because first it gets converted by PrimeFaces' built-in client-side converter for the `java.lang.Integer` data type. We only have to check whether the value is positive and has a valid length. A valid length depends on the selected card in the `p:selectOneMenu` menu that can be accessed by the PrimeFaces JavaScript API as `PrimeFaces.expressions.SearchExpressionFacade.resolveComponentsAsSelector(selector)`, where `selector` is any PrimeFaces selector, which, in our case, is `@(.card)`. If validation fails, we throw an exception by invoking `throw PrimeFaces.util.ValidationContext.getMessage(text, parameter)`.

Client-side validation is triggered by setting `validateClient="true"` on `p:commandButton`.

There's more...

You can also use third-party constraints from other libraries with CSV Framework. Use PrimeFaces' `BeanValidationMetadataMapper` to register third-party annotations with `ClientValidationConstraint`. Removing registered annotations is possible as well. The following code shows this:

```
BeanValidationMetadataMapper.registerConstraintMapping(
    Class<? extends Annotation> constraint,
    ClientValidationConstraint clientValidationConstraint);

BeanValidationMetadataMapper.removeConstraintMapping(
    Class<? extends Annotation> constraint);
```

See also

Extending CSV with JSF validators is the topic of the previous recipe, *Extending CSV with JSF*.

PrimeFaces Cookbook Showcase application

This recipe is available in the demo web application on GitHub (`https://github.com/ova2/primefaces-cookbook/tree/second-edition`). Clone the project if you have not done it yet, explore the project structure, and build and deploy the WAR file on application servers compatible with Servlet 3.x, such as *JBoss WildFly* and *Apache TomEE*.

The showcase for the recipe is available at `http://localhost:8080/pf-cookbook/views/chapter10/extendBvCsv.jsf`.

11
Miscellaneous Advanced Use Cases

In this chapter, we will cover the following topics:

- ▶ Programmatic updating and scrolling with RequestContext
- ▶ Two ways of triggering the JavaScript execution
- ▶ Adding AJAX callback parameters – validation within a dialog
- ▶ Opening external pages in dynamically generated dialogs
- ▶ Polling – sending periodical AJAX requests
- ▶ Blocking page pieces during long-running AJAX calls
- ▶ Controlling form submission using defaultCommand
- ▶ Clever focus management in forms
- ▶ Layout pitfalls of menus and dialogs
- ▶ Targetable messages with severity levels
- ▶ Conditional coloring in dataTable
- ▶ Sticking a component when scrolling
- ▶ Reducing page load time using content caching
- ▶ Possibilities for exception handling in PrimeFaces

Introduction

PrimeFaces has an impressive number of components that are usually suitable for both common and advanced use cases. It is almost impossible to cover all scenarios in just one book and discuss all solutions for each case. The key aspect of this chapter consists in giving users tips that can be applied quickly for often-raised questions. In this chapter, we will go beyond the basics and introduce more interesting features of the PrimeFaces library. We will learn about `RequestContext`, a helpful utility that allows you to mark components as updatable targets at runtime, add AJAX callback parameters; open external pages in dynamically generated dialogs—*Dialog Framework*—and much more. We will also develop a couple of real-world samples for common tasks such as blocking UI during AJAX calls, controlling form submission, periodic polling, focus handling, menus within the layout units and nested panels, targetable messages, sticky components, cached content, and exception handling.

Programmatic updating and scrolling with RequestContext

`RequestContext` is an easy-to-use utility class that provides useful features. `RequestContext` is available for AJAX as well as non-AJAX calls. The most important features will be revealed in this book.

In this recipe, we will see how to specify components to be updated at runtime rather than specifying update targets at compile time declaratively. We will also see how to scroll to any component after the current AJAX request completes. Scrolling to the given component with AJAX updates is very handy when dealing with long pages and can increase the website's usability.

How to do it...

In the first example, we will develop a counter that will be incremented in an action listener. The current counter value will be displayed in two output components `h:outputText`. A decision as to which `h:outputText` component is responsible for the output is provided by the `p:selectBooleanCheckbox` checkbox. The user can decide at runtime whether they would like to update the first or the second output component. Here's the code for the first example:

```
<p:selectBooleanCheckbox id="checkbox"
  itemLabel="Update first output"
  value="#{requestContextBean.firstOutput}"/>
```

```
<h:panelGrid columns="2" style="margin-top:10px;">
  <h:outputText value="First Output"/>
  <h:outputText id="firstOutput"
    value="#{requestContextBean.counter}"/>

  <h:outputText value="Second Output"/>
  <h:outputText id="secondOutput"
    value="#{requestContextBean.counter}"/>

  <f:facet name="footer">
    <p:commandButton value="Increment counter"
      actionListener="#{requestContextBean.incrementWithUpdate}"
      process="@form" style="margin:10px 0 10px 0;"/>
  </f:facet>
</h:panelGrid>
```

In the next example, we will take the same counter that is displayed by `h:outputText` and a very long text output so that the browser's scrollbars appear. At the end of the text output, we will place a command button that increments the counter and scrolls to the counter's output when the AJAX response comes back. The logic for scrolling is implemented inside the button's action listener. Here's the code for this example:

```
<h:panelGrid id="counter" columns="2"
  style="font-weight:bold;">
  <h:outputText value="Counter"/>
    <h:outputText value="#{requestContextBean.counter}"/>
</h:panelGrid>

<p>Some text</p>
...
<p>Some text</p>

<p:commandButton value="Increment counter"
  process="@form" update="counter"
  actionListener="#{requestContextBean.incrementWithScroll}"
  style="margin:10px;"/>
```

The `ViewScoped` bean, with the `incrementWithUpdate()` and `incrementWithScroll()` action listeners, mentioned in the preceding code snippets, looks as shown here:

```
@Named
@ViewScoped
public class RequestContextBean implements Serializable {
```

```java
    private boolean firstOutput = true;
    private int counter = 0;

    public void incrementWithUpdate(ActionEvent ae) {
      counter++;

      RequestContext requestContext =
        RequestContext.getCurrentInstance();

      if (firstOutput) {
        requestContext.update("firstOutput");
      } else {
        requestContext.update("secondOutput");
      }
    }

    public void incrementWithScroll(ActionEvent ae) {
      counter++;

      RequestContext requestContext =
        RequestContext.getCurrentInstance();
      requestContext.scrollTo("counter");
    }

    // getters / setters
    ...
}
```

The following screenshot shows a snapshot result of the first example:

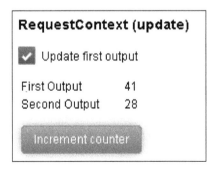

How it works...

The `RequestContext` instance can be obtained as `RequestContext.getCurrentInstance()` in a manner similar to that for `FacesContext`. The `update()` method of the `RequestContext` instance expects the client IDs of the components to be updated. These components are `firstOutput` and `secondOutput`. Depending on the user's checkbox selection (Boolean variable `firstOutput`), either the first or the second `h:outputText` component will be updated.

Scrolling to a given component is done by the `scrollTo()` method. This method expects a client ID of the component that we want to scroll to. The `requestContext.scrollTo("counter")` call ensures that the user will see the counter value after clicking on the **Increment counter** button.

There's more...

The client-side API for scrolling is also available to use directly in JavaScript, as shown here:

```
PrimeFaces.scrollTo("clientId")
```

PrimeFaces Cookbook Showcase application

This recipe is available in the demo web application on GitHub (`https://github.com/ova2/primefaces-cookbook/tree/second-edition`). Clone the project if you have not done it yet, explore the project structure, and build and deploy the WAR file on application servers compatible with Servlet 3.x, such as *JBoss WildFly* and *Apache TomEE*.

The showcase for the recipe is available at `http://localhost:8080/pf-cookbook/views/chapter11/requestContext.jsf`.

Two ways of triggering the JavaScript execution

The `RequestContext` utility class provides an easy way to execute any JavaScript code after the current AJAX request completes. The JavaScript block has to be coded in Java and can be executed by passing it to the `execute()` method. An alternative approach would be to update a script block on a page and trigger the script execution manually. In this case, the JavaScript block is coded directly into a page.

In this recipe, we will see both solutions for JavaScript execution. For this purpose, we will develop a `menu` component and toggle the enabling/disabling of menu items with two command buttons. The first command button should toggle enabling/disabling with the server-side approach and the second one with the client-side approach.

How to do it...

Let's write a p:menu tag with three menu items. We also need two p:commandButton tags with appropriate action listeners:

```
<h:outputText id="indicator"
  value="Enabled? - #{javaScriptExecBean.enabled}"/>

<p:menu id="menu" style="margin:20px 0 10px 0;">
  <p:submenu label="JavaScript Libraries">
    <p:menuitem value="jQuery" url="http://jquery.com"/>
    <p:menuitem value="Yahoo UI" url="http://yuilibrary.com"/>
    <p:menuitem value="Prototype" url="http://prototypejs.org"/>
  </p:submenu>
</p:menu>

<p:commandButton id="toggle1" value="Toggle Menuitems (server-
  side)"
    process="@this" update="indicator"
    actionListener="#{javaScriptExecBean.toggleMenuitems}"/>

<p:commandButton id="toggle2" value="Toggle Menuitems (client-
  side)"
    process="@this" update="indicator toggleScriptWrapper"
    actionListener="#{javaScriptExecBean.toggleEnabled}"/>

<h:panelGroup id="toggleScriptWrapper">
  <script type="text/javascript">
  if (#{facesContext.partialViewContext.ajaxRequest}) {
    $('#menu').find('a').each(function() {
      var $this = $(this);
        if ($this.attr('href')) {
          // disable item
          $this.attr('data-href', $this.attr('href'))
          .removeAttr('href')
          .addClass('ui-state-disabled');
        } else {
          // enable item
          $this.attr('href', $this.attr('data-href'))
          .removeAttr('data-href')
          .removeClass('ui-state-disabled');
        }
      });
    }
```

```
    </script>
  </h:panelGroup>
```

The `panelGroup` component with the `toggleScriptWrapper` ID contains the script logic that is executed after each update on this `panelGroup` component. The bean packs the same logic in a `String` variable `script` and executes it with `requestContext.execute(script)`:

```
@Named
@ViewScoped
public class JavaScriptExecBean implements Serializable {

  private boolean enabled = true;

  public void toggleMenuitems(ActionEvent ae) {
    RequestContext requestContext =
      RequestContext.getCurrentInstance();

    String script;
    if (enabled) {
      script =
        "$('#menu a').each(function() {"
        + "$(this).attr('data-href', $(this).attr('href'))"
        + ".removeAttr('href')"
        + ".addClass('ui-state-disabled');});";
    } else {
      script =
        "$('#menu a').each(function() {"
        + "$(this).attr('href', $(this).attr('data-href'))"
        + ".removeAttr('data-href')"
        + ".removeClass('ui-state-disabled');});";
    }

    requestContext.execute(script);
    enabled = !enabled;
  }

  public void toggleEnabled(ActionEvent ae) {
    enabled = !enabled;
  }

  public boolean isEnabled() {
    return enabled;
  }
}
```

The following screenshot shows what the disabled menu items look like:

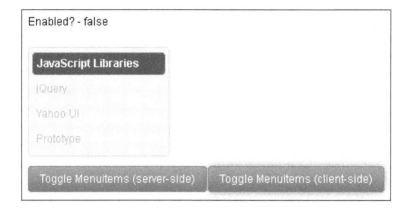

How it works...

Both client-side and server-side scripts implement the same logic. To disable a menu item, its URL has to be copied from the anchor's `href` attribute to a `data-href` attribute. The `href` attribute should be removed then, and the link should be styled with a proper jQuery ThemeRoller class, `ui-state-disabled`. This style class makes elements appear disabled. To enable a menu item, its URL has to be restored from the `data-href` attribute and assigned to `href`. The style class, `ui-state-disabled`, should be removed.

Also, consider the `if` statement with the EL expression, `#{facesContext.partialViewContext.ajaxRequest}`. This statement prevents an initial script execution on page load (the `GET` request).

PrimeFaces Cookbook Showcase application

This recipe is available in the demo web application on GitHub (`https://github.com/ova2/primefaces-cookbook/tree/second-edition`). Clone the project if you have not done it yet, explore the project structure, and build and deploy the WAR file on application servers compatible with Servlet 3.x, such as *JBoss WildFly* and *Apache TomEE*.

The showcase for the recipe is available at `http://localhost:8080/pf-cookbook/views/chapter11/javaScriptExec.jsf`.

Adding AJAX callback parameters – validation within a dialog

This recipe will continue with the discussion on `RequestContext` that we began in the previous recipes. There may be cases where we need values from backing beans in AJAX callbacks. Let's suppose we have a form in a dialog; when the user submits the form, the dialog should stay open to display any validation errors and it should be closed otherwise.

In this recipe, we will learn how the described task can be done with AJAX callback parameters. We will develop an `oncomplete` callback for a command button within `p:dialog`.

How to do it...

The developed page contains a `Dialog` component with an input field. The dialog will be visible when the page is loaded. There is only one valid input value, `PrimeFaces Cookbook`. When the user inputs this value and clicks on the **Save** button, the dialog should be closed. In any other case, it should stay open. The `p:commandButton` button defines `handleComplete(xhr, status, args)`, an `oncomplete` callback. It gets processed when the AJAX request completes. There, we check `args.validName` and close the dialog if this value is `true`. Here's the code for this discussion:

```
<p:growl id="growl" autoUpdate="true"/>

<p:dialog header="What is the name of this book?"
  visible="true" widgetVar="dlgWidget">
  <p:inputText id="name" value="#{ajaxCallbackParamBean.name}"/>

  <p:commandButton id="save" value="Save" style="margin:10px;"
    process="@this name" update="name"
    actionListener="#{ajaxCallbackParamBean.save}"
    oncomplete="handleComplete(xhr, status, args)"/>
</p:dialog>

<h:outputScript id="handleCompleteScript" target="body">
  function handleComplete(xhr, status, args) {
    if (args && args.validName) {
      PF('dlgWidget').hide();
    }
  }
</h:outputScript>
```

The corresponding CDI bean compares the input value with the valid one and creates either an information message or an error message for the `growl` component. Furthermore, it adds a callback parameter, `validName`, with the value `true` for a valid input and `false` otherwise. Here's the code that encapsulates this discussion:

```
@Named
@ViewScoped
public class AjaxCallbackParamBean implements Serializable {

  private String name;

  public void save(ActionEvent ae) {
    RequestContext requestContext =
      RequestContext.getCurrentInstance();

    String message;
    FacesMessage.Severity severity;
    UIInput input = (UIInput) ae.getComponent().
      findComponent("name");

    if ("PrimeFaces Cookbook".equals(name)) {
      message = "All right!";
      severity = FacesMessage.SEVERITY_INFO;

      requestContext.addCallbackParam("validName", true);
      input.setValid(true);
    } else {
      message = "Name is wrong, try again";
      severity = FacesMessage.SEVERITY_ERROR;

      requestContext.addCallbackParam("validName", false);
      input.setValid(false);
    }

    FacesMessage msg = new FacesMessage(severity, message, null);
    FacesContext.getCurrentInstance().addMessage(null, msg);
  }

  // getters / setters
  ...
}
```

The following screenshot shows the dialog and the growl notification that is created when there is an error:

How it works...

The `oncomplete` callback function takes three arguments: `XMLHttpRequest`, status string, and optional parameters provided by the `RequestContext` API. Parameters can be added by the `addCallbackParam(key, value)` method. They are serialized to **JavaScript Object Notation** (**JSON**) and can be accessed in AJAX callbacks by the `args` argument. In the example, we accessed the value of the `validName` callback parameter by `args. validName`. We can add as many callback parameters as we want. Primitive values are supported as well as **Plain Old Java Objects** (**POJOs**). POJOs are serialized to JSON as well.

> By default, the `validationFailed` callback parameter is added implicitly if JSF validation fails so that it is possible to check the failed validation with an if statement: `if (args.validationFailed == true)`.

In the bean, we set the `valid` flag on the input component to `false` when the book's name is wrong. Making the input component invalid leads to red borders around the input field in the UI.

There's more...

If we had the standard `h:inputText` component instead of the PrimeFaces' one, the `input.setValid(false)` setting on the input component would not lead to red borders around the input field in the UI. In this case, we could highlight the invalid input field anyway by adding the `ui-state-error` style class via JavaScript. Here's the code we are discussing:

```
function handleComplete(xhr, status, args) {
    if (args && args.validName) {
```

```
      PF('dlgWidget').hide();
    } else {
      $('#name').addClass('ui-state-error');
    }
  }
}
```

PrimeFaces Cookbook Showcase application

This recipe is available in the demo web application on GitHub (`https://github.com/ova2/primefaces-cookbook/tree/second-edition`). Clone the project if you have not done it yet, explore the project structure, and build and deploy the WAR file on application servers compatible with Servlet 3.x, such as *JBoss WildFly* and *Apache TomEE*.

The showcase for the recipe is available at `http://localhost:8080/pf-cookbook/views/chapter11/ajaxCallbacks.jsf`.

Opening external pages in dynamically generated dialogs

The regular usage of PrimeFaces' dialog is a declarative approach with `p:dialog`. Besides this declarative approach, there is a programmatic approach as well. The programmatic approach is based on a programmatic API where dialogs are created and destroyed at runtime. It is called Dialog Framework. Dialog Framework is used to open external pages in dynamically generated dialogs. The usage is quite simple; `RequestContext` provides two methods—`openDialog` and `closeDialog`—that allow the opening and closing of dynamic dialogs. Furthermore, Dialog Framework makes it possible to pass data back from the page displayed in the dialog to the caller page.

In this recipe, we will demonstrate all features available in Dialog Framework. We will open a dialog with options programmatically and pass parameters to the page displayed in this dialog. We will also meet the possibility of communicating between the source (caller) page and the dialog.

Getting ready

Dialog Framework requires the following configuration in `faces-config.xml`:

```
<application>
  <action-listener>
    org.primefaces.application.DialogActionListener
  </action-listener>
  <navigation-handler>
    org.primefaces.application.DialogNavigationHandler
  </navigation-handler>
```

```
   <view-handler>
      org.primefaces.application.DialogViewHandler
   </view-handler>
</application>
```

How to do it...

We will develop a page with radio buttons to select an available PrimeFaces' book for rating as follows. The rating itself happens in a dialog after a click on the **Rate the selected book** button.

The XHTML snippet for the preceding screenshot is shown here:

```
<p:messages id="messages"
  showSummary="true" showDetail="false"/>

<p:selectOneRadio id="books" layout="pageDirection"
  value="#{dialogFrameworkBean.bookName}">
  <f:selectItem itemLabel="PrimeFaces Cookbook"
    itemValue="PrimeFaces Cookbook"/>
  <f:selectItem itemLabel="PrimeFaces Starter"
    itemValue="PrimeFaces Starter"/>
  <f:selectItem itemLabel="PrimeFaces Beginner's Guide"
    itemValue="PrimeFaces Beginner's Guide"/>
  <f:selectItem itemLabel="PrimeFaces Blueprints"
    itemValue="PrimeFaces Blueprints"/>
</p:selectOneRadio>

<p:commandButton value="Rate the selected book"
  process="@this books"
  actionListener="#{dialogFrameworkBean.showRatingDialog}"
  style="margin-top: 15px">
  <p:ajax event="dialogReturn" update="messages"
```

```
        listener="#{dialogFrameworkBean.onDialogReturn}"/>
    </p:commandButton>
```

The page in the dialog is a full bookRating.xhtml page with a rating component,
p:rating. It also shows the name of the book selected for rating. Here's the code to obtain
the desired results:

```
<!DOCTYPE html>
<html xmlns="http://www.w3.org/1999/xhtml"
  xmlns:f="http://xmlns.jcp.org/jsf/core"
  xmlns:h="http://xmlns.jcp.org/jsf/html"
  xmlns:p="http://primefaces.org/ui">
<f:view contentType="text/html" locale="en">
  <f:metadata>
    <f:viewParam name="bookName"
      value="#{bookRatingBean.bookName}"/>
  </f:metadata>
  <h:head>
    <title>Rate the book!</title>
  </h:head>
  <h:body>
    <h:form>
      What is your rating for the book
      <strong>#{bookRatingBean.bookName}</strong>?

      <p/>

      <p:rating id="rating">
        <p:ajax event="rate"
          listener="#{bookRatingBean.onrate}"/>
        <p:ajax event="cancel"
          listener="#{bookRatingBean.oncancel}"/>
      </p:rating>
    </h:form>
  </h:body>
</f:view>
</html>
```

The next screenshot demonstrates how the dialog looks:

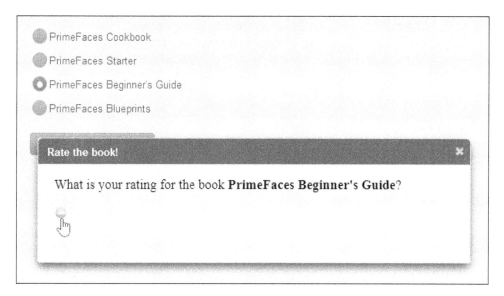

A click on a rating star or the cancel symbol closes the dialog. The source (caller) page displays a message with the selected rating value in the range 0–5:

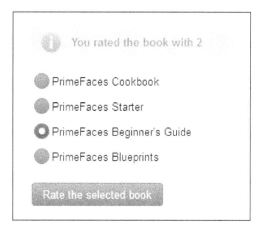

The most interesting part is the logic in beans. The `DialogFrameworkBean` bean opens the rating page within the dialog by invoking the `openDialog()` method with the outcome, options, and POST parameters on a `RequestContext` instance. Furthermore, the bean defines the `onDialogReturn()` AJAX listener, which is invoked when the data (selected rating) is returned from the dialog after it was closed. The following code encapsulates this discussion:

```java
@Named
@ViewScoped
public class DialogFrameworkBean implements Serializable {

    private String bookName;

    public void showRatingDialog() {
        Map<String, Object> options =
            new HashMap<String, Object>();
        options.put("modal", true);
        options.put("draggable", false);
        options.put("resizable", false);
        options.put("contentWidth", 500);
        options.put("contentHeight", 100);
        options.put("includeViewParams", true);

        Map<String, List<String>> params =
            new HashMap<String, List<String>>();
        List<String> values = new ArrayList<String>();
        values.add(bookName);
        params.put("bookName", values);

        RequestContext.getCurrentInstance().openDialog(
            "/views/chapter11/bookRating", options, params);
    }

    public void onDialogReturn(SelectEvent event) {
        Object rating = event.getObject();
        FacesMessage message = new FacesMessage(
            FacesMessage.SEVERITY_INFO,
            "You rated the book with " + rating,
            null);

        FacesContext.getCurrentInstance().addMessage(
            null, message);
    }
```

```
   // getters / setters
   ...
}
```

The `BookRatingBean` bean defines two listeners for the `rating` component. They are invoked when the user clicks on a star and the cancel symbol, respectively. We call `closeDialog()` on a `RequestContext` instance to trigger dialog closing and to pass the current rating value to the `onDialogReturn()` listener:

```
@Named
@RequestScoped
public class BookRatingBean {

  private String bookName;

  public void onrate(RateEvent rateEvent) {
    RequestContext.getCurrentInstance()
      .closeDialog(rateEvent.getRating());
  }

  public void oncancel() {
    RequestContext.getCurrentInstance()
      .closeDialog(0);
  }

  // getters / setters
  ...
}
```

How it works...

`RequestContext` provides two methods of the same name, `openDialog`, to open a dialog dynamically at runtime. The first one only has one parameter—the logical outcome used to resolve a navigation case. The second one has three parameters—outcome, dialog configuration options, and parameters that are sent to the view displayed in the dialog. We used the second variant in the example. The options are put into `Map` as key-value pairs. The parameters are put into `Map` too. In our case, we put the name of the selected book. After that, the name is received in the dialog's `bookRating.xhtml` page via the `f:viewParam`. The transferred parameter is set into `BookRatingBean` by `f:viewParam` so that it is available in the heading above the `Rating` component.

Refer to the PrimeFaces User's Guide (http://primefaces.org/documentation.html) to see a full list of the supported dialog's configuration options.

Let's go through the request-response life cycle. Once the response is received from the request caused by the command button, a dialog gets created with an iframe tag inside. The URL of iframe points to the full page, which, in our case, is bookRating.xhtml. The page will be streamed down and shown in the dialog. As you can see, there are always two requests: the initial POST and the second GET sent by iframe. Note that Dialog Framework only works with initial AJAX requests. Non-AJAX requests are ignored.

The title of the dialog is taken from the HTML title element.

As mentioned earlier, the dialog can be closed programmatically by invoking the closeDialog method on a RequestContext instance. On the caller page, the button that triggers the dialog needs to have an AJAX listener for the dialogReturn event to be able to receive any data from the dialog. The data is passed as a parameter to the closeDialog(Object data) method. In the example, we pass either a positive integer value rateEvent.getRating() or 0.

There's more...

Dialog Framework also provides a convenient way to display FacesMessage in a dynamically generated dialog. This can be achieved by invoking the showMessageInDialog(FacesMessage message) method on a RequestContext instance.

Refer to PrimeFaces User's Guide (http://primefaces.org/documentation.html) and the *Dialog Framework* chapter to see how displaying messages in a dialog works.

PrimeFaces Cookbook Showcase application

This recipe is available in the demo web application on GitHub (https://github.com/ova2/primefaces-cookbook/tree/second-edition). Clone the project if you have not done it yet, explore the project structure, and build and deploy the WAR file on application servers compatible with Servlet 3.x, such as *JBoss WildFly* and *Apache TomEE*.

The showcase for the recipe is available at http://localhost:8080/pf-cookbook/views/chapter11/dialogFramework.jsf.

Polling – sending periodical AJAX requests

Polling is a way to poll a server periodically in order to trigger server-side changes or update parts of a web page. The polling technology in PrimeFaces is represented by the `poll` component. It is an AJAX-ified component that has the ability to send periodical AJAX requests.

In this recipe, we will update a feed reader periodically to show current sports news. A `growl` component will be updated with the same interval too in order to show the time of the last feed update.

How to do it...

The `p:poll` component in the following code snippet invokes the `showMessage()` listener method every 10 seconds and updates a feed reader and a growl. The listener method generates the current time. Furthermore, we will define a `widget` variable in order to stop or start polling using the client-side API. This occurs via command buttons. Take a look at the code for this discussion:

```
<p:growl id="growl"/>

<p:poll id="poll" listener="#{pollingBean.showMessage}"
  update="sportFeed growl"
  interval="10" widgetVar="pollWidget"/>

<p:commandButton type="button" value="Stop Polling"
  style="margin:15px 5px 15px 0;"
  onclick="PF('pollWidget').stop();"/>
<p:commandButton type="button" value="Start Polling"
  style="margin:15px 0 15px 0;"
  onclick="PF('pollWidget').start();"/>

<h:panelGroup id="sportFeed" layout="block">
  <p:feedReader value="http://rss.news.yahoo.com/rss/sports"
    var="feed" size="10">
    <h:outputText value="#{feed.title}"
      style="font-weight: bold"/>
    <br/>
    <h:outputText value="#{feed.description.value}"
      escape="false"/>
    <p:separator/>
  </p:feedReader>
</h:panelGroup>
```

The corresponding screenshot illustrates an update with `p:poll`:

 Refer to the *Setting up and configuring the PrimeFaces library* recipe of *Chapter 1, Getting Started with PrimeFaces*, to see mandatory dependencies for the `feedReader` component.

How it works...

The `interval` attribute of `p:poll` defines the time interval, in seconds, at which to execute periodic AJAX requests. The default value is 2 seconds. In the example, we set it to `10`. Similar to any other AJAX-ified components, we can specify components to be processed and updated partially with the `process` and `update` attributes, respectively. The `update` attribute in the example contains IDs of `p:feedReader` and `p:growl`.

Polling can be stopped and started using the `stop()` and `start()` widget methods respectively. We defined two push buttons to execute `pollWidget.stop()` and `pollWidget.start()` on a click event.

There is also the `stop` attribute. It accepts Boolean values that can be bound to it at any arbitrary time. When the value is `true`, polling will be stopped.

There's more...

`Poll` also supports the `autoStart` mode. By default, polling starts automatically on page load. To prevent this behavior, set the `autoStart` attribute to `false`.

Another useful setting is the `timeout` attribute, which defines a timeout for AJAX requests in milliseconds. The timeout is not set by default. Setting a valid timeout allows breaking off long-running requests.

PrimeFaces Cookbook Showcase application

This recipe is available in the demo web application on GitHub (`https://github.com/ova2/primefaces-cookbook/tree/second-edition`). Clone the project if you have not done it yet, explore the project structure, build and deploy the WAR file on application servers compatible with Servlet 3.x, such as *JBoss WildFly* and *Apache TomEE*.

The showcase for the recipe is available at `http://localhost:8080/pf-cookbook/views/chapter11/polling.jsf`.

Blocking page pieces during long-running AJAX calls

The `blockUI` component allows us to block any piece(s) of a page during AJAX calls. Blocking is initiated by one or more trigger components. The `blockUI` component adds a layer and any custom content over the target elements to be blocked and gives the appearance and behavior of blocking user interaction. It is very handy if you have, for example, a large `dataTable` component, and sorting, filtering, and pagination takes much time. You can block almost everything—even the entire page.

In this recipe, we will implement `p:panel` and `p:dataTable` that are blockable in order to learn all the features of `p:blockUI`.

How to do it...

The `panel` component in the following code snippet gets blocked when the command button is clicked on and gets unblocked when the AJAX response is received. We will see a semitransparent layer over the panel, which blocks user interactions within it. The action listener on the command button simulates a long-running task. The following code encapsulates this discussion:

```
<p:panel id="panel" header="Blockable Panel"
  style="height:90px;">
  Click on Save to block me.

  <p:commandButton id="saveBtn" value="Save"
    actionListener="#{blockUIBean.doSomething}"
    style="margin:10px;"/>
</p:panel>

<p:blockUI block="panel" trigger="saveBtn"/>
```

The following example demonstrates a `dataTable` component that gets blocked on pagination and sorting. The `blockUI` component displays custom content with an animated image and the text **Please wait, data is being processed...**:

```
<p:dataTable id="dataTable" var="message"
  value="#{blockUIBean.messages}"
  paginator="true" rows="5" ...>
  <p:ajax event="page" listener="#{blockUIBean.doSomething}"/>
  <p:ajax event="sort" listener="#{blockUIBean.doSomething}"/>
  <p:column sortBy="#{message.subject}">
    <f:facet name="header">
      <h:outputText value="Subject"/>
    </f:facet>
    <h:outputText value="#{message.subject}"/>
  </p:column>
  <p:column sortBy="#{message.text}">
    <f:facet name="header">
      <h:outputText value="Text"/>
    </f:facet>
    <h:outputText value="#{message.text}"/>
  </p:column>
</p:dataTable>
```

```
<p:blockUI block="dataTable" trigger="dataTable">
  <h:panelGrid id="blockContent" columns="2"
    style="table-layout:auto;">
    <h:graphicImage library="images" name="ajax-loader.gif"
      style="margin-right:12px; vertical-align:middle;"/>
    <h:outputText value="Please wait, data is being processed..."
      style="white-space:nowrap;"/>
  </h:panelGrid>
</p:blockUI>
```

The following screenshot shows the blocked `dataTable` component when the user has clicked on page 2:

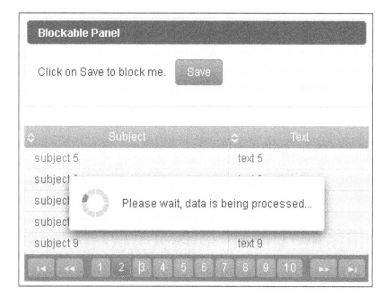

How it works...

`BlockUI` requires the `trigger` and `block` attributes to be defined. The `trigger` attribute defines a **search expression** for the component that sends an AJAX request and blocks triggers. The `block` attribute defines a **search expression** for the component to be blocked.

Chapter 1, Getting Started with PrimeFaces, provides more details on search expressions.

In the first code snippet, we pointed the `trigger` attribute to the button's ID, `saveBtn`, and in the second one to the table's ID, `dataTable`. The `block` attribute points to the panel's ID, `panel` and to the table's ID, `dataTable`, respectively. In the case of `dataTable` blocking, we placed custom content inside the `p:blockUI` tag. In this way, we can display any content we want.

 BlockUI does not support absolute or fixed-positioned components, for example, `dialog`.

There's more...

There are two widget methods to be used on the client side. The `show()` method blocks the specified component and the `hide()` method unblocks it. They can be used in the `onstart` and `oncomplete` callbacks respectively.

PrimeFaces Cookbook Showcase application

This recipe is available in the demo web application on GitHub (`https://github.com/ova2/primefaces-cookbook/tree/second-edition`). Clone the project if you have not done it yet, explore the project structure, and build and deploy the WAR file on application servers compatible with Servlet 3.x, such as *JBoss WildFly* and *Apache TomEE*.

The showcase for the recipe is available at `http://localhost:8080/pf-cookbook/views/chapter11/blockUI.jsf`.

Controlling form submission using defaultCommand

The *Enter* key makes form submission so easy that users always tend to use it. The most intuitive way is that the user can enter some text or make some changes to the existing text and then hit the *Enter* key to submit the form. But what command component will submit the form if we have more than one of them? Browsers, especially Internet Explorer, behave differently here. The `defaultCommand` component solves this problem by normalizing the command (for example, `button` or `link`) that submits the form when the *Enter* key is hit.

In this recipe, we will discuss `p:defaultCommand` in detail. We will implement `p:selectOneMenu` for dynamic selection of the command button used for form submission when the *Enter* key is hit.

How to do it...

We intend to save the chosen command button used for form submission in a backing bean. To achieve this, we need `p:selectOneMenu` with listed command buttons (their IDs) and an attached `p:ajax` behavior event. Such an AJAX-ified `p:selectOneMenu` component should update `p:defaultCommand` on a change event automatically so that the chosen command button will be used in `p:defaultCommand`. A `p:inputText` component should take input and a corresponding `h:outputText` component should display the same input when the *Enter* key is hit. Furthermore, we want to display the pressed button as a growl notification. The following code captures this discussion:

```
<p:growl id="growl" autoUpdate="true"/>

<h:panelGrid columns="2" cellpadding="5">
  <h:outputLabel for="btnSelect" value="Select default button:"/>
  <p:selectOneMenu id="btnSelect"
    value="#{defaultCommandBean.btn}">
    <p:ajax update="@form"/>
    <f:selectItem itemValue="btn1" itemLabel="Button 1"/>
    <f:selectItem itemValue="btn2" itemLabel="Button 2"/>
    <f:selectItem itemValue="btn3" itemLabel="Button 3"/>
  </p:selectOneMenu>
</h:panelGrid>

<h:panelGrid columns="3" cellpadding="5"
  style="margin:15px 0 15px 0;">
  <h:outputLabel for="text" value="Text:"/>
  <p:inputText id="text" value="#{defaultCommandBean.text}"/>
  <h:outputText id="display" value="#{defaultCommandBean.text}"/>
</h:panelGrid>

<p:commandButton id="btn1" value="Button1" update="display"
  actionListener="#{defaultCommandBean.showMessage('Button1')}"/>
<p:commandButton id="btn2" value="Button2" update="display"
  actionListener="#{defaultCommandBean.showMessage('Button2')}"/>
<p:commandButton id="btn3" value="Button3" update="display"
  actionListener="#{defaultCommandBean.showMessage('Button3')}"/>

<p:defaultCommand id="defCommand"
  target="#{defaultCommandBean.btn}"/>
```

The following screenshot shows what happens when the second button is chosen as default and the user enters `sometext` and hits the *Enter* key:

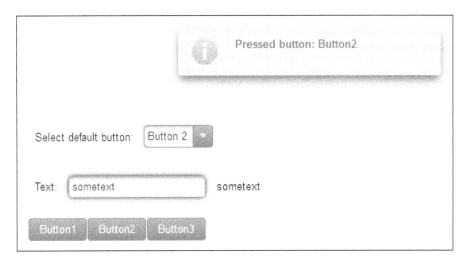

How it works...

`DefaultCommand` must be in a form in order to work, and the `target` attribute is required to refer to an identifier of a clickable command component. The `target` attribute in this example references such an identifier via the EL expression `#{defaultCommandBean.btn}`. The possible identifiers are `btn1`, `btn2`, and `btn3`. The button with the identifier in the `target` attribute is used as default. That means it gets clicked and submits the form when the user enters something into the input field and presses the *Enter* key. In addition, the action listener `showMessage` generates a message text for `p:growl`.

 To perform form submission on a key press, an input field must be focused due to the browser's nature.

There's more...

Besides `target`, there is also the `scope` attribute, which is needed for multiple default commands on the same page. The `scope` attribute restricts the area for handling the *Enter* key. It refers to the ancestor component of the input field considered by this `p:defaultCommand`.

PrimeFaces Cookbook Showcase application

This recipe is available in the demo web application on GitHub (`https://github.com/ova2/primefaces-cookbook/tree/second-edition`). Clone the project if you have not done it yet, explore the project structure, and build and deploy the WAR file on application servers compatible with Servlet 3.x, such as *JBoss WildFly* and *Apache TomEE*.

The showcase for the recipe is available at `http://localhost:8080/pf-cookbook/views/chapter11/defaultCommand.jsf`.

Clever focus management in forms

`Focus` is a component that makes it easy to manage the focus setting on a JSF page. By default, the `focus` component finds the first enabled (editable) and visible input component on the page and applies focus. Typically, input components are associated with HTML elements, such as `input`, `textarea`, and `select`.

In this recipe, we will learn about the default and advanced behaviors of the `Focus` component. We will develop two `h:panelGrid` components with several input components in order to demonstrate the behavior of `p:focus` in detail.

How to do it...

The XHTML code snippet contains a total of three `p:inputText` components:

```
<p:messages/>

<p:focus context="secondGrid"/>

<h:panelGrid columns="2" style="margin-bottom:10px;">
  <h:outputLabel value="Dummy"/>
  <p:inputText/>
</h:panelGrid>

<h:panelGrid id="secondGrid" columns="2">
  <h:outputLabel for="firstname" value="Firstname *"/>
  <p:inputText id="firstname" required="true" label="Firstname"/>

  <h:outputLabel for="surname" value="Surname *"/>
  <p:inputText id="surname" required="true" label="Surname"/>
</h:panelGrid>

<br/>

<p:commandButton value="Submit" update="@form"/>
```

The following screenshot shows a focus set for the **Surname** field after a form is submitted. We entered something in the **Firstname** field but left the **Surname** field empty.

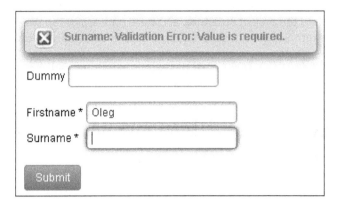

How it works...

The default behavior of the `focus` component can be restricted by the `context` attribute. This attribute defines a **search expression** for the `root` component from which the Focus component starts to search for input components.

> *Chapter 1, Getting Started with PrimeFaces*, provides more details on search expressions.

In the example, `context` points to the ID of the second `h:panelGrid` component. That means although we have two `h:panelGrid` components, only the second will be considered for `p:focus`. The content of the first `h:panelGrid` component gets ignored. If there are no validation errors, the focus is set implicitly on the first editable and visible input field within the second `h:panelGrid` component. This is the **Firstname** field. If there are any validation errors, the first invalid input component will receive the focus. This is the **Surname** field in the preceding screenshot.

> To get this feature working on AJAX requests, you need to update the `p:focus` component as well.

There's more...

If we want to set focus explicitly on an input component, we can use the `for` attribute that specifies exactly this input component.

Another feature is the `minSeverity` attribute. It specifies the message's minimum severity level to be used when finding the first invalid component. The default value is `error`. If you set it, for example, to `info`, the focus will not be normally set on the first invalid component due to the higher severity level of the created validation message matching this threshold. In this case, the default behavior is applied—the focus is set on the first enabled and visible input component.

PrimeFaces Cookbook Showcase application

This recipe is available in the demo web application on GitHub (`https://github.com/ova2/primefaces-cookbook/tree/second-edition`). Clone the project if you have not done it yet, explore the project structure, and build and deploy the WAR file on application servers compatible with Servlet 3.x, such as *JBoss WildFly* and *Apache TomEE*.

The showcase for the recipe is available at `http://localhost:8080/pf-cookbook/views/chapter11/focusManagement.jsf`.

Layout pitfalls of menus and dialogs

When working with the `layout` component, we should be aware of the pitfalls of menus and dialogs inside layout units. Beginners often face overlap issues and try to find several workarounds. In fact, there are easy solutions available.

In this recipe, we will show how to overcome these issues. We will integrate `p:menubar` and `p:dialog` into layout units.

How to do it...

Let's assume that we have a full-page layout with two layout units, `center` and `north`. The `north` unit contains a `menubar` component with quite normal options:

```
<p:layout fullPage="true">
  <p:layoutUnit position="center">
    Center
  </p:layoutUnit>
  <p:layoutUnit position="north" size="80" resizable="false">
    <h:form>
      <p:menubar>
```

```
        <p:submenu label="JavaScript Libraries">
          <p:menuitem value="jQuery" url="#"/>
          <p:menuitem value="Yahoo UI" url="#"/>
          <p:menuitem value="Prototype" url="#"/>
        </p:submenu>
        <p:menuitem value="Go Back" url="#"/>
      </p:menubar>
    </h:form>
  </p:layoutUnit>
</p:layout>
```

If we try to open the menu, it gets partially hidden by the layout unit, as shown in the following screenshot. We can see scrollbars on the right-hand side as well.

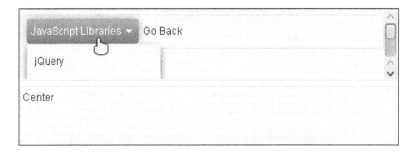

To overcome this wrong appearance, we will set `overflow` to `visible` for the content container (the `div` element) of the `north` layout unit. This CSS setting can be placed within `h:head`. The following code encapsulates this discussion:

```css
<style type="text/css">
  .ui-layout-pane-north .ui-layout-unit-content {
    overflow: visible;
  }
</style>
```

The menu now appears correctly, as shown in the following screenshot. It overlaps the layout unit when we click on it.

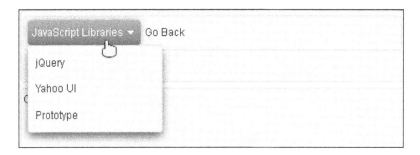

The second potential problem is the modal dialog inside a layout unit. Let's assume we place such a dialog with default options inside the `center` layout unit. The semitransparent layer of the modal dialog overlaps the dialog and prevents any interactions with it. This is shown in the following screenshot:

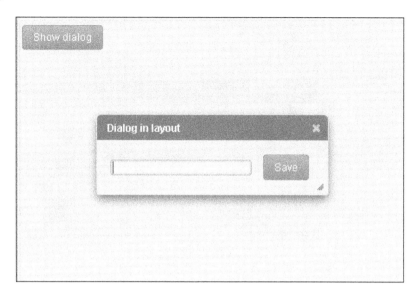

To overcome this issue, we need to set the `appendTo` attribute to the `@(body)` value, as shown here:

```
<p:layoutUnit position="center">
  <p:dialog header="Dialog in layout" modal="true"
    widgetVar="dlgWidget" appendTo="@(body)">
    <h:form>
      <h:inputText/>
      <p:commandButton value="Save"
        style="margin:10px;"/>
    </h:form>
  </p:dialog>

  <p:commandButton value="Show dialog" type="button"
    onclick="PF('dlgWidget').show()"/>
</p:layoutUnit>
```

Now, the semitransparent layer is placed behind the dialog, as shown in the following screenshot:

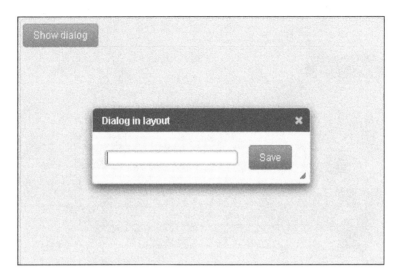

How it works...

Drop-down and pop-up menus often need to overlap adjacent layout units (panes). An ideal solution would be to append the menu elements to the body tag. In this case, no additional effort is needed to use PrimeFaces menus with `layout`. When this is not possible for some reason, there is an option to handle the menus. If a menu appears in a nonscrolling layout unit, we should give the unit's content container the CSS property `overflow: visible` and ensure it is the last unit in the HTML markup. By making it the last unit, it has a naturally higher stack order.

Setting the `appendTo` attribute to `@(body)` appends the dialog as a child of the document body. The `@(body)` value is a search expression in terms of **PrimeFaces Selectors** (**PFS**) to reference the HTML body element.

The preceding argument is valid for the overlay panel. Set `appendTo="@(body)"` when `overlayPanel` is in another panel component, such as `layout` and/or `dialog`.

Components with `appendTo="@(body)"` need a `h:form` tag inside when they communicate with the server. But, avoid nested `h:form` tags. Nested forms bring unexpected behavior and JavaScript errors.

See also

The `Layout` component is discussed extensively in the *Creating complex layouts* recipe in *Chapter 4*, *Grouping Content with Panels*.

PrimeFaces Cookbook Showcase application

This recipe is available in the demo web application on GitHub (`https://github.com/ova2/primefaces-cookbook/tree/second-edition`). Clone the project if you have not done it yet, explore the project structure, and build and deploy the WAR file on application servers compatible with Servlet 3.x, such as *JBoss WildFly* and *Apache TomEE*.

The showcase for the recipe is available at `http://localhost:8080/pf-cookbook/views/chapter11/layoutPitfalls.jsf`.

Targetable messages with severity levels

We sometimes need to target a `FacesMessage` instance to a specific component. For example, suppose we have `p:growl` and `p:messages`/`p:message` tags on the same page and need to display some messages as `p:growl` and some as `p:message`. PrimeFaces has a grouping feature for messages to associate a notification component to specific command components so that messages created as a result of an action will be displayed in the associated messages or the growl tags.

In this recipe, we will develop samples for targetable messages. Furthermore, we will discuss the `severity` attribute. By means of `severity`, we can display messages depending on their severities.

How to do it...

Let's use one `p:messages` tag and two `p:growl` tags, as shown in the following code snippet:

```
<h:panelGroup id="msg1">
  <p:messages for="save" showDetail="true"/>
  <p:growl for="change" showDetail="true"/>
  <p:growl globalOnly="true" showDetail="true"/>
</h:panelGroup>

<p:commandButton value="Save" update="msg1"
  action="#{targetableMessagesBean.addSaveMessage}"/>
<p:commandButton value="Change" update="@form"
  action="#{targetableMessagesBean.addChangeMessage}"/>
<p:commandButton value="Delete" update="@form"
  action="#{targetableMessagesBean.addDeleteMessage}"/>
```

Three command buttons create `FacesMessage` instances. The first button creates two messages that are displayed only by the `p:messages` tag. The second command button creates one message that is displayed only by the first `p:growl` tag with the `for` attribute set to `change`. The message created by the third command button is displayed only by the second `p:growl` tag with `globalOnly` set to `true`. The action methods look as follows:

```
public String addSaveMessage() {
  addMessage("save", FacesMessage.SEVERITY_INFO,
    "Sample info message",
    "First data was successfully saved");
  addMessage("save", FacesMessage.SEVERITY_INFO,
    "Sample info message",
    "Second data was successfully saved");

  return null;
}

public String addChangeMessage() {
  addMessage("change", FacesMessage.SEVERITY_INFO,
    "Sample info message",
    "Data was successfully changed");

  return null;
}

public String addDeleteMessage() {
  addMessage(null, FacesMessage.SEVERITY_INFO,
    "Sample info message",
    "Data was successfully deleted");

  return null;
}

private void addMessage(String key,
  FacesMessage.Severity severity,
  String message, String detail) {
  FacesMessage msg = new FacesMessage(severity, message, detail);
  FacesContext.getCurrentInstance().addMessage(key, msg);
}
```

Let's now use the `p:messages` and `p:growl` tags without the `for` attribute but with a `severity` attribute:

```
<h:panelGroup id="msg2">
  <p:messages severity="error" showDetail="true"/>
  <p:growl severity="info, warn" showDetail="true"/>
  <p:growl showDetail="true"/>
</h:panelGroup>

<p:commandButton value="Generate error message" update="msg2"
  action="#{targetableMessagesBean.addErrorMessage}"/>
```

The command button should create an error message with the `severity` error:

```
public String addErrorMessage() {
  addMessage(null, FacesMessage.SEVERITY_ERROR,
    "Sample error message",
    "Operation failed");

  return null;
}
```

The message created is only displayed by the `p:messages` tag with `severity="error"` and by the second `p:growl` tag without a `severity` attribute.

How it works...

The key of an added `FacesMessage` instance should match the `for` attribute of the `p:growl`, `p:messages`, or `p:message` components to be displayed. If the `for` attribute is missing, all added `FacesMessage` instances will be accepted. If a notification component has set the `globalOnly` flag (`globalOnly="true"`), only the `FacesMessage` instances without a defined key (key is `null`) will be displayed.

 PrimeFaces utilizes the component's `clientId` parameter as the key.

The `severity` attribute of a notification component defines exactly which severities can be displayed by this component. It accepts a comma-separated list. The possible values are `info`, `warn`, `error`, and `fatal`. They match the Java constants, `FacesMessage.SEVERITY_INFO`, `FacesMessage.SEVERITY_WARN`, `FacesMessage.SEVERITY_ERROR`, and `FacesMessage.SEVERITY_FATAL`, respectively. If the `severity` attribute is missing, messages with any severity will be displayed.

PrimeFaces Cookbook Showcase application

This recipe is available in the demo web application on GitHub (`https://github.com/ova2/primefaces-cookbook/tree/second-edition`). Clone the project if you have not done it yet, explore the project structure, and build and deploy the WAR file on application servers compatible with Servlet 3.x, such as *JBoss WildFly* and *Apache TomEE*.

The showcase for the recipe is available at `http://localhost:8080/pf-cookbook/views/chapter11/targetableMessages.jsf`.

Conditional coloring in dataTable

The `dataTable` component provides conditional coloring on rows, which can be styled based on conditions. The row styling utilizes the `rowStyleClass` attribute that has a condition as the EL expression.

In this recipe, we will demonstrate the conditional coloring on rows for countries with **GDP** (**gross domestic product**) less than $3,500,000.

How to do it...

A basic definition of a color-coded table that displays a list of countries with their GDPs is given here:

```
<p:dataTable value="#{dataTableColoringBean.countryGdpList}"
  var="countryGdp"
  rowStyleClass="#{countryGdp.gdp le 3500000 ? 'colored' : ''}">
  <p:column headerText="Name" sortBy="#{countryGdp.name}">
    #{countryGdp.name}
  </p:column>
  <p:column headerText="GDP (Millions of US $)">
    #{countryGdp.gdp}
  </p:column>
</p:dataTable>
```

The colored style definition used in `rowStyleClass` could be as simple as the following:

```
<style type="text/css">
  .colored {
    background-color: #FF0000;
    color: #FFFFFF;
  }
</style>
```

After sorting by name, the end result shows four colored rows here:

Name ▲	GDP (Millions of US $)
Brazil	2190000
China	9330000
France	2739000
Germany	3593000
Japan	5007000
Russia	2113000
United Kingdom	2490000
United States	16720000

How it works...

With the `rowStyleClass` attribute, a style class can be defined for each row according to the country's GDP as `rowStyleClass="#{countryGdp.gdp le 3500000 ? 'colored' : ''}"`. Arithmetic, logical, or relational operators of JSF Expression Language can be used to define the condition.

PrimeFaces Cookbook Showcase application

This recipe is available in the demo web application on GitHub (`https://github.com/ova2/primefaces-cookbook/tree/second-edition`). Clone the project if you have not done it yet, explore the project structure, and build and deploy the WAR file on application servers compatible with Servlet 3.x, such as *JBoss WildFly* and *Apache TomEE*.

The showcase for the recipe is available at `http://localhost:8080/pf-cookbook/views/chapter11/dataTableColoring.jsf`.

Sticking a component when scrolling

The `Sticky` component is used to make another component *stick* to the top of the page once a user has scrolled past it. Hence, the `sticky` component requires a target component to keep it in the viewport on scroll.

In this recipe, we will demonstrate the usage of the `p:sticky` tag.

How to do it...

We would like to stick a select menu with a label as shown in this screenshot:

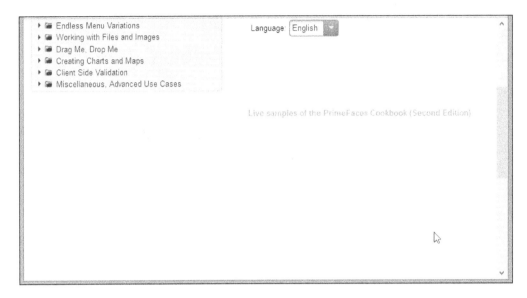

The select menu and the label are placed within h:panelGrid, which acts as the target component:

```
<h:panelGrid id="langGrid" columns="2"
  style="box-shadow: none;">
  <p:outputLabel for="lang" value="Language: "/>
  <p:selectOneMenu id="lang">
    <f:selectItem itemLabel="English" itemValue="en"/>
    <f:selectItem itemLabel="German" itemValue="de"/>
    <f:selectItem itemLabel="French" itemValue="fr"/>
  </p:selectOneMenu>
</h:panelGrid>

...

<p:sticky target="langGrid"/>
```

How it works...

The component to be sticked is referenced via the `target` attribute. In the example, the `target` attribute points to the ID of `h:panelGrid`. If the component sticks, its position is changed to fixed by setting the `position: fixed` style. This happens automatically on scrolling down. The fixed position gets removed on scrolling up when the component is visible at its original location.

 There are no visual styles of sticky; however, the `ui-shadow` and `ui-sticky` classes are applied to the target when the position is fixed. Therefore, we set `box-shadow: none` on `h:panelGrid` in order to remove the visible shadow around the grid.

There is also the `margin` attribute. It defines the offset between the sticked component and the top of the page. The default value is `0`.

There's more...

The header of `p:dataTable` can also be fixed at the top of the visible viewport when scrolling:

```
<p:dataTable stickyHeader="true" ...>
   ...
</p:dataTable>
```

PrimeFaces Cookbook Showcase application

This recipe is available in the demo web application on GitHub (`https://github.com/ova2/primefaces-cookbook/tree/second-edition`). Clone the project if you have not done it yet, explore the project structure, and build and deploy the WAR file on application servers compatible with Servlet 3.x, such as *JBoss WildFly* and *Apache TomEE*.

The showcase for the recipe is available at `http://localhost:8080/pf-cookbook/views/chapter11/sticking.jsf`.

Reducing page load time using content caching

Reducing the page load time can be done by caching the HTML content after initial rendering. PrimeFaces' `cache` component can be used to cache the content. It supports two providers that enable content management in a cache store. The first provider is for *Ehcache* (`http://ehcache.org`) and the second one for *Hazelcast* (`http://hazelcast.com/products/hazelcast`).

In this recipe, we will use *Ehcache*—an open source, standard-based cache used to boost performance, offload the database, and simplify scalability. We will explain how the `cache` component works in an example with a feed reader wrapped inside the `p:cache` tag.

Getting ready

The cache provider is configured via a context parameter in `web.xml`. The provider for *Ehcache* is configured here:

```
<context-param>
  <param-name>primefaces.CACHE_PROVIDER</param-name>
  <param-value>org.primefaces.cache.EHCacheProvider</param-value>
</context-param>
```

A dependency for *Ehcache* in `pom.xml` is required as well:

```
<dependency>
  <groupId>net.sf.ehcache</groupId>
  <artifactId>ehcache</artifactId>
  <version>2.9.0</version>
</dependency>
```

By default, the *Ehcache* implementation looks for a file called `ehcache.xml` at the top level of the classpath. If *Ehcache* does not find that file, it takes the `ehcache-failsafe.xml` file that is packaged in the *Ehcache* JAR. For WAR projects, the `ehcache.xml` file should be placed below the `src/main/resources` folder. It contains a configuration for cache regions. You can imagine a region as a `Map` object with key-value pairs. The value is the cached content then. The cache region in this recipe has the name `appCache`. This is shown in the following code:

```
<?xml version="1.0" encoding="UTF-8"?>
<ehcache xmlns:xsi="http://www.w3.org/2001/XMLSchema-instance"
  xsi:noNamespaceSchemaLocation="ehcache.xsd"
  updateCheck="true" monitoring="autodetect"
  dynamicConfig="true">
```

. . .

```
<cache name="appCache"
    maxEntriesLocalHeap="10000"
    eternal="false"
    timeToIdleSeconds="120"
    timeToLiveSeconds="120"
    diskSpoolBufferSizeMB="30"
    maxEntriesLocalDisk="10000000"
    diskExpiryThreadIntervalSeconds="120"
    memoryStoreEvictionPolicy="LRU">
  </cache>
</ehcache>
```

 See the configuration details in the official *Ehcache* documentation (`http://ehcache.org/documentation`).

How to do it...

We will develop a feed reader that is encircled by `p:cache`. The feed reader fetches podcasts from JSF Central (`www.jsfcentral.com`). This is shown in the following code:

```
<p:cache region="appCache" key="jsfcentral">
  <p:feedReader value="http://www.jsfcentral.com/resources/
    jsfcentralpodcasts/?feed=rss"
    var="feed" size="10">
    <h:outputText value="#{feed.title}"
      style="font-weight: bold"/>
    <br/>
    <h:outputText value="#{feed.description.value}"
      escape="false"/>
    <p:separator/>
  </p:feedReader>
</p:cache>
```

How much can `p:cache` speed up page-loading time? The measured time for the occurrence of the `window onload` event depends on the existence of `p:cache`. The page with the wrapped feed reader inside the `p:cache` tag needs approximately **700–740 milliseconds** until the `onload` event occurs. The page with the feed reader without `p:cache` needs approximately **1.4–1.8 milliseconds**. The tests were performed on a computer with Window 8.1 and Firefox 34.

How it works...

Once the page is loaded initially, the content inside p:cache is cached inside the cache region of the cache provider. GET or POST requests on the same page or page fragment retrieve the output from the cache instead of rendering the content regularly.

The content within the cache region is identified by the key attribute of the p:cache tag. EL expressions such as key="some_#{userBean.language}" are supported too so that key can be done dynamic.

> The getter and other methods from beans inside p:cache are not invoked when the content is fetched from the cache. When the cache expires at the specified time (the timeToIdleSeconds and timeToLiveSeconds options in ehcache.xml), the content will be rendered by JSF renderers and cached again for subsequent calls.

There's more...

The cache provider can be accessed programmatically via the following code:

```
RequestContext.getCurrentInstance().
  getApplicationContext().getCacheProvider()
```

All cache regions can be cleared then with the clear() method. There are also the get, put, and remove methods to get, put, and remove the content of the specific region and the specific key.

PrimeFaces Cookbook Showcase application

This recipe is available in the demo web application on GitHub (https://github.com/ova2/primefaces-cookbook/tree/second-edition). Clone the project if you have not done it yet, explore the project structure, and build and deploy the WAR file on application servers compatible with Servlet 3.x, such as *JBoss WildFly* and *Apache TomEE*.

The showcase for the recipe is available at http://localhost:8080/pf-cookbook/views/chapter11/caching.jsf.

Possibilities for exception handling in PrimeFaces

PrimeFaces provides powerful exception handling for AJAX and non-AJAX requests out of the box. The mapping between error pages and exception types is configured via the `error-page` ability in `web.xml`. Exceptions for AJAX requests can also be configured via the special `p:ajaxExceptionHandler` tag in order for them to be shown on the same page where they occurred. An implicit object, `pfExceptionHandler`, provides useful information about exception details.

In this recipe, we will give helpful tips about configuration details and demonstrate PrimeFaces' exception handling for AJAX and non-AJAX requests.

Getting ready

In order to be able use the exception handling, a special EL resolver and a factory class for 'ExceptionHandler of PrimeFaces should be registered in `faces-config.xml`:

```
<application>
  <el-resolver>
    org.primefaces.application.
      exceptionhandler.PrimeExceptionHandlerELResolver
  </el-resolver>
</application>

<factory>
  <exception-handler-factory>
    org.primefaces.application.
      exceptionhandler.PrimeExceptionHandlerFactory
  </exception-handler-factory>
</factory>
```

PrimeFaces parses the `web.xml` file on application startup to figure out an appropriate page to redirect to when an exception of a certain type occurs. The `web.xml` file of the showcase contains three `error-page` entries:

```
<error-page>
  <exception-type>
    java.lang.Throwable
  </exception-type>
```

```
    <location>
       /views/chapter11/errors/throwable.jsf
    </location>
  </error-page>
  <error-page>
    <exception-type>
     java.lang.IllegalStateException
    </exception-type>
    <location>
       /views/chapter11/errors/illegalState.jsf
    </location>
  </error-page>
  <error-page>
    <exception-type>
       javax.faces.application.ViewExpiredException
    </exception-type>
    <location>
       /views/chapter11/errors/viewExpired.jsf
    </location>
  </error-page>
```

There are two pages for the special exception types, `IllegalStateException` and `ViewExpiredException`, and one generic page for all other kind of exceptions.

In addition to this, you can set the `javax.faces.FACELETS_BUFFER_SIZE` context parameter in `web.xml` to support exception handling in the *RENDER_RESPONSE* phase. Otherwise, you will probably **see javax.servlet.ServletException: Response already committed**. This is shown in the following code:

```
<context-param>
  <param-name>javax.faces.FACELETS_BUFFER_SIZE</param-name>
  <param-value>65535</param-value>
</context-param>
```

How to do it...

We will develop three AJAX-ified `p:commandButton` components and three others to send non-AJAX requests. All buttons invoke actions, which throw different exceptions. We will also have a `p:ajaxExceptionHandler` tag for `ViewExpiredException`. This kind of exception mostly occurs when the session expires. In this case, we would like to update and show a dialog with the exception details and a **Reload** button. This is shown in the following code:

```
<h3 style="margin-top:0">AJAX requests</h3>

<p:commandButton value="Throw NullPointerException"
  action="#{exceptionHandlerBean.throwNullPointerException}"/>
<p:commandButton value="Throw IllegalStateException"
  action="#{exceptionHandlerBean.throwIllegalStateException}"/>
<p:commandButton value="Throw ViewExpiredException"
  action="#{exceptionHandlerBean.throwViewExpiredException}"/>

<h3 style="margin-top:20px">Non-AJAX requests</h3>

<p:commandButton ajax="false" value="Throw NullPointerException"
  action="#{exceptionHandlerBean.throwNullPointerException}"/>
<p:commandButton ajax="false" value="Throw IllegalStateException"
  action="#{exceptionHandlerBean.throwIllegalStateException}"/>
<p:commandButton ajax="false" value="Throw ViewExpiredException"
  action="#{exceptionHandlerBean.throwViewExpiredException}"/>

<p:ajaxExceptionHandler update="expDialog"
  type="javax.faces.application.ViewExpiredException"
  onexception="PF('exceptionDialog').show();"/>

<p:dialog id="expDialog" header="#{pfExceptionHandler.type}
  occured!"
  widgetVar="exceptionDialog" height="500px">
  Message: #{pfExceptionHandler.message}
  <br/>
  Timestamp: #{pfExceptionHandler.formattedTimestamp}
  <br/>
  StackTrace:
  <h:outputText value="#{pfExceptionHandler.formattedStackTrace}"
    escape="false"/>

  <p:button value="Reload the application!"
    style="margin:20px 5px 20px 5px"
    onclick="document.location.href = document.location.href;"/>
</p:dialog>
```

The dialog is quite useful if you do not want to create a separate error page, as shown in the following screenshot:

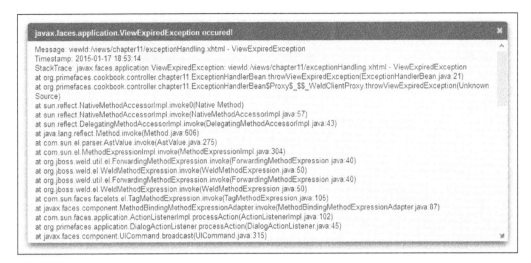

The separate error pages, `viewExpired.jsf`, `illegalState.jsf`, and `throwable.jsf`, have some common information about the exception thrown. For instance, the `throwable.jsf` page looks like this:

```
<h3 style="margin-top:0">
  <strong>Oops, an unexpected error occured</strong>
</h3>

Message: #{pfExceptionHandler.message}
<br/>
Timestamp: #{pfExceptionHandler.formattedTimestamp}
<br/>
StackTrace:
<h:outputText value="#{pfExceptionHandler.formattedStackTrace}"
  escape="false"/>
```

The following screenshot shows the exact output of this page:

Oops, an unexpected error occured

Message: NullPointerException
Timestamp: 2015-01-17 18:51:18
StackTrace: java.lang.NullPointerException: NullPointerException
at org.primefaces.cookbook.controller.chapter11.ExceptionHandlerBean.throwNullPointerException(ExceptionHandlerBean.java:13)
at org.primefaces.cookbook.controller.chapter11.ExceptionHandlerBean$Proxy$_$$_WeldClientProxy.throwNullPointerException(Unknown Source)
at sun.reflect.NativeMethodAccessorImpl.invoke0(Native Method)
at sun.reflect.NativeMethodAccessorImpl.invoke(NativeMethodAccessorImpl.java:57)
at sun.reflect.DelegatingMethodAccessorImpl.invoke(DelegatingMethodAccessorImpl.java:43)
at java.lang.reflect.Method.invoke(Method.java:606)
at com.sun.el.parser.AstValue.invoke(AstValue.java:275)
at com.sun.el.MethodExpressionImpl.invoke(MethodExpressionImpl.java:304)
at org.jboss.weld.util.el.ForwardingMethodExpression.invoke(ForwardingMethodExpression.java:40)
at org.jboss.weld.el.WeldMethodExpression.invoke(WeldMethodExpression.java:50)
at org.jboss.weld.util.el.ForwardingMethodExpression.invoke(ForwardingMethodExpression.java:40)
at org.jboss.weld.el.WeldMethodExpression.invoke(WeldMethodExpression.java:50)
at com.sun.faces.facelets.el.TagMethodExpression.invoke(TagMethodExpression.java:105)
at javax.faces.component.MethodBindingMethodExpressionAdapter.invoke(MethodBindingMethodExpressionAdapter.java:87)
at com.sun.faces.application.ActionListenerImpl.processAction(ActionListenerImpl.java:102)
at org.primefaces.application.DialogActionListener.processAction(DialogActionListener.java:45)
at javax.faces.component.UICommand.broadcast(UICommand.java:315)

How it works...

The `viewExpired.jsf` and `illegalState.jsf` error pages are configured for exceptions of the types `ViewExpiredException` and `IllegalStateException`, respectively. Any other exceptions are caught by the `java.lang.Throwable` type and will be redirected to the `throwable.jsf` page.

The `p:ajaxExceptionHandler` exception handler component provides a way to update other components on the same page and execute the `onexception` callback on the client side after that. Be aware that the `p:ajaxExceptionHandler` component is only valid for AJAX requests. It does not have any effect on non-AJAX requests. In the example, `ViewExpiredException` is shown on a separate page for non-AJAX requests.

 Place `p:ajaxExceptionHandler` in your Facelets master template so that it will be included in every page.

Information about the exception is provided via the keyword, `pfExceptionHandler`, and can be accessed on a page by EL expressions such as `#{pfExceptionHandler.message}`. All exposed properties are listed here:

Property	Description
`exception`	This is an exception instance
`type`	This is the type of the exception
`message`	This is the exception message
`stackTrace`	This is an array of `java.lang.StackTraceElement` instances
`formattedStackTrace`	This sets stack trace as a presentable string
`timestamp`	This sets a timestamp as a date
`formattedTimestamp`	This sets a timestamp as a presentable string

PrimeFaces Cookbook Showcase application

This recipe is available in the demo web application on GitHub (`https://github.com/ova2/primefaces-cookbook/tree/second-edition`). Clone the project if you have not done it yet, explore the project structure, and build and deploy the WAR file on application servers compatible with Servlet 3.x, such as *JBoss WildFly* and *Apache TomEE*.

The showcase for the recipe is available at `http://localhost:8080/pf-cookbook/views/chapter11/exceptionHandling.jsf`.

Index

Thank you for buying
PrimeFaces Cookbook
Second Edition

About Packt Publishing

Packt, pronounced 'packed', published its first book, *Mastering phpMyAdmin for Effective MySQL Management*, in April 2004, and subsequently continued to specialize in publishing highly focused books on specific technologies and solutions.

Our books and publications share the experiences of your fellow IT professionals in adapting and customizing today's systems, applications, and frameworks. Our solution-based books give you the knowledge and power to customize the software and technologies you're using to get the job done. Packt books are more specific and less general than the IT books you have seen in the past. Our unique business model allows us to bring you more focused information, giving you more of what you need to know, and less of what you don't.

Packt is a modern yet unique publishing company that focuses on producing quality, cutting-edge books for communities of developers, administrators, and newbies alike. For more information, please visit our website at www.packtpub.com.

About Packt Open Source

In 2010, Packt launched two new brands, Packt Open Source and Packt Enterprise, in order to continue its focus on specialization. This book is part of the Packt open source brand, home to books published on software built around open source licenses, and offering information to anybody from advanced developers to budding web designers. The Open Source brand also runs Packt's open source Royalty Scheme, by which Packt gives a royalty to each open source project about whose software a book is sold.

Writing for Packt

We welcome all inquiries from people who are interested in authoring. Book proposals should be sent to author@packtpub.com. If your book idea is still at an early stage and you would like to discuss it first before writing a formal book proposal, then please contact us; one of our commissioning editors will get in touch with you.

We're not just looking for published authors; if you have strong technical skills but no writing experience, our experienced editors can help you develop a writing career, or simply get some additional reward for your expertise.

Mastering PrimeFaces

Josh Juneau

[PACKT]

Mastering PrimeFaces [Video]

ISBN: 978-1-78398-806-8   Duration: 05:04 hours

Master the PrimeFaces Component framework and quickly develop sophisticated web applications

1. Develop sophisticated user interfaces for your Java EE applications utilizing the Ajax core components.

2. Master the PrimeFaces powerful JSF component library to build your application.

3. Portray outstanding visual dashboards for your data.

4. Use the PrimeFaces mobile framework to provide a top-notch mobile front-end interface for your application users.

PrimeFaces Blueprints

Create your very own portfolio of customized web applications with PrimeFaces

Sudheer Jonna
Ramkumar Pillai

PACKT

PrimeFaces Blueprints

ISBN: 978-1-78398-322-3   Paperback: 310 pages

Create your very own portfolio of customized web applications with PrimeFaces

1. Learn how to use the rich UI components of PrimeFaces.

2. Explore all the major features of PrimeFaces with real-world examples.

3. Step-by-step guide with precise explanations of code and functionalities.

Please check **www.PacktPub.com** for information on our titles

Learning PrimeFaces
Extensions Development

ISBN: 978-1-78398-324-7   Paperback: 192 pages

Develop advanced frontend applications using
PrimeFaces Extensions components and plugins

1. Learn how to utilize the enhanced Extensions'
    components in the existing or newly created
    PrimeFaces based applications.

2. Explore all the components major features with
    lots of example scenarios.

3. Features a systematic approach to teach a wide
    range of Extensions component features with the
    JobHub web application development.

PrimeFaces Cookbook

ISBN: 978-1-84951-928-1   Paperback: 328 pages

Over 90 practical recipes to learn PrimeFaces-the rapidly
evolving, leading JSF component suite

1. The first PrimeFaces book that concentrates
    on practical approaches rather than the
    theoretical ones.

2. Readers will gain all the PrimeFaces insights
    required to complete their JSF projects
    successfully.

3. Written in a clear, comprehensible style
    and addresses a wide audience on modern,
    trend-setting Java/JEE web development.

Please check **www.PacktPub.com** for information on our titles

www.ingramcontent.com/pod-product-compliance
Lightning Source LLC
Chambersburg PA
CBHW081504050326
40690CB00015B/2924